INTRODUCTION TO
PRIVATE INVESTIGATION

ABOUT THE AUTHOR

Joseph Anthony Travers, C.P.I., holds a Bachelor's Degree in Criminal Justice from the California State University at Long Beach and has been advanced to candidate for a Master's of Science Degree in Criminal Justice at the Graduate School of Criminal Justice, C.S.U.L.B.

An Honorably Discharged Veteran from the United States Navy, Mr. Travers has a total of six years of experience in Law Enforcement, specifically in Criminal Investigations and Police Training and Supervision. He possesses professional certificates in California State Peace Officer Standards and Training; Basic, Intermediate, Advanced Officer Training, Hostage Negotiations, and Field Training Officer Certificates. In addition, Mr. Travers has experience in Loss Prevention and Private and Personnel Security, having served as the former Manager of Security, Southern California, for McDonnell Douglas Corporation.

Mr. Travers has been a California State Licensed Investigator since 1983 and his investigative work has been chronicled in *People* magazine, various cable networks, and on television stations such as KCBS, KNBC, KABC, KTTV, KCOP, KHJ, and KTLA. His work has also been recognized in front-page headlines of newspapers around the country, including *The Los Angeles Times, The New York Times, The Sacramento Bee,* and *The Orange County Register.*

For three years, Mr. Travers has taught Private Investigations, and is currently the Director of Education at Private Investigative Research Company in Rancho Cucamonga, California. He has testified as an expert witness and conducted investigations on Police Practices and Investigative Technique in California State and United States Federal Courts.

INTRODUCTION TO PRIVATE INVESTIGATION

Essential Knowledge and Procedures for the Private Investigator

By

JOSEPH ANTHONY TRAVERS, C.P.I.

CHARLES C THOMAS • PUBLISHER
Springfield • Illinois • U.S.A.

Published and Distributed Throughout the World by

CHARLES C THOMAS • PUBLISHER
2600 South First Street
Springfield, Illinois 62794-9265

© *1995 by* CHARLES C THOMAS • PUBLISHER
ISBN 0-398-06527-6   (cloth)
ISBN 0-398-06528-4   (paper)
Library of Congress Catalog Card Number: 95-10754

Printed in the United States of America
SC-R-3

Library of Congress Cataloging-in-Publication Data

Travers, Joseph Anthony.
    Introduction to private investigation : essential knowledge and
procedures for the private investigator / by Joseph Anthony Travers.
        p.   cm.
    Includes bibliographical references and index.
    ISBN 0-398-06527-6. — ISBN 0-398-06528-4 (pbk.)
    1. Private investigators—United States—Handbooks, manuals, etc.
I. Title.
HV8093.T73   1995
363.2'89—dc20   95-10754
                                                                    CIP

For
My Son
Joshua,
Forever Young.

FOREWORD

Over the years, the most curious phenomenon that I have encountered in my work as a Private Investigator is the misconceptions of what a P.I. does, and the "glamorous" lifestyle we lead! Our public image is so far off the mark; it was refreshing for me to see a book introduced that helped to clear up this distortion, and also, to bring us closer to the 21st century! Joseph Travers' *Introduction to Private Investigation* creates a realistic account of just what is expected of a P.I., and what types of people are cut out for this type of work. Also, we are brought up to date on laws, technology, equipment, and case studies that are more pertinent to the 90's, and to the types of challenges facing the P.I.'s of today.

Our world is changing at such a rapid pace, and it is difficult to keep up with that pace. It is equally difficult to choose a career that is both rewarding and financially lucrative. The good news is that the field of investigation is becoming more and more diverse, offering opportunity in every direction, not just from the standpoint of law enforcement, but in the private sector as well. Mr. Travers' book deals with material that has never been touched on before in a book designed to educate private investigators about their craft. His information is accurate, current, and practicable.

I am personally a strong believer in specialization. My advice would be to find a niche that you enjoy, educate yourself to the level of "expert," and design and implement a marketing plan, to begin your journey into this exciting field. *Introduction to Private Investigation* opens the door to that journey. I highly recommend anyone presently involved in or considering a career change into the field of professional investigation to allow this book to help guide the way.

GLEN S. GOODMAN
Chairman
California Institute for Professional Investigators

FOREWORD

The private investigation industry has changed dramatically in the past half-century. From a time when the typical P.I. had the reputation of being a booze-slugging, woman-chasing roughneck—to today's investigators, professional men and women dedicated to preserving justice in the public and private sectors.

Investigators play an important role in the civil and criminal justice systems in this country. Their contribution to the war on crime is largely unknown and unrecognized. Today's investigators search out the facts for many crimes, including insurance fraud, arson, industrial espionage, theft, and drug abuse. Their clients include insurance companies, attorneys, private employers, and government agencies.

The science of investigation is a learned profession. *Webster's Dictionary* describes the word "investigate" as "to observe or study by close examination and systematic inquiry." And "learned" is "to gain knowledge of understanding or skill in by study, instruction, or experience." Therein lies the purpose of this book. There is a constant need for up-to-date technical information to assist professional investigators in their quest for the truth.

This book will enable the professional investigator or apprentice to sharpen the skills they use every day. Be it undercover, surveillance, interviewing, case preparation, or courtroom testimony, even the most seasoned veterans understand the need to be on top of their game in order to provide clients with the best possible results.

We have seen the need for specialized education in the investigation field in order to serve our clients in the private sector. While many investigators have a law enforcement background, and received training to deal with the public and criminal activities, the private sector must play by a different set of rules. Today, sexual harassment and violence in the workplace top the headlines, and require investigations that ferret out civil liability, not just criminal intent. The need for specialized skills has developed into schools that teach the art of private investigation, how to avoid invasion of privacy, the ability to search public records, and so on.

I applaud the efforts of Joe Travers to write an easy-to-read textbook for investigators. It is filled with practical information and stories which will provide extremely valuable training for us all.

MARK A. McCLAIN, C.P.I.
President
California Association of Licensed Investigators

PREFACE

Introduction to Private Investigation is designed to provide the essential knowledge and procedure needed to operate successfully as a private investigator. It is both an instructional textbook for those individuals desiring a career as a private investigator, and a resource manual that can be an invaluable tool for later reference. The approach is a direct, concise style, which facilitates comprehension by novices as well as experienced private investigators, and makes possible competent and professional performance of all types of private investigation. The purpose for writing this book is to fill the existing need within the field for a precise, comprehensive text detailing the development of skills necessary for professional investigative work. In addition, there is a lack of recent, up-to-date textbooks currently available to individuals wishing to learn about private investigation. *Introduction to Private Investigation* will help fill this void.

The text material has been class-tested from an accredited curriculum approved by the California Education Department for Post-Secondary Vocational Education. This curriculum has been taught by Educational Designs Institute of Commerce, California, and by Private Investigative Research Company School of Investigation of Rancho Cucamonga, California.

Introduction to Private Investigation is intended for both the individual without prior investigative experience and the newly licensed private investigator who lacks formal education in a private investigations vocational school. It is also written for those persons possessing background in police or law enforcement.

One unique attribute of *Introduction to Private Investigation* is its commitment to the practice of private investigation in the private business sector (i.e., auto clubs, law firms, etc.) as opposed to the police sector (i.e., police and law enforcement). Another notable quality is its concern with both the portrayal of private investigation as a legitimate professional discipline and the subsequent degradation of the popular, media-propagated misconceptions of private investigators.

JOSEPH A. TRAVERS, C.P.I.

ACKNOWLEDGMENTS

Introduction to Private Investigation is a result of many years of education and experience. I have not "reinvented the wheel" so-to-speak, but with the help of many colleagues I have only attempted to improve upon the profession of investigation.

I owe a debt of gratitude to many in the field of academia, to those who promote open-minded thought. Among the many I have gained inspiration from include Dr. Rodolfo Torrez, Professor of Public Policy and Administration, C.S.U.L.B., and Dr. Albert C. Germann, Professor Emeritus Criminal Justice, C.S.U.L.B.

Professionally, I have acquired many skills and techniques from many investigators—all too many to mention. Among these include James F. Broder, C.P.P., Vice President of Confidential Management Services, Inc.; Mark A. McClain, C.P.I., President of California Association of Licensed Investigators, and Vice President of Krout and Schneider Investigations; Dana D. Griffith of Griffith Investigations; Joel C. Villasenor, C.P.P., CIC Investigations; Vern Horst, Investigator for Riverside County Sheriff's Department; Albert Rusas, Detective for Maywood Police Department; and Samuel J. D'Amico, Regional Vice President for American Protective Services, Inc.

A sincere appreciation for technical assistance goes to two of my former students and graduates of Private Investigative Research Company School of Investigations, Julia Cosmides, currently a graduate student at the University of Notre Dame, and Bernadette Marquez, who plans to attend law school. A special thanks to my office manager, Carol Gonzalez. Without their contribution this could not have been possible.

Finally, the continued moral support of my business partner, Michael G. Mendoza, President of Private Investigative Research Company, has allowed me the time and opportunity to complete this endeavor.

CONTENTS

INTRODUCTION TO
PRIVATE INVESTIGATION

Chapter 1

INVESTIGATION CONCEPTS

Courage

Why is it that most men's lives are controlled by small and petty circumstances? I am saddened as I watch people love the good and great things that are within their reach and could be theirs with "BUT A LITTLE ACT OF COURAGE!"

The mediocre man, "Average Man," is the one I speak of here. He is the one who has so little self-esteem that he cannot trust his own thoughts and judgments, but in the final analysis must rely upon outside sources for his decisions. This is the man who is ruled by the mob, or who accepts all that he reads as truth and finally becomes like the mob. This is the man who has some degree of success only when he is caught upon the crest of a wave generated by the few exceptional self-directed individuals.

This is the man who has a positive attitude for that moment he is in the presence of positive individuals, but when left alone, "falls to his negative knees." This is the man who sells his birthrights (commitment to his own thoughts) for fear of what he thinks his neighbor might think. This is the man who stands tall as he is prompted by the actions of the mob, but is terrified with the silence of his own presence.

This is the man who follows and fears to lead. This is the man who hides his deeds in the cloak of nobility, since his dishonesty prevents him from dealing with truth and reality. This is the man who cries "foul" when life has passed him by.

This is the man who is ruled by circumstance.

Strong men create circumstances which serve their needs and desires. If you are a man of circumstance, the cure for this disease is courage.

Courage is the most beautiful of all human expressions. Courage as I see it is "an act in the face of fear." We only need courage when we are afraid, which means that we need courage almost all of the time, because we are afraid of something all of the time.

I have discovered that fear becomes a coward when faced with but a small act of courage, and further, that the muscle of courage will grow strong with continued use.

My advice to myself is, "do those things which you fear, and keep doing them until you are no longer afraid, and then you will have become the master of your fate."

I have studied the deeds of men both great and small, and I have studied those men who are great and small. In this study there appears to be many differences. All of the differences which count have at their base, one single thing—COURAGE.

Courage is that one ingredient which separates the weak from the strong, the successful from the weak, the great from the average.

All the things you desire in life have one common handle, which is made for the hand of the man of courage.

To be afraid is to be alive. To act against that fear is to be a man. William Penn Patrick once said, "I HAD RATHER DIE ON MY FEET THAN LIVE ON MY KNEES."

WILLIAM PENN PATRICK

Private Investigations is a field that requires a great deal of courage. It is one which you as the investigator will be called upon to make quick decisions, create inventive solutions to problems and deal with a wide range of people and situations. It is one that requires both skill and experience; no amount of "book learning" or head knowledge can take the place of actual hands-on, practical experience in investigation. As Edward Smith in his book *Practical Guide for Private Investigators* has pointed out, proficiency in private investigation can be compared to acquiring proficiency at the piano[1] you can't just read a book on music theory and expect to step out upon the world's stage as a concert pianist without spending hours practicing on the piano.

In this chapter, you will be given an introduction to private investigation. You will be provided with a brief overview of the history of investigations, the criminal justice process, and civil law. Finally, you will be shown the relevant legislation about private investigators, the code of ethics for professionals in the field, and the necessary tools for skillful report writing.

DEFINITION OF PRIVATE INVESTIGATION

Charles Sennewald, the former Security Director of Broadway Department Stores, defines investigation thusly: "An investigation is the examination, study, searching, tracking and gathering of factual information that answers questions or solves problems."[2] In addition to mere fact gathering, the private investigator is also called upon to formulate logical hypotheses and conclusions that are based upon the available

---

[1]Smith, Edward. *Practical Guide for Private Investigators.* Boulder: Paladin Press, 1990.

[2]Sennewald, Charles A. *The Process of Investigation.* Boston: Butterworth-Heinemann, 1981, p. 3.

information. Thus, the desired result of an investigation is "the factual explanation of what transpired."[3]

It would be more than simplistic to say that an investigator deals exclusively with facts—it would be untrue. While he or she is concerned with uncovering the actual details of a particular event or situation, there is also the need to determine *why* such things went on, how they are all related, and what relevancy each piece of information provides the case at hand. The facts themselves are useless if you are unable to apply logic, discern connections, and arrive at the correct conclusion.

The Investigator's Code

Every thorough investigation answers the following basic questions:

1. Who?
2. What?
3. When?
4. Where?
5. Why?
6. How?

When looking to determine the "who" portion of an investigation, some types of questions that you might ask include who discovered the crime, who reported it, or who saw or heard anything. You might also ask who had a motive for committing the crime, who did it, and who helped, if there were any others involved.

Some examples of "what" questions are to find out what exactly happened, what crime was committed, what the actions of the suspect were, and what weapons were used in the commission of the crime. Find out what evidence exists to support or refute the claims of the suspect, what the witnesses know or don't know, and what the motive behind the crime was.

Some possible "where" questions include: where was the witness, where was the evidence found, where is the subject now, and where did the incident happen? You could also find out where the suspects were seen, where the victim was found, and where the suspect was apprehended.

"When" questions are similarly straightforward: when did the incident happen, when was it discovered, when was anyone notified as to its

---

[3]Ibid.

occurrence, and when did help arrive? Also ascertain when the victim was last seen and when the suspect was taken into custody.

When trying to answer the "how" of an investigation, you should be concerned with the "modus operandi," or the "method of operation." Namely, find out how the crime was committed: how the suspect got to the scene of the crime, how he or she left it, how did he or she obtain the tools or weapons necessary to execute the crime, how much damage was done, and how much property was stolen, etc. Basically, you are interested in developing a "blueprint" of the incident, learning all the details so that you may accurately portray just exactly how the incident came about.

The final question in the Investigator's Code is "Why?" Even though it is usually the first question most people ask upon learning that a crime has been committed—"I can't believe he would do such a thing!"—for the purposes of private investigation, it is probably the least crucial of all six questions. But, since a portion of the investigator's work does involve the drawing of logical conclusions based upon the facts already gathered, you should ask yourself why an incident occurred and why the particular method of implementation was used.

Obviously, if you are involved in a noncriminal investigation, you will need to tailor your questions to fit the particular case on which you are working. For example, if you are hired by a woman who is concerned that her husband may be cheating on her, you won't necessarily be asking who committed the crime or who had a motive for the crime. Instead, you might want to find out with whom the husband spends a great deal of time, who else knows about any outside affiliations this man might have, and to whom he might have confided in regarding his philandering.

TRIAL RUN

In the following story, I present a fictitious account of a woman who has an investigation done on the man with whom she is romantically involved. As you read this story, try to answer the six questions of the Investigator's Code—Who, What, Where, When, How, and Why.

It was an unlikely place to meet the man of her dreams. Roaming the frozen food aisle at the grocery store with her two-year-old daughter, Margot did not expect to meet Harrison Reid Ashbery, II. Nor did she expect him to strike up a conversation with her, thoroughly charm and delight her, and offer to take both her and her daughter out for an ice cream cone later that afternoon. She learned that he was the sole owner of a thriving mail order firm, had a lovely home in an affluent neighborhood not far from her own, and had just recently purchased a red Mercedes convertible. He had been engaged once before but never married, had no children of his own but professed a great affection for them, and was quite the gourmet cook. When Margot revealed that she, too, owned her own business, lived in a fairly up-scale home and was very handy in the kitchen, Harrison seemed convinced that fate had brought them together.

Margot's friends, however, were much more cautious about the whole affair and encouraged Margot to be careful. Even though Harrison appeared to be a wealthy, articulate, and successful man, there was always the possibility that things were not as they appeared. As Margot's mother was fond of saying, "If something looks too good to be true, it probably is too good to be true." So, more to appease her friends than out of any real suspicion of her own, Margot hired a private investigative agency to look into Harrison's background.

It did not take them long to uncover some startling statistics. Harrison Reid Ashbery II was actually Harry Osborne of Green Bay, Wisconsin, and had declared bankruptcy two years previous after being indicted for mail order fraud. His former wife, mother of their three children, had once threatened to file charges against him for child abuse. His probate records indicated that he had never owned property. The house belonged to a friend who was out of town on an extended leave of absence and had asked Harry to check in occasionally and water the plants. The Mercedes belonged to this friend as well.

The rest, as they say, is history. Margot's mother tried very hard not to say "I told you so," and four months after Harry had disappeared, set Margot up with a handsome, young CPA.

Even though this is a fictionalized account, such investigations do occur. Jerry Palaca and Tim Bartlett, both retired New York City detectives, operate an investigative agency called Check-a-Mate that thoroughly checks into the backgrounds of potential spouses, as well as people who are merely dating on a regular basis with no intention to marry in the future. How they conduct these investigations is to look into prior marriages, criminal records, business colleagues, and financial records, among others. They say that

> These days, the most common concerns are whether a person has a criminal record, AIDS, is on the verge of bankruptcy, or is a child molester. That last is particularly frightening to divorced or widowed women with small children. And the notoriety that such deviants have been getting has pushed the issue to the forefront in the minds of many people.[4]

There are many different types of businesses and organizations that utilize investigative services, and many various duties that investigators

---

[4]"Checking Out Prospective Mates." *USA Today,* Dec. 1990, Vol. 119, No. 2547, p. 5.

may perform. Some examples include law firms, for which private investigators can conduct claims and divorce investigations, locate missing persons, and run criminal investigations. For banks, there are credit and background investigations. Department stores often have need of undercover investigators to uncover shoplifting or internal theft, as well as credit and background investigations. Restaurants, food stores, industrial plants, and insurance companies may also employ investigators. And, of course, you may go to work for a detective agency, for which you may be called upon to perform any and all types of investigation.

HISTORY OF PRIVATE INVESTIGATION/SECURITY

The pursuit and administration of justice have not always been as they are today. While no one can deny that even in our modern courts and policing system, inequities exist, we do at least espouse the theory that "justice is blind," that all individuals are innocent until proven guilty, and that everyone is entitled to a fair and speedy trial before a jury of their peers.

Such was not always the case.

In seventeenth century England, there was one source of justice: the king. King Charles, who reigned from 1625 to 1645, acted as judge, jury, and executioner. Later that same century, however, with the reign of King Charles II, Parliament was allowed to administer the laws, thereby taking some of the absolute power away from the monarchy and establishing a system of greater accountability. Habeas corpus—which is Latin for "bring me the body"—was introduced, which established the concept of a preliminary hearing or arraignment. In 1663, constables began patrolling the streets to keep order; the night watch system went into implementation, and the first police were installed. In the 1700s, Harry Fielding began the "Bow Street Runners," which were the country's first plain-clothed detectives.

It wasn't until the 1800s that England's first metropolitan police force was created, at the now almost legendary Scotland Yard in London. Sir Robert Peel, who is considered to be the father of modern policing, developed the first police force that was quasi-military in its structure, administration, and implementation. Because of his influence, policemen were called "bobbies" for many years after, although I have been told that only tourists to England call police officers by that name today.

In America, the first police force did not come into being until 1844. Allan Pinkerton was the first American detective, founding the Pinkerton National Detective Agency in 1850. It is from the Pinkertons that the slang referent for private investigators originated: their trademark was "the Eye that Never Sleeps," from which it was easy to derive the term "Private Eye." When an assassination attempt on President Lincoln was made as Lincoln was traveling to his Inauguration, Pinkerton was there to protect him. His sons went into private investigating with him and together they provided security for railroads and fought against western bandits and the pervasive anarchy that characterized the American west. A lasting legacy from the Pinkertons includes many criminal investigation procedures and communication systems between law enforcement agencies that are the foundation of existing operations.[5]

CRIMINAL JUSTICE PROCESS

The California Penal Code defines crime as any act, whether in omission or commission, that violates a law forbidding or commanding it, and the consequence of which is some kind of punishment. In the criminal justice system as we know it today, there are basically three types of crime: infraction, misdemeanor, and felony. The degree of punishment is what distinguishes the crime. For example, when you are going ninety-five miles an hour in a forty-five zone and a California Highway Patrol officer pulls you over, you have been caught committing an infraction. You will have to pay a large sum of money. Thus, an infraction is a crime that is punishable by fine only. If you are charged with an infraction, you are not entitled to a jury trial; if convicted, you do not go to jail. A misdemeanor, on the other hand, is a crime that is punishable by fine and/or up to one year of imprisonment in a county jail. In California, they are considered to be "in-between" crimes that are neither infractions nor felonies. A felony, then, is a crime which is punishable by fine and/or imprisonment in a state penitentiary, or death. Obviously, felonies are the most serious crimes: murder, which is defined as killing with malice; manslaughter, or killing without malice; and robbery, which is theft by threat or force, are all examples of felonies.

---

[5]"Private Investigator's Influence on American History." C.I.P.I. Journal, summer 1993, Vol. 1, No. 1, pp. 1, 4.

There are two elements that need to be present before an act can be considered a crime. First of all, there needs to be the act itself—a murder, a robbery, etc. The second element that must be present is the intent to commit the crime. Intent can be specific, which means that the individual specifically intended to commit the crime against the person to whom it actually happened. For example, if two people were having an argument and one pulled out a gun and shot the other, the intent is fairly self-obvious. There can also be what is called "general intent," which is rather like a catch-all for those cases where specific intent may be too difficult to prove. An example of a general intent crime is where an individual strikes and kills a pedestrian with her car after having consumed enough alcohol to give her a blood alcohol content of .10. Although the specific intent to run the pedestrian down and kill her was not present in the motorist's mind, driving drunk is in itself evidence of a general and dangerous disregard of public safety and the law.

The third form of intent is transferred intent. This means that the person may well have intended to commit a crime against one individual but actually ended up committing it against another. Such cases would be where an individual walks into a drug store and points a gun at the cashier, demanding all the money in the drawer and every package of cigarettes in the store. When the cashier refuses to comply, the wielder of the gun tries to shoot her but misses and shoots the twelve-year-old boy who is hiding in the candy aisle. Although the specific intent was not to kill the twelve-year-old boy, the shooter is still guilty of having committed that crime.

The court system in which crimes are tried is made up of five distinct levels: district, municipal, superior, appellate, and finally, the Supreme Court. The district court is the lower division of municipal court, in which are tried misdemeanors and infractions. The superior court is where felonies are tried, or where appeals from lower courts are tried. The appellate court hears appeals from the lower courts, which are cases that are being retried on some point of law and not on the facts themselves. And, finally, the Supreme Court, which is the highest court in the country, is where cases go that are appealing decisions made in the appellate court.

In our criminal justice system, the process begins when you are accused of a crime. If it is a misdemeanor or a felony, a complaint is filed by a district attorney or a city attorney, and a grand jury is called to determine whether there is sufficient evidence stacked up against you, often there is an arrest made and you as the defendant are then "booked," which means that a permanent record of your arrest and all the surrounding details is made. At this point, you are usually entitled to "post bail," or provide some kind of monetary assurance that you will appear in court at your appointed date. The United States Constitution provides that bail amounts will not be unreasonably high, so that people are most often able to come up with the needed collateral. In some cases where the court determines that there is not a high risk of flight, the defendant will be released on his or her own recognizance, in which instance no amount of bail will need to be paid.

Arraignment before the judge usually follows fairly rapidly, in which you will be advised fully of the charges that are being brought against you and given the opportunity to enter a plea. Entering a plea entails asserting that you are not guilty of the crime you are accused of having committed, guilty, or nolo contendere, which means that you will not contest the charge being brought against you. A plea of nolo contendere essentially means that you are pleading guilty in the criminal court, but that you cannot be held liable for any civil liabilities that arise as a consequence of your criminal act.

On a side note, I would like to point out a frequent error made in newspaper articles when the subject matter is a criminal trial. Often, the reporter will state that "Mr. Ty Rant pled innocent to the charge of killing his wife, three children, and dog." While one does like to believe that Mr. Rant is innocent until proven guilty, he cannot plead innocence in a court of law. In the recent O.J. Simpson trial, for instance, when asked how he pled, Mr. Simpson did not say "innocent." He said, "not guilty."

After the arraignment, misdemeanors generally go right to trial, but with felonies there is first the preliminary hearing, or "prelim," at which the district attorney must demonstrate that there is probable cause to show that the defendant committed the crime. For the defense, it is usually just an opportunity to find out what kind of case the prosecution will be bringing against the client. Most often, the client is not allowed to testify during the preliminary hearing.

The trial then moves to Superior Court, in which the defendant again enters his or her plea. In cases where the D.A. is not certain that sufficient evidence exists to convict the defendant on all charges, or perhaps simply to avoid the expense and time of a long, drawn-out trial, the prosecuting attorney and the D.A. will enter a plea bargain, which is an agreement between the two lawyers in which some of the charges against the defendant will be dropped or reduced in exchange for a guilty plea to other and usually lesser charges. For example, former Olympic ice skater Tonya Harding avoided some potentially disastrous charges by accepting a plea bargain for obstruction of justice and received little more than a slap on the wrist for her alleged role in the attack on rival skater Nancy Kerrigan. Although stripped of her National Championship, she is now enjoying relative success in other endeavors.

Unless a defendant waives or relinquishes the right to be tried before a jury, trials in the Superior Court are handled before a competent jury of twelve men and women who have been selected and mutually agreed upon by both members of counsel. Conviction can only come if the jury is convinced *beyond a reasonable doubt* that the defendant is indeed guilty of the charged crime. Unanimous decisions from the jury are needed to convict or acquit, or absolve someone of guilt. If even one juror harbors a lingering and reasonable uncertainty of the absolute guilt of the defendant, then we have what is called a hung jury and the judge must either order the jury back to reconsider or declare a mistrial, upon which occurrence there will usually be a retrial.

If a verdict of guilty is handed down by the jury, the judge refers the defendant to a probation officer for evaluation. Probation officers are "the eyes and ears" of the court, and it is their job to investigate the defendant's background and possibly determine whether or not the individual may serve all or part of the sentencing on probation, or out of prison. For persons who are sent to prison and then released for good behavior, there is a time of parole, in which they will be monitored by a corrections officer. Pardons are acts by executive officers of government, either governors or presidents, that essentially erase a crime or the conviction of it. Dramatic last-minute pardons of people destined for the gas chamber are the stuff of made-for-television movies and documentaries. The most notable pardon in history thus far has been that of President Gerald Ford toward former President Richard Nixon for his role in the Watergate scandal.

Ideally, trial by jury enables the defendant to receive a fair and impartial hearing by a competent tribunal of his or her peers. Ideally, such a jury weighs all the evidence carefully and renders a judgment free of bias and hidden agendas. However, since all juries are made up of fallible and impressionable human beings, such nondiscriminatory justice is often hard to come by, as Art Buchwald points out in the following commentary:

The Rationale Approach to Justice

One of the most interesting legal judgments . . . has the business world agog. Penzoil, a maker of motor oil, sued Texaco for improperly trying to acquire Getty Oil Co.

How naughty was Texaco? According to a verdict handed down by a Houston jury, Texaco behaved badly enough to have to cough up $11 billion.

The question that many people are asking is how the jury arrived at the $11 billion figure. Why not $9 billion or $15 billion?

I have a hunch that this is what happened.

First, it was by no means a simple lawsuit. It involved charges or intrigue, double-crossing and many horrendous white-collar crimes that cannot be mentioned in a family newspaper. Suffice to say that Penzoil had agreement to purchase Getty Oil and Texaco moved in to sabotage the deal.

Thus Penzoil brought Texaco to court, where a jury of 12 humble citizens was asked to rule on a case that 95% of all the judges in Texas would have trouble understanding.

The jurors listened with rapt attention to the witnesses and read page upon page of evidence. They also had to bone up on antitrust law, petroleum law, punitive damages, merger and acquisition rulings and Robert's Rules of Order.

Finally, after hearing the complicated presentations of both sides, the jury retired to discuss the verdict.

The first juror rendered his opinion. "I've heard the evidence and I would just like to say one thing. Five years ago I drove into a Texaco station and the attendant would not wipe my windshield. So I say we give the Penzoil Company $1 billion."

A second juror said, "I tried to get air from a Texaco station for my bike when I was a kid and the man with the hat told me to buzz off. Let's fine Texaco $2 billion."

"The owner of a Texaco station in Louisiana wouldn't let me use the men's room because I didn't buy any gas. If that isn't worth a billion dollars I don't know what is."

Each juror had a different reason for raising the penalty. One happened to be a happy Penzoil consumer. He said he and his family had been using their oil for years and found that quality outstanding. He stated, "It's so good you can drink it."

Another juror socked it to the defendant because the Texaco station near him closes at nine o'clock.

The damages added up to $12 billion. But the 12th juror had not been heard from.

He stood up and said, "Aren't you ashamed of yourselves? You are all punishing Texaco for slights, real or imagined, committed against you. Our job is to judge the merits of the case. We have to ask ourselves, was Texaco guilty of dirty tricks, or are the Penzoil people just a bunch of sore losers? Forget your personal vendettas and let justice be done. Let's have some charity in our hearts and not force a poor multinational to go begging at this time of year."

There were tears in many jurors' eyes after hearing the plea.

The foreman got up. "You are right. We were trying to get revenge when we should judge this case of the evidence. Let's start over again and decide what penalty to assess without rancor."

The foreman passed a pad around the room. Each person wrote a number on it. The paper came back to the foreman who said, "This is more like it. The final figure is $10 billion."

The 12th juror jumped up and said, "Hey, guys, why not make it $11 billion, so we can get into the Guinness Book of World Records.

INTRODUCTION TO CIVIL LAW

The civil court system is set up almost exactly the same way that the criminal courts are, except that the lowest level of civil court is called small claims as opposed to district. Thus, it goes from small claims court to municipal, superior, appellate and, ultimately, the supreme court.

Just as crimes are tried in the criminal court system, torts or civil wrongs are tried in the civil courts. A tort is simply a wrongful act or damage done, excluding a breach of contract, for which the injured person is due compensation. An example of a tort would be if the proprietor of a business did not keep her floors swept free of debris which could induce a fall, and someone ends up breaking a bone as a result of falling over this debris. This tort is an example of negligence and is eligible for trial in a civil court.

The five courts are separated from one another on a monetary basis. That is, suits in which the damages being sought are between $1.00 and $5,000 are tried in small claims court. In municipal court, the suits run between $5,001 and $25,000. Superior court hears suits that are $25,001 and up. Appellate court listens to appeals, and supreme court is the highest court of appeals for all civil as well as criminal cases.

PRIVATE INVESTIGATOR'S ACT

Private investigation is a field that requires a substantial working knowledge of the law. It is itself subject to fairly strict regulation, delineating exactly what a private investigator may and may not do. For example, the Private Investigator Act forbids anyone to perform the duties of a private investigator without a license to do so. Also, private investigators may not wear badges or masquerade as peace officers. They cannot divulge any information gained during the course of an investigation to anyone other than the client for whom the information was gathered, unless that information pertains to a criminal offense—at which case, the investigator may reveal it to a law enforcement official or district attorney.

In California, private investigators are regulated by the Bureau of Security and Investigative Services, which is a bureau in the Department of Consumer Affairs. The laws governing private investigators in the state of California are set forth in the Private Investigator Act, which appears in the Appendix. You should read it carefully to familiarize yourself with the stipulations and prohibitions it contains.

INFORMATION ABOUT LICENSING

In order to be a candidate for receiving your license, there are a number of conditions and requirements that you must meet. A criminal history check is made on all applicants for licensure, and a person may be denied a license if he or she has been convicted of a crime that is substantially related to the functions or duties of private investigating. If you have committed any act involving dishonesty, fraud or deceit with the specific intention of either greatly improving your own circumstances or injuring someone else, you may well be denied a license. Other possible grounds for being refused a license would be if you had performed some activity prior to receiving a license that only licensed individuals are legally allowed to perform.

Before applying for a license, one must have at least three years, with a total of 2,000 hours each year, of compensated experience. This includes, among others, policemen, military police, insurance adjusters, and those individuals who are employed by a licensed private investigator. People who have an associate of arts degree in police science, criminal law, or justice from an accredited institution will receive credit for 1,000 hours of investigative work, or six months. People with a bachelor's degree in the same courses, or those with a law degree, will get credit for 2,000 hours, or one year.

Experience that does not count toward qualifying hours includes that gained as an independent contractor, a server of legal process, or as someone who searches public records to find people or information. People who transport criminals, conduct investigations for attorneys, or repossess property are also not eligible to receive compensatory credit for the hours spent in those activities.

CODE OF ETHICS

For physicians, it's the Hippocratic Oath. They solemnly swear to preserve the sanctity of human life and to act at all times with the best interest of the patient in mind. For private investigators, there is no one standardized list but rather a collection of traits and goals that, taken together, comprise the professional investigator's code of ethics.

Because the public often has a jaundiced and rather skeptical view of private investigators, it is absolutely critical that professionals in this field conduct themselves in an irreproachable manner. Too many books and movies—the recent blockbuster, *The Client,* being no exception—portray private investigators as seedy, rapacious, and morally reprehensible. They do not show the dedication, creative ability, and hard work that really go into a successful career as an investigator. Therefore, it is vital that we as investigators make every effort to present ourselves as professionals of integrity in a viable and worthwhile field.

Edward Smith breaks down these ethical obligations into five general principles:

1. Perform investigations in a professional, moral and ethical manner.
2. Work within the framework of the law.
3. Conduct investigations in a lawful manner.
4. Protect confidential information.
5. Tell the whole truth when presenting information.[6]

While this list does encapsulate the ideals and principles we should all espouse, a more detailed rendering is useful in providing more explicit

---

[6]Smith, p. 2.

guidelines for behavior. The following is intended to give you a clear picture of what your ethical obligations should look like.

I WILL STRIVE TO KEEP MYSELF INFORMED OF DEVELOPMENTS AND TECHNIQUES AFFECTING MY PROFESSION.

I WILL CONDUCT MYSELF IN A BUSINESS-LIKE MANNER BEFITTING A PROFESSIONAL.

I WILL MAKE NO CLAIMS TO QUALIFICATIONS I DO NOT POSSESS.

I WILL BE LOYAL TO MY CLIENT AND DIVULGE THE INFORMATION I OBTAIN ONLY TO HIM/HER OR THEIR REPRESENTATIVE.

I WILL NOT INVOLVE MYSELF IN INVESTIGATIONS ON BEHALF OF A CLIENT WITH THE INTENT TO BREAK THE LAW OR TO USE THE INFORMATION UNETHICALLY.

I WILL NOT PROVIDE MY CLIENTS WITH ADVICE OR COUNSEL OF A DISCIPLINE IN WHICH I AM NOT QUALIFIED.

I WILL NOT USE MY POSITION OF TRUST FOR UNETHICAL GAINS.

I WILL NOT ACCEPT INVESTIGATIONS WHICH CONFLICT WITH PREVIOUS OR CURRENT INVESTIGATIONS.

I WILL BE HONEST, ACCURATE, FACTUAL, AND COMPLETE IN MY REPORTING.

I WILL NOT REPRESENT MYSELF AS A MEMBER OF LAW ENFORCEMENT.

I WILL CHARGE MY CLIENT ACCORDING TO OUR AGREEMENT.

I WILL HONOR MY VERBAL AGREEMENTS AS IF THEY WERE IN WRITING.

Unfortunately, even if the private investigator is beyond reproach in his or her ethical intentions, not every client is as scrupulous. There was one instance in which an individual procured the services of an investigator to determine whether or not the people up the street from him were involved in illicit drug trafficking and other misdeeds. The investigator conducted a background check on these neighbors, did surveillance, and eventually determined that yes indeed, these people were up to no good. The investigator then returned to the client with this information and the investigation was concluded. However, the client later decided to march up to those neighbors with a shotgun and kill them. Does this mean that the investigator was somehow liable for the role he played in the unfortunate incident? Not at all. He acted in good faith, doing his job within the confines of the law, and reporting the desired information back to the person who had paid him for it. It was not his place to determine why such information was being sought. However, if he had known beforehand that the client wanted the information specifically for the intent of murdering the neighbors, then the investigator would have been ethically and legally bound to refuse the investigation.

Finally, the California Association of Licensed Investigators has issued their own statement concerning the ethical standard by which a private investigator should be bound:

CODE OF ETHICS

Each and every member of the California Association of Licensed Investigators, Inc., subscribes to and circumscribes his or her activities set out in the Code of Ethics.

Duties of the Investigator in Civil and Criminal Cases

The primary duty of an investigator engaged in either civil or criminal cases is to determine the true facts and to render honest, unbiased reports in reference thereto.

Duty to a Client

The best interests of a client may be served by maintaining a high standard of work and reporting to a client the full facts ascertained as a result of the work and effort expended whether they be advantageous or detrimental to the interests of the client, and that nothing be withheld from said client save by the dictates of the law. It should be borne in mind at all times that the duties of the investigator should be within the bounds of the law or any manner of fraud.

Duty to the Public and to the Profession

An investigator or security professional should at all times maintain a high standard of conduct, personally and professionally, that may serve as a good example to others.

Confidence of a Client

The duty to preserve the client's confidence outlasts the employment of an investigator, and extends as well to his or her employees; and neither of them should accept employment which involves the disclosure or use of the confidence for the private advantage of the client without his or her knowledge and consent, even though there are other available sources of information. An investigator should not continue employment when he or she discovers that this obligation prevents the performance of his or her full duty to his or her former or new client.

Advertising

The most worthy and effective advertising possible is the establishment of a well-merited reputation for professional capacity and fidelity to trust. This can only be built by character and conduct. The solicitation of business by misleading advertising is unprofessional and is prohibited.

Retainers and Fees

Controversies with clients concerning compensation can best be avoided by the protection of some form of written agreement of letter. It should never be forgotten that the investigation business is a profession and all financial dealings with clients should be handled on that basis.

REPORT WRITING

Earlier this chapter I described the primary duty of the private investigator as the gathering of facts and the drawing of logical conclusions from those facts. The work product of an investigator, therefore, is the presentation of data gained as a result of his or her investigation, which is the report. A well-written report accomplishes three things: it provides the reader with a clear, comprehensible picture of the incident; it influences the attitude of the reader; and it guides the reader toward further action. In addition, a well-written report reflects the writer's level of professionalism—or, indeed, a poorly written report illustrates a *lack* of professionalism. Therefore, it is very important that you learn how to present your facts clearly, thoroughly, and concisely. The standard of your work will be judged not by how many hours you spend sitting in a surveillance van or how "cool" you look in a slouch hat and overcoat, but by how well your reports are written.

A good report, then, is one that enables any person, investigator or otherwise, to understand clearly the known facts regarding what happened, the steps that have been taken in response to the incident. After reading the report, the reader should be as well informed about the matter and all its relevant facts as the person who was actually present during the occurrence and who wrote the report.

The report should be clear, written with simple and easy to understand language in a logical and/or chronological order. You may well have an exhaustive and impressive vocabulary full of words that sound wonderful and mean virtually nothing to most people on the street. Your intent in writing the report is not to dazzle the reader by how verbose and well-phrased you are. Your intent is to communicate information in a manner that will leave no room for doubt or misunderstanding. Therefore, you should write as though you could see each event happening before you.

Concise reports are absolutely essential. Relay only the necessary facts, which basically means that your report should answer the six basic questions of the Investigator's Code: who, what, when, where, how, and why. Avoid giving opinions or personal conclusions unless they are clearly identified as such and are relevant to the report. In other words, don't present your opinion as fact just because you are completely convinced that it is. Stick to the facts.

Thirdly, your report should be correct, which means that all the information contained in it is accurate and objective. Stay away from emotional statements or words that may color the facts. Make sure that, to the best of your ability, all grammar, spelling, and punctuation is correct.

Finally, make sure the report is complete and covers all relevant areas pertaining to the incident under scrutiny. If the reader has any questions after reviewing your report, then it is incomplete.

The basic element of all reports is, once again, to communicate information. A report describes an incident, situation or condition, both to your department and to other concerned departments, persons, or agencies. Keep these audiences in mind when you write your report.

The most difficult portion of any report is the narrative, or that part that actually tells the story of what happened. This entails that you will not only need to be able to express yourself succinctly in writing, but that you will have to know how to conduct a good investigation in order to produce the information that will be contained in the narrative. Investigation and reporting, then, are intrinsically related to one another. While there are many reasons for conducting an investigation, all of them have the same ultimate goal: to discover the truth. You need to be able to ask the right questions in order to receive the right answers.

In addition to answering all the right questions, your report must be written in chronological order. Everything that happens has a beginning and an end within a certain span of time. You should begin your report at the start of what happened and relay each subsequent event in the order that it occurred, until your narrative is concluded. This may seem self-obvious, but it is an essential element of organization that provides coherence and logical progression to your report; without it, your report will be disjointed, hard to follow, and certainly unprofessional.

Since detail and accuracy are so crucial in writing your report, you will need to know how to give a good "portrait parle" of the people and vehicles you are describing in your report. A portrait parle is a "spoken picture," or a verbal description of a person or thing's physical appearance. For a person, you should provide these seven traits, in order: gender, ethnicity, hair color, eye color, age, height, and weight. For a vehicle, you should give these five traits in order: VIN number, license plate, make, model, and color. There are other traits for both people and vehicles that you may report on, but we will get to those in later chapters. For now, you should just get into the habit of identifying these traits on people you meet and know, and cars that you see as you drive. Practice will increase your ability to swiftly and accurately identify people and vehicles, so that when you are in the field on an investigation you will not have trouble describing to your client all that you see in great detail.

In order to write good reports, then, no skill is more important than the ability to observe or perceive the facts. Toward that end, you, as the investigator, will need to be able to relate your observations with completeness and accuracy. Spell names and places correctly, always give the correct time, and make sure that your writing is legible. When giving the time, use the 24-hour military time instead of the 12-hour. For example, instead of 3:00 PM, you would write 1500 hours. For 4:00 AM, you would write 0400 hours. Midnight is 2400 hours, 11:00 AM is 1100 hours, noon is 1200 hours, and 1:00 PM is 1300 hours. Also, when writing reports, always print in block letters using all capitals, in black ink.

The most important thing to remember, finally, about writing reports, is that this is the product upon which your whole investigation will be judged. Take pride in your work. Be meticulous, accurate and methodical, and the satisfaction of your client will be an added bonus to the inward satisfaction you will feel from a job well done.

REVIEW

1. What is the definition of "investigation"?
2. Give the Investigator's Code.
3. Name three firms for which private investigators are often employed.
4. What is "habeas corpus"?
5. Who was Harry Fielding?
6. What are the bobbies?
7. Where did the term "Private Eye" originate?
8. Give the three types of crime and the punishment for them.
9. True or False: There are only two types of intent: specific and general.
10. Name the five criminal court levels.
11. Name the five civil court levels and give the monetary limitations of each.
12. What does it mean to be released on one's own recognizance?

13. What is a plea bargain?
14. What do probation officers do?
15. What is the bureau that regulates private investigators in the state of California?
16. How many hours of compensated experience do you need before you may apply for a license? How many years?
17. How many hours of credit does someone with an associate's degree in police science receive?
18. Give five ethical standards by which private investigators should abide.
19. What are the seven traits that go into a portrait parle of an individual?
20. Why should reports be written in chronological order?

Chapter 2

NARCOTICS

Professor Emeritus Albert C. Germann tells a story that goes something like this:

You and your partner are police officers on foot patrol sometime during the late 1920's. On this particular evening, you and your partner—we'll call him Nick—walk into a restaurant on your beat and find a couple and their young child enjoying a dinner of spaghetti and meatballs. As you get closer to the table, you see that both the man and his wife are drinking a glass of red wine with their pasta. Now, times being what they are, and the two of you being the dutiful policemen that you are, you place the couple under arrest and take their child into protective custody.

After work, you and Nick go unwind with other officers of your department in that ritual known to policemen as "choir practice." As you stand around discussing the events of your day and all the arrests you made, you and Nick, still in uniform light up two marijuana cigarettes and tell your buddies about that poor couple you arrested just a few hours previous. Does this make you and Nick hypocrites? Not at all; in the late 1920's, marijuana was not illegal. Nor, for that matter, was cocaine.

Now suppose it is 1994. You and Nick, who have somehow managed to arrive at this present time without aging, are out again on patrol and wander into this same restaurant—which, despite a few remodelings and a name change to "Rubio's Pasta Palace," has remained essentially unchanged. And there, also untouched by age, is the couple and their child. Except this time, instead of enjoying a glass of red wine together, the man and woman are sharing a marijuana cigarette. As dutiful as ever, you and Nick arrest the couple, take their child into protective custody, and tell your buddies about this ill-fated couple while all of you sit around at a local bar drinking a few beers.

Because, as everyone knows, marijuana is illegal in 1995.

INTRODUCTION

If you were to ask most people whether or not it is a crime to be under the influence of a drug, chances are they would tell you "yes." And yet if you ask these same people if it is a crime to enjoy a wine cooler or a shot of tequila, they would probably laugh at you. Certainly, in 1995, at least, it is *not* a crime to be under the influence of alcohol, or of caffeine, nicotine, diet pills, etc. To most people, the word "drug" links up instantaneously with cocaine, or heroin, or other "controlled substances" about which the American populace has heard so much. For our purposes, "drug" shall be defined to be any substance that is ingested into the body and produces an effect. Some examples of nondangerous, but still habit-forming drugs are caffeine, as in the coffee (or tea) you have to have in the morning in order to face the day, and chocolate.

A word that has become synonymous with drugs is "narcotics." Even though people often use these words interchangeably, they are in fact qualitatively distinct. A narcotic is clinically defined to be any derivative of opium, which is an extract from poppies that induces sleep, relieves pain, and can become incredibly addictive. Thus, heroin, morphine, and opium, and all their derivatives, are narcotics. A handy way to differentiate between "drugs" and "narcotics" is to remember that all narcotics are drugs, whereas all drugs are *not* narcotics.

Drug-related deaths are becoming increasingly common. By some estimates, drug abuse ranks as the third most common way to die in the United States, with cancer being first and AIDS coming in second. Because of the prevalence and seriousness of drug abuse in our country, it is important for the private investigator to be familiar with some of the most common drugs and how to identify them, the legislation surrounding drugs, and those controlled substances commonly found in the workplace.

COMMON DRUGS AND IDENTIFYING THEM

The following descriptions of drugs and their effects are in no way intended to be taken as complete and definitive. They are provided to give you as a private investigator a working knowledge of some of the more common drugs you might encounter as you go through your career. For more precise explanations of the effects of drugs and how to identify them, you should certainly do some more in-depth research on your own.

Heroin

Heroin is a narcotic which, as already stated, means that it is a derivative of opium. However, it can be up to three times more powerful in effect than morphine, which is another opium derivative, and much more addictive. Bitter and odorless, heroin ranges in color from white to brown, depending upon the origin of the drug and whatever additives were used in the refining process. For example, heroin from Mexico tends to be tan or brown, whereas from the Far East it is usually white. It belongs to the general category of drugs known as "depressants," because it serves to lower the rate of vital activities. In other words, it acts as a sedative upon the central nervous system and the resultant effects upon the user include slower movements and speech, constricted or shrunken pupils and drowsiness, among others.

The methods of ingesting heroin include swallowing, sniffing, and smoking, but the most common by far is injecting. A heroin addict, generally referred to as a junkie, is notorious for the often unsanitary or even primitive means with which he or she acquires the "fix," and of course, the use of dirty needles has widely propagated the AIDS virus. The typical drug "kit" or paraphernalia of heroin abusers includes three essential items: a syringe, a spoon or bottle cap, and some kind of heat source, whether a match, lighter, torch, or whatever. Many kits will also contain a belt or rubber tube or some kind of ligament to be used as a tourniquet. Injecting the drug directly into the vein is called "mainlining," whereas "skin popping" refers to the less effective method of shooting into any fleshy part of the body.

Before the drug can be injected, a quantity of it is first diluted with a small amount of water, in a teaspoon or bottle cap, which are commonly referred to as "cookers." The match or lighter is then applied to dissolve the drug, which is sucked into the syringe and injected directly into the user's vein. Injection is the preferred method of ingestion because none of the drug is wasted; smoking allows a significant quantity of the heroin to dissipate into the air and thus some of the potential high is lost. Also, the initial effects of the drug are greater via mainlining as opposed to other means of ingestion, because it goes directly into the bloodstream.

Some of the common names you may encounter in reference to heroin are junk, Mexican mud, brown sugar, horse, smack, dope, and joy powder, among others. Slang referents to drugs change rapidly, so this is by no means a fixed or exhaustive list.

There are many ways to determine whether a person is under the influence of heroin. As already mentioned, heroin is a depressant, which means that it slows down bodily processes. Hence, movements will be slower, speech will be slower, and reaction will be delayed. Whereas with alcoholic intoxication you often find a stagger or lurch in a person's walk, a heroin user typically glides or seems to be almost "floating" when they walk. If you happen upon someone who has very recently injected him or herself with the drug, you may notice that his or her mind appears to be somewhere else; when asked a direct question, he or she may come up with an unrelated response, or seem to have difficulty focusing on you. Perhaps they are scratching a lot—heroin effects and induces a tingly, pervasive itch. Also, their skin may appear clammy or damp, as heroin stimulates the skin's sweat glands. As a result, chronic abuse of heroin dehydrates the body to such an extent that the addict often has brittle nails and dry mouth and skin, and can develop a craving for sweets or soft drinks. Of course, this isn't to say that everyone who drinks a six-pack of Pepsi™ soda every day is a heroin addict!

Perhaps the most tell-tale sign of heroin abuse is track marks, which are the scars left behind after intravenous injections. Typically, these marks will be in the arms, directly over the veins. A fresh mark, that originates from an extremely recent injection, will appear to be an oozing red dot, whereas marks that are a little older will show as slightly elevated orange scabs with red borders. Further along in the healing process, the color changes to light or dark brown. Very old and almost fully healed marks show signs of rejuvenated skin, which look like silver blue streaks. It is important to remember, however, that heroin addicts *know* that track marks are dead giveaways, and so they will go to great lengths to hide them. A common tactic is the use of tattoos. Other methods include shooting up in less visible parts of the body, such as the hands, behind the neck, under the arms, or even for males, in the scrotum.

Initial users of heroin may feel nauseous, or even vomit, but after adjustment to the drug will experience an intense euphoria. The "rush" lasts from four to six hours, during the course of which the user may become drowsy and lethargic, sometimes even lapsing into a semiconscious state. His pupils constrict to generally below 2.9 mm, which normal pupil size being between 2.9 and 6.5 mm, depending upon the individual and the lighting conditions. Long-term abusers often have little or no desire for food, and their libido decreases markedly.

Heroin is a dramatically, physically-addictive drug; it and cocaine are the only two drugs animals will self-administer until they die. Because of the extreme physical dependence users develop upon heroin, the withdrawal symptoms are quite excruciating. They can include, among others, delirium, physical pain, hot flashes, sweating, nausea, diarrhea, fever, and even seizures. In fact, the term "kicking the habit" originated from the involuntary twitching that ensues after a forty-eight hour period of withdrawal from heroin.

One school of thought maintains that once a person is addicted to heroin, he or she never fully "recover." In other words, "once an addict, always an addict." In Great Britain, for example, it is accepted that persons who are addicted to heroin will remain so for the rest of their lives, and thus a program has been implemented whereby junkies are given their weekly and/or daily injections of heroin by medically-trained personnel. By having government workers administer the drug, the unhygienic practice of sharing needles or "shooting up" in unsafe and unsanitary conditions is abolished, and the government is able to monitor the amount of drug the junkie ingests. While some people may have a moral objection to this practice, arguing that it tacitly condones drug abuse, it is also arguable that it is a means of containment and regulation of a problem that in all likelihood will never entirely disappear.

Cocaine

Another widely abused drug is cocaine. Even though people commonly associate it with heroin, it is in fact fundamentally different in that it is a stimulant and serves to increase energy levels, libido, and drive. It delivers a short-lived euphoria, ranging from one to two hours, and can be smoked, inhaled, injected, or even taken orally, through application to the gums, palate, or underside of the tongue. When absorbed into the blood, cocaine is a very powerful drug indeed; a tiny amount (from 1 to 3 milligrams) releases a chemical called norepinephrine from the body's nerve endings, which has a profound stimulating effect on the brain. Because it has become the drug of choice for "white-collar" users, such as lawyers, doctors, and other professionals, and for Hollywood personalities, cocaine is extremely expensive. It may come in a variety of forms: rock chunks, commonly called "crack;" a white, odorless, and bitter powder; or even a liquid that is injected into the bloodstream. As little as one gram, taken at one sitting, has been known to cause overdose, which can cause increased body temperature, hallucinations, convulsions, and even respiratory failure, which in turn can lead to cardiac arrest and death.

As a stimulant, cocaine induces a marked mood elevation in which the user reports a feeling of euphoria, heightened energy, and augmented physical and mental capabilities. Medically, cocaine is an anesthetic, which means that it relieves pain; fatigue disappears; the user feels imminently capable, smarter, more alert. However, some unwanted effects of cocaine use include restlessness, hallucinations, or even a form of paranoia in which the user may feel that insects or snakes are crawling beneath their skin. Some of the physical effects of cocaine use are an elevated pulse rate, dilated pupils, rapid heartbeat, higher blood pressure, insomnia, and loss of appetite. The person becomes excitable, more talkative, and experiences a sense of heightened mental acuity. Even more so than intoxicated individuals, cocaine abusers' eyes may be red and watery, with a dilated pupil size of over 6.5 mm (recall that normal pupil size ranges between 2.9 and 6.5 mm). Generally, this translates into a pupil that is more than one-half the distance to the outer edge of the iris.

Unlike heroin, cocaine induces predominantly psychological dependence. While there is the potential for physical dependence, it is not nearly as great as that with heroin. Withdrawal symptoms are not the violently physical ones of the heroin junkie but rather can be depression, anxiety, nervousness, irritability, and headaches. Cocaine abuse creates behavioral dependence: a strong craving in the brain to duplicate the surge of euphoria, and of course, to avoid the let-down that invariably follows the rush.

One of the most common means of ingesting cocaine is to inhale it, or "snort" it. As a result, a possible means of detecting the chronic cocaine abuser is to look at the individual's nose, which will typically be red or swollen. Snorting destroys the sensitive mucous membrane of the nose and can even cause perforation of the nasal septum, which is the narrow cartilaginous strip separating the nostrils. A nose that is constantly runny or even bleeding, on an individual that does not have allergies or any other medical condition that would legitimize a chronic sinus problem, may be a pretty good sign that the person you see before you is a cocaine addict.

An interesting article in the *National Geographic* about how cocaine is made and the effects of its manufacture upon the environment discusses how the rain forests of Peru, Columbia, and Bolivia are becoming contaminated with all the toxic process by which the finished product is obtained. First, the coca leaves are soaked in sulfuric acid. Next, they are strained from the liquid, which will then be mixed with such chemicals as kerosene, lime, and ammonia to make cocaine base. After further refinement with acetone, ether, and hydrochloric acid, the base becomes cocaine hydrochloride, which is the drug itself.

The article goes on to report that approximately 308 tons of cocaine were confiscated around the world in 1993. To make that much cocaine, 38 million gallons of kerosene, 1.1 million gallons of solvents, 295,000 gallons of sulfuric acid, 18,500 gallons of hydrochloric acid, and 3,700 gallons of ammonia were used. A huge percentage of these chemicals are being dumped into river systems, causing widespread pollution and destroying aquatic life. Thus, cocaine and its use poses more than just a societal problem: it has become an environmental hazard as well.

Marijuana

Just as cocaine comes from coca leaves, marijuana is a derivative of the hardy Indian hemp plant *Cannabis Sativa*. In unprocessed form marijuana is the dried and crushed leaves of the cannabis plant, resembling the small granules of oregano or tea leaves. Some common names for it include grass, pot, weed, smoke, Jane, and reefer. Marijuana, as indicated in the opening anecdote, is a drug whose status in the legal system of the United States has been in a state of flux. Although it is at present illegal in this country, it was not always outlawed, and as you probably know there is currently a large and heated debate raging about whether or not hemp/marijuana should in fact be legalized. A lot of the controversy surrounding this particular drug stems from the seemingly contradictory medical information concerning the addictiveness of marijuana, the possibility of long-term and/or permanent damage as a result of using the drug, and any potential medicinal benefits of its use. And, of course, you have the hippie holdouts who claim that hemp is the cure-all for what ails the world, touting it as the next best fuel source, the most logical material out of which to make paper, or even as the solution to world hunger.

For our purposes, we will focus exclusively on those properties of marijuana which have earned it its classification as a controlled substance. So, as a controlled substance, marijuana belongs to the class of drugs known as hallucinogens. Typically, the effects of marijuana last from between two to four hours, during which are experienced feelings of mild euphoria, distortions in the way time and space are perceived, and relaxation. Memory can be slightly impaired, physical functions and motor coordination suffer, and reactions become slower. The most notice-able physical reaction is a reddening of the eyes, and there is also a very slight dilation of the pupils. Users report a keener sense of hearing, which is explained by the fact that all their other senses are suppressed, so that their hearing, by comparison, seems sharper. Under larger doses, users have reported that they experience vivid, visual imagery, some-times even to the extent of hallucinations. Marijuana is popular at parties because it tends to make even the mundane seem extraordinarily amusing. It also promotes wakefulness in social settings, so people can be extraordinarily amused longer into the night. When used in isolation, however, marijuana can have just the opposite effect and make the user feel drowsy or somewhat lethargic.

The most common way to ingest marijuana is to smoke it, either in pipes or "bongs," or in small hand-rolled cigarettes called joints. Of course, it can also be taken orally—people have been known to bake it into brownies, for instance. Because it is generally fairly inexpensive—the cost varies from state to state, but it is usually under $1,000 per pound—and can also be grown quite easily in one's backyard or even on inconspicuous window sills, it is an easy drug to obtain, and the National Institute on Drug Abuse has said that one out of every ten high school seniors smokes pot every day. These same statistics indicate that possibly 55 million Americans have tried marijuana and 23 million use it regularly.

Of the more than 400 known chemical compounds in marijuana, it is delta-9-tetrahydrocannabinol, or THC, that produces the mind-altering effects. It is a thick, sticky resin plentiful in the upper leaves and flowers of the plant. In unprocessed form, marijuana consists of the dried leaves of the cannabis plant and contains a THC concentration of roughly $1\frac{1}{2}$ to $2\frac{1}{2}$ percent. Some studies have shown that THC is fat soluble, which means that it clings to fat cells and therefore is not processed by the body's natural detoxifiers, namely the liver and kidneys. Because of this, it is possible for THC to accumulate in the body, which can cause noticeable apathy, listlessness, loss of ambition and drive, increased narcissism, moodiness, irritability, and a loss of concern for personal hygiene. A variety of research has also linked the build-up of THC with brain damage, lung cancer, sterility, decreased sperm counts, chromo-somal abnormalities, and even breakdown of the body's natural immune system, which in turn results in higher susceptibility to infection. Other side effects of this accumulation of marijuana in the system could include spontaneous recurrence, also known as "flashbacks," which have been reported by some users days or even weeks after having last used marijuana. It is important to remember that THC, the active ingredient in marijuana, can be detected in the blood and urine for at least a week, and usually from ten to thirty-five days.

The medical evidence that exists concerning marijuana is contradictory and, in comparison with what we know about alcohol and tobacco, very sketchy. As mentioned above, marijuana use has been linked to brain damage and other serious somatic ailments, while other studies have shown that the long-term effects of marijuana are negligible when compared with those of cigarette smoking or alcohol use. It is unarguable that smoking anything, whether pot or cigarettes or whatever else people choose to put a match to, can cause respiratory damage. However, people like Mark Kleiman, associate professor at Harvard's John F. Kennedy School of Government, claims in his work *Against Excess* that "the quarter century since large numbers of Americans began to use marijuana has produced remarkably little laboratory or epidemiological evidence of serious health damage done by the drug." Kleiman faces opponents like Dr. Michael Horwitz of Cedars-Sinai Medical Center, who asserts that chronic users of marijuana may develop mental disorders such as acute panic of long-term memory deficiencies, or other impairments including brain atrophy, infertility, and emphysema. Horwitz says that the problem with marijuana is that the adverse consequences may not appear overtly dangerous; unlike with alcoholism, which will eventually destroy the liver and cause the eyes to turn yellow from jaundice—an extremely attention-getting indication that something is wrong.

Another issue under debate is whether or not marijuana is addictive, and if it is, whether it is physical or psychological. With drugs like heroin, there is no question about its addictiveness and the profound physical dependence users develop. Dr. Hoffman believes that people who do become physically dependent upon marijuana may not realize it because the withdrawal symptoms—irritability, insomnia, stomach cramps, and headaches, among others—take several weeks to manifest. Roger Roffman, associate professor at University of Washington, also believes that habitual smoking can produce the physical craving to continue doing so; but even he, who has been studying the effects of long-term marijuana smoking since 1986, has to agree that "marijuana dependence is not very well understood, and there haven't been many efforts to study it or treat it." ["Danger? Debate Smolders" Irene Lacher, LA Times, Sept. 8, 1993].

Sinsemilla

Sinsemilla literally means "without seeds" and refers to the female marijuana plant, specifically the heavy, flowering tops which are richly endowed with THC. The cultivation of sinsemilla involves the identification and removal of male *Cannabis Sativa* plants before pollination of the female plants can take place. In comparison with marijuana, which typically has a THC concentration of under 2 percent, sinsemilla can have up to 10 percent.

The effects of sinsemilla are similar to marijuana, as are the methods of its ingestion, due to its higher concentration of THC content, and because of the more labor-intensive cultivation. Commonly, it is believed that one person cannot adequately care for more than 50 plants at one time.

Hashish

Yet another derivative of the ubiquitous cannabis plant, hashish is the dried and pressed resin that is mixed with some of the plant's fiber to form a hard rock-like lump. Depending upon the amount of resin in the mixture, hashish can range in color from light brown to black. The usual method of ingestion is to smoke it in a pipe, whether a commercially sold "hash pipe" made of wood and metal, or the more exotic "waterpipes," which help regulate intake while cooling the smoke. Another method is to sprinkle it atop tobacco and smoke it that way.

The THC content of hashish is higher than that of either sinsemilla or marijuana, ranging from anywhere from 5 to 10 percent. As such, the effects of smoking hashish are even more intense.

Hash Oil

The most potent extract of the cannabis plant is hash oil, or liquid hashish. Not always a liquid per se, hash oil can sometimes have the consistency of honey or tar and can come in a variety of colors: clear, yellow, red, dark brown, or black. It is obtained through the use of a high-vacuum distillation process in which marijuana leaves are boiled and any sediment is filtered out from the ensuing resin. The THC content of hash oil is very high, between 20 to 60 percent—three to ten times the content of marijuana or hash. Therefore, hash oil can be quite expensive, with one pint costing $7,000 and up; because of both the expense and the potency, one ounce of hash oil will often be stretched into 2,000 doses or more.

The usual means of ingestion is to place one drop of the oil on a marijuana cigarette or even a regular tobacco cigarette, resulting in an increase of potency. It can also be smoked in an opium pipe, or even mixed with such liquids as coffee or wine so that it may be taken orally. Again, the effects are similar to those produced by marijuana, hashish and sinsemilla, except they are greatly intensified.

Because the oil is often packaged in small and innocuous vials, it is often hard for law enforcement personnel to detect. It, like heroin and cocaine, has no distinctive odor, but is easier to illicitly transport because of the many ways in which it can be concealed. Some examples of this include storing it in prophylactic sheaths or dissolving it in liquor, perfumes, and aftershave lotions.

LSD

Whereas marijuana and its sister cannabis derivatives are fairly mild hallucinogens, LSD, or lysergic acid diethylamide, is a much more explosive and potentially dangerous mind-altering drug. The primary effect of LSD on the user is to exaggerate emotional reactions and perceptions, because it has an overstimulating effect upon the section of the brain that controls vision and perception. Colors will seem brighter, objects will appear luminous, often with an "aura" or "halo" about them. The user will appear to overreact to ordinary objects, due to an altered perception of reality. He or she will be utterly enthralled by what he or she sees; or else be very depressed and unreasonably disturbed.

Physically, LSD precipitates a rise in bodily temperature, causing the user's face to appear flushed. Pupils dilate; dizziness and visual disturbance are common. The heart rate increases, while muscular coordination decreases, often resulting in a fine tremor in the user's fingertips. Facial contortions and a decreased urge to urinate are other common physical indicators of LSD use.

Perhaps the most distinguishing characteristic of LSD is that it always causes flashbacks, in which the user's body releases stored-up quantities of LSD and experiences all over again the mind-altering effects of the drug. Studies have shown that LSD, like marijuana, is not fat-soluble and adheres to the fat cells in the body, so that as these fat cells are metabolized, LSD is released into the bloodstream, eventually reaching the brain. Often these flashbacks are particularly trying for the user, because they take him or her by surprise and can sometimes be what is called a "bad trip," in which the person's relationship with the outside world can be totally shattered. An example of this is where the person's body image seems to change right before his or her eyes. Hallucinatory images of dismemberment or even of experiencing one's own death are not uncommon. It is important to remember that in practically no other psychological condition do people undergo such dramatic fluctuations in bodily image. Should you encounter someone who is in the grips of a "bad trip," the most effective way to handle that is to calmly reassure that person that he or she is all right, and that the effects of the trip will in fact wear off.

PCP

Another example of a drug that produces strong or even violent reactions in people who use it is PCP, or phencyclidine. Originally introduced as an anesthetic for large animals, such as horses and cows, PCP primarily effects the nervous and cardiovascular systems. It can be taken in a number of ways, such as smoking, snorting, injecting, and swallowing, because it comes in an array of forms, from solid to liquid; perhaps you have heard of "Super Cools," which were one method of ingestion in which Cool cigarettes were dipped in liquid PCP and then smoked to produce the desired high. However, because the PCP discolored the cigarettes to such an extent that they were easily detected by informed law enforcement officials, users turned to commercially-manufactured, dark cigarettes known as "shermans," because they would not noticeably darken after being dipped into the liquid PCP.

There are multifarious names for PCP on the street, some of which are angel dust, hog, goon, crystal joints, Crystal-T, cyclones, DOA, Cadillac, CJ, KJ, killer, dummy/monkey dust, Sherms, animal tranquilizer or "trank," rocket fuel, scuffle, supergrass, superweed, ozone, etc. Because there are constant shifts and adaptations in the way people refer to their drug, this list is by no means complete.

Initial effects of PCP usually come within one to five minutes after smoking it, and the high peaks after about thirty minutes. The duration of the high continues for some time after that, however, often lasting as long as six hours, and it is normally twenty-four to forty-eight hours later before the user is completely him or herself again. If the drug is taken regularly or in high doses, the effects can last for several weeks or even months.

A person on PCP typically feels an almost superhuman control of his surroundings. Because PCP is hallucinogenic in nature, it creates the impression in the user that he or she can change the shape of objects or people. Persons under the influence of this drug have described auditory and visual hallucinations, feelings of weightlessness, a sense of omnipotence, profound distortions of space and time, invulnerability, and out-of-body experiences. Some of the manifestations of PCP use include difficulty in standing and an exaggerated, deliberate gait, in which the user walks as if uncertain the ground below him isn't about to shift suddenly and cause him to lose his balance. Coordination becomes a difficult and intricate process, and speech is slurred. The individual has trouble concentrating, and the things said by him or her seem illogical or out of place. Blood pressure is elevated, up to 140/85 or greater, and bodily temperature rises, resulting in an increased pulse and amount of perspiration. Pupils are nonreactive; often there is a blank stare, almost as if the person is looking right through you. Muscles exhibit signs of spasticity or tension, and the person will often be grimacing or grinding his teeth. PCP affects perception and can cause delusions; often the person is grimacing because he may feel he is being attacked by insects or other vermin. In addition, users exhibit a condition known as nystagmus, in which the eyes jerk or bounce as they follow the progress of an object. For example, when you hold a pencil before their eyes and ask them to follow it as you move it across their field of vision, their eyes will jerk instead of following it in a smooth motion. This condition, known as horizontal nystagmus, in which the eyes bounce up and down while following an object, is almost exclusive to PCP users: only if his blood alcohol content is extremely high will a drunk person show signs of vertical nystagmus.

The most common characteristic of PCP influence is bizarre and unpredictable behavior. Because PCP is an anesthetic, it deadens a person's ability to perceive pain, thus adding to his or her belief that he or she is invincible. Mercurial shifts in mood and consciousness mean that you can never tell whether the person will be cooperative and communicative, or aggressive and violent; such shifts in behavior can occur in the span of a few seconds.

Another symptom of PCP use is the irresistible urge to remove clothing.

Because PCP causes an elevation in body temperature, clothes can become restrictive and uncomfortable. Users can also have violent reactions to sudden or bright light, loud noises or sharp unexpected movement. One way to try and subdue a PCP "tripper" is to reduce the amount of visual, auditory, and physical stimulation he or she receives.

When I was a police officer, I had a number of encounters with persons under the influence of PCP. I was out on patrol one night when a woman drove up alongside my patrol car and told me that some teenaged boy had just tried to carjack her. So I circled around and drove to where she said the incident had happened, but as I cruised down the street I could see no one around. I was just about to leave the neighborhood when I heard something crash onto the roof of my car. Now, even though people tell you not to lock all your car doors if you think there's a possibility you might get accosted, how many of us can resist that initial panic and keep from locking those doors? I couldn't. I locked my doors.

Pretty soon a face appeared, dangling down over my windshield. It was a kid I knew, Squeaky or Squiggy or something like that, a gang kid I'd dealt with before. Well, at this point I didn't know the kid was on PCP, so I turned on my lights to try and get him off my car. Wrong thing to do. He went ballistic on me and started trying to tear the light bar off the roof of the car. By this time it occurred to me that just maybe this kid was stoned, and having heard that PCP users were known to exhibit superhuman strength, I wasn't entirely sure that he wouldn't be able to rip that light bar right off the roof. So, while he was engaged in trying to destroy my car, I got out and made my way to one of the apartment complexes where I knew a friend of his lived. Luckily this guy was home, and when I told him that his buddy Squeaky was up on the roof of my car, this guy came out and talked him down. He was then arrested and taken to jail. My light bar, by the way, weathered the attack just fine.

Another incident happened to a friend, a police officer who works for the city of Pasadena. It was late one night after a party, and my friend, who had been drinking, decided that he really wasn't in the best shape for driving. So he pulled off the freeway onto the shoulder and was going to take a nap and just sleep it off. Well, not too long after he'd fallen asleep, a California Highway Patrol officer drove up and told my friend that he'd have to take him into the station. They were arguing about this for a few moments when they suddenly saw a naked man running toward them in the fast lane. Of course, this is California, and people might think things like this happen all the time. They don't. So the CHP officer went running after this man—fortunately for all concerned, traffic was at a minimum—caught up with him, and they both tumbled to the ground. In the scuffle, the man knocked the CHP officer out and it looked like things were not going to go the way of law and order. My friend managed to subdue the naked PCP user, got him into handcuffs, and put him in the back of the CHP officer's patrol car. Then, his duty done, he went back to his own car and went back to sleep. I think he later received a commendation for his part in the arrest of the PCP user.

Ethanol

The most widely abused drug in the United States is alcohol. Just look at all the alcohol-related traffic accidents and you will understand that it is a grave and growing concern for our society. However, alcoholism doesn't just affect an individual's driving ability; it can spill over into their work life as well. Peyton Schur and James Broder report that alcoholism cost the U.S. economy $117 billion in 1983 alone [Investigations of Substance Abuse in the Workplace]. Alcoholism leads to absenteeism, reduced production, greater potential for work-related accidents, and high medical costs.

The active ingredient in alcohol is ethanol. The concentration of ethanol varies depending upon what kind of alcoholic beverage you are consuming. For example, a glass of wine has a concentration of 22 percent ethanol, or 44 proof. Beer contains 3 to 5 percent ethanol, or 6 to 10 proof. Thus, "proof" is achieved by doubling the percentage, so that hard liquor, which has an ethanol concentration of 40 percent, has a proof of 80. One drink of wine is considered to be four ounces; one drink of beer is twelve ounces; and one drink of hard liquor, one and one-fourth ounces.

Alcohol is a depressant, which means it lowers the inhibitions, slows down metabolic processes, and delays reaction time. Pupils constrict. Nerve endings in the extremities become numb—mouth, fingers, toes, etc. The initial feeling of warmth that people experience occurs when blood rushes to the skin, creating an illusion of warmth when in actuality the internal organs are being deprived of their normal supply of blood. This superficial warming is what accounts for the appearance of flushed skin when people drink. Alcohol also acts as a dehydrating agent, robbing the body of its essential fluids.

It takes approximately twenty to forty minutes after taking that first drink for a person to feel the effects of alcohol, even though people might believe the effect to be instantaneous. You might say that your mind tricks you into believing that the effects come sooner. If you are an experienced drinker, you know what it feels like to be under the influence of alcohol, and so your mind accommodates and produces the feelings well before the actual physiological effects kick in. Also, because the liver only metabolizes one ounce per hour, it takes twenty-four hours for the body to completely flush itself of alcohol. If a person has consumed more alcohol than the body can fully absorb, alcohol poisoning occurs.

The effects of alcohol on a person may be influenced by whether or not they ate prior to consuming alcohol, the amount of sleep they had, fatigue, illness, emotional state, if they mixed it with prescribed medications, and if they mixed it with illegal drugs. Mixing alcohol with other drugs is a recipe for disaster. Most prescription labels specifically prohibit the drinking of alcoholic beverages while taking the medication, because such a combination can severely impair a person's ability to function. Mixing alcohol with other depressants, like barbiturates, can induce coma or even death. This is what happened to Kurt Cobain, for example, when he apparently drank champagne after having taken tranquilizers. He went into a coma and was only revived after the timely intervention of his wife and trained medical personnel.

Because alcohol is at present legal and readily available in our society, social drinking is not only uncommon but is actually culturally acceptable. Whether or not social drinking leads to abuse or alcoholism is still in debate, however our job as investigators is not to report the level of a person's alcohol level, but the facts of its use.

Amphetamine

Amphetamine, methamphetamine, and dextroamphetamine are, for all intents and purposes, synonymous. As a class of drug, they are stimulants, which means that they produce a sense of euphoria, cause the pupils to dilate, and increase the heartbeat and pulse. They may be snorted, injected, or taken orally.

At one time, amphetamines were prescribed for a variety of medical conditions, such as narcolepsy and Parkinsonism, and they have been used as a treatment for obesity. Even though the effectiveness of amphetamines in the maintenance of weight loss has been questioned, there are still a number of diet pills on the market, like Dexatrim™ or Acutrim™.

Amphetamines give users a sense of increased physical strength and heightened mental capacity, as well as sharpened alertness and a loss of fatigue. Feelings of self-confidence and competence are enhanced. Users become more energetic, almost manic, and have a difficulty sitting still. They can become excessively active and argumentative, irritable, or nervous. A prime indicator of amphetamine use is the person's repeated expressions that they have little or no need for food or sleep. Thus, malnutrition is associated with higher levels of consistent amphetamine abuse: it is not unheard of for abusers to lose ten to thirty pounds of body weight. Also, an individual on amphetamines may have a compulsive desire to take apart mechanical objects and put them back together—often unsuccessfully. Now, just because your neighbor may have a fondness for Volkswagen bugs and you see several of them sitting around his driveway in various states of disrepair, don't automatically assume that he must be an amphetamine addict. For all you know, he could have every intention and every *capability* of putting them back together successfully!

It is important to keep in mind that amphetamines in high doses can produce unpredictable behavior and extreme paranoia. Suspiciousness, auditory hallucinations, and a compulsive touching or picking at the extremities can also occur. Long-time users often go into "runs," in which they may go for four or five days at a time without eating or sleeping until they "crash," or succumb to exhaustion and sleep for extended periods of time. During these runs, it is not uncommon for "special freaks," as amphetamine abusers are often called, to inject as much as 1,000 mg. of amphetamines every two to three hours, whereas the usual prescribed dosage is somewhere between 2.5 and 15 mg. *per day.* Because it is possible for tolerance to develop, the user has to keep increasing the dosage in order to achieve the same high as when he or she first began using the drug.

Ice

Ice is methamphetamine in rock form, with a purity of ninety to one hundred percent, and acts as a stimulant to the central nervous system. Highly addictive, ice is colorless and odorless and resembles rock salt or even a chip of ice. It is sold in various forms, including cigarette paper that has been saturated with methamphetamine base; glass vials; paper bundles or clear heat-sealed cellophane packets; and, more recently, in pieces of plastic straws which have been heat-sealed at both ends. The usual method of ingestion is to smoke it, producing a euphoric rush that lasts from four to fifteen hours. When you compare this to the much shorter duration of cocaine effects—20 minutes for smoking it and 60 minutes from snorting cocaine—it is easy to see why ice is such an irresistible drug, even though it is quite expensive. For example, as of 1990, one-tenth of a gram of ice cost $50, with one ounce costing $3,600 to $7,000.

As already mentioned, ice is a highly addictive and potent form of methamphetamine. Because the drug is usually smoked, the effects are felt almost immediately: the gaseous form of the drug is absorbed directly into the bloodstream through the lungs. Some of the symptoms of ice include increased alertness, enhanced feelings of well-being, excitation, dilated pupils, elevated blood pressure and pulse rate, insomnia, and loss of appetite. Overdose can bring on agitation, fever, hallucinations, psychosis, convulsions, cardiac arrest, and even death. Withdrawal from ice causes depression, apathy, long heavy sleep, disorientation, and in some cases, suicidal tendencies. Some experts contend that ice is more deadly and dangerous than cocaine, because of its purity and the bizarre, unpredictable behavior it can instigate in those who abuse it.

The first state in this country is to acquire ice on any significant scale was Hawaii. It is believed that ice is being mass-produced in Korea and then shipped to the Philippine Islands, and from there to Hawaii, where it is then distributed throughout the continental United States.

Names to be aware of are crystal, which is rock amphetamine; crank, which is powdered methamphetamine; and the various terms for ice, which include hot ice, super ice, glass, or crystal.

Barbiturates

Barbiturates are depressants and belong to that class of drug most frequently prescribed as sedatives and sleep-inducers. There are four general classifications of barbiturates "ultrashort," "short," "intermediate," and "long-acting," depending upon the length of effect. The most heavily abused barbiturates tend to fall into the "short-acting" and "intermediate-acting" categories.

Some common names of barbiturates include sleeping pills, downers, and barbs. Because these pills often come in colorful capsules, some names have evolved around the various colors, such as blue devils for blue pills, reds or pinks for red-colored pills, rainbows or double trouble for red-and-blue colored pills, and yellow jackets or yellow bullets for yellow pills. A goofball is a combination of barbiturate and amphetamine, usually taken after a person has been "strung-out" on amphetamines and wishes to "come down," and so he takes a barbiturate to counteract the energizing effects of amphetamine.

Barbiturates can induce difficulty with coordination, nystagmus, strabismus (lack of eye parallelism), and slurred speech. Sluggishness, poor comprehension and memory, and stymied cognitive processing are also common, as are irritability and a tendency toward picking quarrels. Overdose can bring on clammy skin, weak and rapid pulse, coma, or possible death.

It is possible for barbiturates to become just as addictive as heroin. Some heroin addicts use barbiturates in substitution when their drug of choice is unavailable. Sleeping pills, the most widely-known barbiturate, accounts for more than 20 million prescriptions each year. And while therapeutic doses of common sedatives range between 100 to 200 mg. per day, addicts may take more than 800 mg. a day. Because they are so easily obtained, either by real or falsified prescriptions, dependence upon sleeping pills and other barbiturates is becoming increasingly prevalent.

Methaqualone

Methaqualone, most commonly referred to as Quaalude, is a hypnotic sedative that is nonetheless not classified as a barbiturate. Generally, it comes in a white crystalline powder that is bitter and either odorless or very nearly so. It can be taken in pill form and mixed with other drugs, such as aspirin, Valium®, and alcohol. In combination with alcohol, methaqualone's sedative and depressant effects are increased dramatically.

Quaaludes are known for their sedative/hypnotic, anesthetic, and antihistamine properties. Some of the effects of methaqualone on users include drowsiness, confusion, delirium, slurred speech, and drunken behavior without exhibiting the odor of alcohol. Overdose symptoms are shallow respiration, cold and clammy skin, weak and rapid pulse, convulsions, coma, and possible death. At one time, Quaaludes were prescribed by medical doctors as tranquilizers and pain relievers, but because of their high potential for abuse, it was declared illegal to prescribe or possess them in the United States. The drug is intensely physically and psychologically addictive, and some experts on drug abuse believe that the potential for addiction and abuse of methaqualone is as serious as that of heroin.

Toluene

By far the most addictive drug is toluene, the chemical component found in many aerosol paints, glues, or solvents. Toluene is sniffed or "huffed," and has been shown to be the most effective killer of brain cells than any other drug. The practice of huffing has become alarmingly popular among American's young people, because the drug is easily and legally obtained—there is no legal age limit placed upon the purchase of model airplane glue, for example—and the effects are almost immediate.

Toluene induces an intoxication almost like that of alcohol. Drowsiness, light-headedness, and hallucinations are some of the common effects of huffing, as are stupor and ringing in the ears. Huffing causes the user's eyes to become red and watery. Vision becomes blurred or doubled, and there is arrogation of the mucous membranes of the nose and mouth.

It is usually easy to spot someone who is a chronic huffer. For one thing, the odor is retained on the breath and clothes, and it is distinctly unlike the odor of alcohol. In addition, the huffer carries with him or her rags or paper bags or some kind of plastic bag in which the substance that is being inhaled is carried. Another telltale sign is paint or other unusual residue about the mouth and hands of the user; often they are too stoned to realize that they are getting paint all over themselves as they inhale.

Inhaling not only damages the brain, but it can also permanently injure the lungs and respiratory tract of the user. In one tragic example, a young man who had supposedly given up the habit of inhaling suddenly collapsed on the sidewalk outside a local store, completely unable to breathe. It turned out that his lungs were so coated with the fabric protectant spray he had been huffing that he was eventually asphyxiated, and there was nothing that anyone could do to help him.

HEALTH AND SAFETY CODES

Now that you have at least a familiarity with some of the more common drugs and their effects, we can move on to a discussion of the legislation that has been passed regarding the control of these substances. As hinted in the opening anecdote of this chapter, the legal community has not been consistent in its stance toward drugs, and it is likely that future drug-related legislation will look markedly different even from today's. For example, if the current debate over the legalization of drugs and their place in society will necessarily come into effect.

As a private investigator, you should make it your business to keep abreast of the changes in drug laws, and the implications of those changes. What we discuss below is an overview of those laws most directly applicable to the general topic of narcotics, concentrating primarily upon the penal code as it exists in the state of California, as an example.

BUSINESS AND PROFESSIONS CODE 4149

This code is designed to monitor who shall and shall not have lawful use of syringes which, as you know, are one of the principal elements in a heroin junkie's "kit." "No person shall possess or have under his or her control any hypodermic needle or syringe except when acquired in accordance with the provisions of this article." Thus, diabetics, health care professionals and other persons who might reasonably be expected to possess a syringe are the only ones who by law are allowed to do so.

CALIFORNIA PENAL CODE 647 (F)

This penal code has to do with disorderly conduct:

> Every person who commits any of the following acts is guilty of disorderly conduct, a misdemeanor:

> ...(f) Who is found in any public place under the influence of intoxicating liquor, any drug, controlled substance, or toluene, or any combination of any intoxicating liquor, drug, controlled substance, or toluene, in such a condition that he or she is unable to exercise care for his or her own safety of the safety of others, or by reason of his or her being under the influence of intoxicating liquor, any drug, controlled substance, toluene, or any combination of any intoxicating liquor, drug, or toluene, interferes with or obstructs or prevents the use of any street, sidewalk, or other public way [Penal Code 1994, Abridged CA. ed., 1994, pp. 231–232].

Thus, there are a few conditions a person must meet before they can be convicted of the misdemeanor of disorderly conduct while under the influence of a drug. First, you must be under the influence, a condition which can be verified by breathalyzers, urinalysis, or other such tests.

Second, you must be in a public place. This may seem self-obvious, and yet is an important element to remember: you cannot be convicted of a misdemeanor for disorderly conduct if you are at your home and under the influence of alcohol. However, if you are falling down drunk off a bar stool in a public bar, then you are free game.

Third, you have to be unable to exercise proper care for yourself and/or the safety of others. This is very important. Being drunk in public is one thing, but creating disturbances in which you or others might feasibly be harmed is grounds for arrest on charges of disorderly conduct.

PENAL CODE 381

This code deals specifically with the most deadly and addictive of drugs, toluene.

(a) Any person who possesses toluene or any substance or material containing toluene, including, but not limited to, glue, cement, dope, paint thinner, paint and any combination of hydrocarbons, either alone or in combination with any substance or material including but not limited to paint, paint thinner, shellac thinner, and solvents, with the intent to breathe, inhale, or ingest for the purposes of . . . intoxication, elation, euphoria, dizziness, stupefaction, or dulling of the senses or for the purposes of, in any manner, changing, distorting, or disturbing the audio, visual or mental processes, or who knowingly and with the intent to do so is under the influence of toluene or any material containing toluene, or any combinations of hydrocarbons is guilty of a misdemeanor.

HEALTH AND SAFETY CODES (H&S CODES)

This next section is intended as a brief sketch of the many health and safety codes concerning drugs, trafficking, possession, and use. It will be broken up into three major groupings: Heroin, Cocaine, Codeine, Mescaline, and Peyote as the first group; Marijuana and Hashish are the second group; and Barbiturates, Amphetamines, LSD, and PCP are the third. Each code will be briefly summarized for you so that you may get the main point. As you read them, you will see that they follow a distinct pattern. For your own information, you should look up each of these codes in the Penal Code.

Heroin, Cocaine, Codeine, Mescaline and Peyote

1. *H&S Code 11350:* Possession of Any of the Above Controlled Substances of their Derivatives, which is a felony.
2. *H&S Code 11351:* Possession for Sale of a Controlled Substance, which is also a felony. Some ways to determine whether an individual is intending to sell the drug are to look at how much of the drug he or she has: the larger the quantity, of course, the more likely it is that it is intended to be sold. Also, the way the drug is packaged may also be indicative of its intended use.
3. *H&S Code 11352:* Sales and Transportation of a Controlled Substance, a felony.
4. *H&S Code 11353:* Sale to a Minor of a Controlled Substance by an Adult, a felony.
5. *H&S Code 11354:* Sale to a Minor of a Controlled Substance by a Minor, which is also a felony.
6. *H&S Code 11355:* Sale of a Controlled Substance in Lieu of a Controlled Substance. In other words, this is when someone tries to sell "bunk," or bad stuff, as the genuine article. Another example is when you as an undercover agent arrange a money transaction in which you give a person money in exchange for some illicit substance, and transaction in which you give a person money in exchange for some illicit substance, and before they give you the drugs they ascertain that you are in fact an agent. To avoid prosecution, they flush the drug down the toilet. However, because you were essentially *sold* the product, even if that product is no longer viable, the individual who sold it to you is still liable.
7. *H&S Code 11363:* Cultivation of Peyote. Peyote is another name for mescal, which is a spineless cactus indigenous to the southwestern United States and northern Mexico. The dried tops of these cacti were chewed by Indians for their narcotic effects, which include hallucinations. Oftentimes my students are unfamiliar with the term peyote until I tell them that the characters in the popular western *Young Guns* chewed peyote while they were out in the desert and got completely blown out of their minds. Somehow they all seem to know what peyote is then!

Marijuana and Hashish

1. *H&S Code 11357(a):* Possession of Hashish, a felony.
2. *H&S Code 11357(b):* Possession of Less than 1 Ounce of Marijuana, an infraction.
3. *H&S Code 11357(c):* Possession of More than 1 Ounce of Marijuana, a misdemeanor.
4. *H&S Code 11358:* Cultivation of Marijuana, a felony.

I would like to take this opportunity to point out one of the many inconsistencies and logic errors inherent in the penal system. Let me paint a brief scenario: You have just purchased a little less than an ounce of marijuana from Joe the Stone, a neighborhood dope dealer that everyone agrees would be better off behind bars. By buying your little-less-than-an-ounce of pot from Joe the Stone, you have contributed to the illicit drug trafficking against which our government has supposedly declared an all-out war. And yet, if Nick, the ever-diligent policeman of our earlier anecdote, were to apprehend you with your illicit purchase burning a hole in your pocket, all he could do is issue you a citation. You would pay a fine, maybe get a little lecture, and been sent on your merry way. And who's to say you wouldn't run out the instant Nick was out of sight, hunt up Joe the Stone, and buy yet another less-than-an-ounce-of-pot?

Now, suppose you are a harmless and fairly reclusive hold-out from the sixties who has very discreetly been cultivating a potted Cannabis Sativa. She calls the police and Nick comes to arrest you and throw you in the state pen.

Just something to think about.

5. *H&S Code 11359:* Possession of Marijuana for Sale, a felony.
6. *H&S Code 11360(a):* Sale or Transportation of Marijuana, a felony.
7. *H&S Code 11361:* Sale of Marijuana to a Minor, a felony.

Barbiturates, Amphetamines, LSD, and PCP

1. *H&S Code 11377(a):* Possession of Any of the Above Controlled Substances of their Derivatives, a felony.
2. *H&S Code 11377(b):* Possession of Quaalude, which is a misdemeanor.
3. *H&S Code 11378:* Possession of Controlled Substance for Sale, a felony.
4. *H&S Code 11379:* Sale of Controlled Substance, a felony.
5. *H&S Code 11380:* Sale to a Minor by an Adult, a felony.
6. *H&S Code 11382:* Sale of a Controlled Substance in Lieu of a Controlled Substance, a felony. That's the "bunk" code again, this time for barbiturates, amphetamines, LSD, and PCP.
7. *H&S Code 11383:* Possession of Chemicals with the Intent to Manufacture Methamphetamine. It is interesting to note that companies that manufacture the chemicals used in clandestine laboratories to make speed are required to provide the FDA with a list of their clientele, so that the FDA will be able to monitor the purchase of these chemicals. Ideally, whenever a large amount of purchases are made of these particular chemicals, the computer will pick up on it and we will be led to another drug arrest. However, the people who make speed are not stupid; their survival depends upon outwitting the people who lay the foolproof plans for their capture. Thus, the way they get around this snare is to employ middlemen who make the initial purchases and then turn around and sell the chemicals again to the people who actually make the drugs.

H&S CODE 11550(a): Unlawful Possession

This code basically makes it illegal for persons to be under the influence of any previously identified controlled substance:

> Except as otherwise provided in this division, every person who possesses (1) any controlled substance specified in subdivision (b) or (c), or paragraph (1) of subdivision (f) of Section 11054, specified in paragraph (14), (15), or (20) of subdivision (d) of Section 11054, or specified in subdivision (b), (c), or (g) of Section 11055, or (2) any controlled substance classified in Schedule III, IV, or V which is a narcotic drug, unless upon written prescription of a physician, dentist, podiatrist, or veterinarian licensed to practice in this state, shall be punished by imprisonment in the state prison.

THE CONTROLLED SUBSTANCES ACT (CSA)

Now that you have a fairly well-organized outline of the Health and Safety Codes concerning drugs, we'll move on to the less comprehensible organization of the Controlled Substances Act, or the CSA, which is legislation that separates the various drugs into five groups or schedules for purposes of categorization. Separation into these schedules is a function of three criteria: the potential the drug carries for abuse, whether or not there is a current accepted medical use for the drug, and the user harm or safety under supervised medical conditions. What is given are generalizations of the specific drugs listed in the various schedules. For more precise information, you should look up H&S Code 11054, H&S Code 11055, H&S Code 11056, H&S Code 11057, and H&S Code 11058.

Schedule I

Schedule I includes, among others, hashish, heroin, marijuana, LSD, mescaline, and all derivatives of the above mentioned substances. For all of these drugs there is a high potential for abuse, and no current accepted medical usage. There is also a lack of current accepted safety for use, even under medical supervision.

Schedule II

Schedule II includes amphetamines, barbiturates, cocaine, codeine, methadone, morphine and opium. With these drugs, as in Schedule I, there is a high potential for abuse. However, these substances all have current accepted medical uses—amphetamines as diet control, barbiturates as sedatives, cocaine as a pain reliever, etc. It is recognized about all of these drugs that abuse may lead to sever physiological and psychological dependence.

Schedule III

In this schedule are included all derivatives of opium, morphine, and codeine. The potential for abuse with these drugs is defined to be less than in Schedules I and II. The drugs do have a current accepted medical use, and abuse may lead to low to moderate physiological and psychological dependence.

Schedule IV

This schedule is perhaps designed as a catch-all for the other three. Simply stated, the drugs in Schedule IV are defined to be other narcotics, depressants, and stimulants not named in the above three schedules. The potential for abuse is lower than in Schedule III. These drugs do have an accepted medical use, but cause limited psychological and physical dependence.

Schedule V

In this schedule fall the narcotics, depressants, and stimulants not included in Schedule IV. The potential for abuse is lower than in Schedule IV, the drugs do have an accepted medical use, and again, there is limited psychological and physical dependence.

Here might be a good time to note that even if it seems that the psychological and physical dependence of the drugs lessens as you go further down the list, it is important to keep in mind that all controlled substances carry with them some kind of psychological and physical dependence. Even if it is limited or moderate or whatever, the danger is still there and you should never tamper or experiment with controlled substances.

DRUGS COMMONLY FOUND IN THE WORKPLACE

A large part of a private investigator's work involves investigations into the workplace. Employee theft, security lapses, improper supervision and conspiracy are just some of the many things you may be asked to investigate throughout the course of your career. A large portion of your work, however, will involve investigating for drug use in the workplace. Federal studies have estimated that between 10 to 20 percent of all U.S. workers use dangerous drugs on the job. Additional research would indicate that people who take drugs regularly—by some estimates, this amounts to about 25 percent of the population—are probably going to use drugs at work [*Investigation of substance abuse in workplace.* p. 12]. Drug-related theft, injury and lost production time have cost the U.S. economy billions of dollars over the last few years. Mandatory drug testing for employees has become a hot issue, with an individual's right to privacy being juxtaposed against the corporate right to a safe working environment. Drugs are endemic and show no signs of abatement.

Because we have already dealt fairly thoroughly with some of the more common drugs, this section is primarily intended as a summary review of the types of drugs you can reasonably expect to encounter in the workplace. The signs and symptoms listed here are intended to help you begin to recognize possible drug users in the work environment.

Opiates: Heroin, Morphine and Codeine

Heroin, morphine and codeine are all derivatives of opium, which is in itself a derivative of the poppy. To produce opium, the poppy is dried and ground into a powder. The powder is then refined and processed to produce morphine, heroin and codeine.

Of these three, morphine and heroin are the most likely candidates to be found in the workplace. The effects of morphine include the alleviation of pain without the subsequent loss of consciousness, drowsiness, mood shifts, loss of relativity in time and space, restlessness, mild anxiety, and nausea. It has a duration of effect ranging from four to five hours and can be injected or taken orally.

Heroin, as already discussed, can be injected or smoked and produces a euphoria that generally subsists four to six hours. Its manufacture and importation into the U.S. is illegal. Some tell-tale signs of heroin influence are moist skin, relaxed muscles and jaws, constricted pupils and a constant scratching.

Amphetamine and Methamphetamine

Both of these are stimulants, which means they promote increased energy, a sense of marked, enhanced physical strength, and a feeling of greater mental capacity. The person will feel little or no need for food and sleep, will exhibit dilated pupils, and may seem suspicious or paranoid. One interesting thing to consider is that addiction to amphetamines can come across as schizophrenia. I can remember one time when I was standing in line to pay some kind of bill, and had been standing in line for probably over an hour. There was an individual behind me exhibiting all the classic signs of speed use: itching, incessant chattering about anything and everything, shifting anxiously back and forth, chain smoking, etc. I became very annoyed with this individual because I felt he was being inappropriate, and couldn't everyone see that this guy was higher than a kite? So we happened to reach pay windows at exactly the same time, and I was just about to say something about this individual to the woman behind the counter when I heard him tell the woman who was helping him that he was sorry he was so wound up, but that he was schizophrenic and he had been standing in line so long that he had missed the proper time to take his medication. I had forgotten the first lesson of private investigators: **NEVER ASSUME.**

Marijuana

Marijuana is the most common extract of the *Cannabis Sativa* plant. It effects the central nervous system and the heart, causing a sense of euphoria and an elevated heart rate of over 140. Pupils become only slightly dilated, but the eyes generally appear red. The person often gets the munchies and has a dry mouth. Because marijuana is usually smoked, there is often a pungent odor about the person that will point strongly to marijuana use.

Cocaine

A stimulant, cocaine generates a restless excitement and a decreased sense of fatigue. Initially, the cocaine user at work might seem like the ideal worker: motivated, ambitious, tireless. However, closer observation might show that your aspiring workaholic is actually a cocaine abuser: the red nose, dilated pupils and often irritable, edgy excitement might be indications of more than stress. Remember that cocaine is extremely psychologically addictive, and can be found in even the highest strata of occupations.

PCP

PCP, or phencyclidine, was originally created to be an animal tranquilizer. The most noticeable effect on users is their misperceptions of reality, often exhibited by fixed concentration on objects or people without really seeming to "see" them. PCP users are prone to sudden violent behavior and unpredictable mood shifts. They may fancy themselves immune to normal restraints and even show signs of superhuman strength. The best thing to do if confronted with an out-of-control PCP tripper is to reduce the amount of stimulation the person receives and attempt to securely restrain him.

LSD

LSD is the acronym for lysergic acid diethylamide. It is a powerful hallucinogen which vividly distorts a person's perceptions of reality. A person on LSD may have facial contortions, dilated pupils and an elevated heart rate. They will also be extremely emotional, overreacting to the most mundane of events or things.

Employee's Right to Privacy

With the issue of drug investigation and testing in the workplace invariably comes the issue of privacy. Just how far does a person's right to privacy extend? Where does private end and public begin? Is it ever okay to invade another person's right to privacy?

These are just some of the questions that arise when the issue of drug testing in the workplace is discussed. Definitions of terms are always helpful in cases like this, so the first thing to do is establish just what is meant by public, and what is meant by private.

Public is defined by Funk and Wagnall's Pocket Dictionary as "of, pertaining to, or affecting the people at large or the community." It also extends to those objects, parks or exhibits which are intended for the use and benefit of all. Private, on the other hand, is defined diametrically opposite: "not for public or common use; individual." Private, therefore, pertains to a particular person or group and is not controlled or influenced by the people. So perhaps when an individual's private interests begin to encroach upon or compromise the interests of the whole, that person's right to privacy may become secondary to the overall interests of the collective society. Obviously, this is a philosophical question that scholars have been debating for centuries and is not about to be resolved here.

As for the question about when an employer may test for drugs, the following criteria must be met: there must be established a reason to believe that the employee is using drugs, by having two independent verifiable sources corroborate that a person may be using drugs; random testing as opposed to selective, preferential or discriminatory testing must be in effect; or the occupation of the employee in question is one that is safety sensitive. In other words, in occupations where the public's safety would be jeopardized should something go wrong, drug testing is permissible. This is a function of the Drug-Free Work Place Act of 1988, which states that any organization which deals with the public or the state must have a drug-training and drug-awareness program.

Undercover Report Writing

For obvious reasons, the bulk of the work you do investigating drug abuse in the workplace will likely be done undercover. And, since the work product of the private investigator is reports, it is important that you know how to write an undercover report.

In the last chapter you were introduced to the basic chronological report: the use of military time, writing in upper-case block letters, using complete thoughts and descriptions. Undercover report writing utilizes the same basic techniques: it is written chronologically, which means that it is a logical explanation of an act given in time sequence. An undercover report is also written without headings—your time increments serve as headings.

One of the most important things to remember about undercover report writing is that it is done in *third person.* First person is when you write in terms of "I." Examples of second person are "You forgot to buy milk at the store yesterday." An example of third person follows: "Joe Travers has a five-year-old son. He likes to wear boots whenever possible. Whenever someone touches Joe Travers' single-cup coffee maker, Joe Travers gets personally offended." Much of this book is written in second person.

When writing your undercover report, use third person because if it should happen to slip out of your grasp and wind up being discovered by one of the very people you are investigating, they won't know that you were the one writing the report.

And, last but not least, an undercover report should be narrative, which means it should tell a story for each act observed. In other words, for everything upon which you are reporting, you should answer the six essential questions of the Investigator's Code: who, what, when, where, why, and how.

You will find that as you read this book, the techniques of report writing will be constantly refined. As has been said before and will be said again, the work product of the private investigator is reports, and part of the purpose of this book is to make sure that you will be able to deliver a satisfactory and professional work product to your employers.

SAMPLE UNDERCOVER REPORT
CONFIDENTIAL

#007 Reports
Los Angeles
Tuesday, April 07, 1993

0730 hours	Employees were observed entering the facility and during the course of the day, the following observations were made: Overheard John, the leadman, telling Albert P. to follow him into the Packing and Shipping Department, where he was introduced to that department's leadman, Frederick. Leadman Frederick's last name is unknown. However, he is described as: Male, Mexican, 40 years of age, 5'6", 165 pounds, salt and pepper hair with matching mustache, brown eyes, wearing a blue cap with red stripes, white short sleeve shirt, green dungaree pants and brown boots. John informed Albert (leadman) that Albert P. was to work in his Department for the duration of the day.
0730–0945 hours	No irregular activity was observed.
0945–0955 hours	No irregular activity was observed.
1015 hours	Observed four male employees passing some type of pill among themselves. It is the Investigator's observation that it appeared to be Benzedrine tablets ("whites"). These four male employees do not work in the Department, and were just walking through.
1025 hours	Overheard Albert, leadman, telling Albert P. to go and help Juan. Juan's last name is unknown; however, he is described as: Male, Mexican, 5'5", 19 years of age, 130 pounds, brown curly hair, brown eyes, white T-shirt, blue denim pants, blue tennis shoes, and a thin brown mustache.

1035 hours	Overheard Juan telling Albert P. that he (Juan) wants help from another department because there were no parts in his department. Juan further stated, "Just look busy, and don't work too fast."
1035–1200 hours	No irregular activity was observed.
1200 hours	Lunch break. Observed employees breaking for lunch. No other irregular activity was observed.
1230 hours	Employees returned to the facility.
1230–1430 hours	No irregular activity was observed.
1430–1440 hours	Afternoon break. No irregular activity was observed.
1600–1655 hours	Employees in the Packing and Shipping Department were observed standing around, doing nothing. Overheard two unknown employees discussing the fact that they need some cardboard to make boxes for shipping tanks.
1700 hours	Employees observed leaving the facility, and no further activity was observed.
	Respectfully submitted. #007

REVIEW

1. True or False: Marijuana was illegal in the 1920s.
2. True or False: It is a crime in this country to be under the influence of a drug.
3. What is the definition of a drug?
4. What are three nondangerous, habit-forming drugs?
5. What are two examples of narcotics?
6. Heroin constricts/dilates the pupils. (circle the correct answer)
7. What are two common names for heroin?
8. True or False: Cocaine is less physically addictive than heroin.
9. Is cocaine a stimulant or a depressant?
10. How long do the effects of marijuana typically last?
11. What is the active ingredient in marijuana?
12. Which is more potent, hash oil or sinsemilla?
13. What is nystagmus?
14. True or False: PCP acts as a sedative upon the user.
15. What is H&S Code 11357(c)?
16. What are the three criteria for division into the five schedules of the CSA?
17. True or False: The effects of ice last longer than the effects of morphine.

18. What are the criteria for allowing employers to perform drug testing in the workplace?
19. Amphetamine addiction can produce a state that resembles which psychological disorder?
20. Give an example of a third-person narrative.

Chapter 3

UNDERCOVER INVESTIGATION

He didn't want to believe it. In fact, he almost *couldn't* believe it. After all, Larry had been on the force for almost fifteen years and had been nothing if not exemplary for every one of those fifteen years. Chief Golding simply was unwilling to believe that his friend and colleagues had become a dirty cop. But he had a tip from a reliable source that Larry had been stealing money from suspects and others, and he knew he would have to look into it. So, after much consideration, Golding organized a sting operation in which Larry would be sent to retrieve a bag full of money and drugs that had supposedly been found on the street by a resident. If Larry turned in the cash, he would be absolved of suspicion. If he kept it, then it wouldn't matter how many beers he had bought Golding over the years—he was finished.

It sounded like a simple enough ruse.

However, when Golding asked for a report a few days later from the sting officer, he found that the wrong patrolman had been sent out by the dispatcher. Incredulous, the chief asked what had happened.

"He kept the cash," they told him.

Suddenly the ruse didn't seem so simple.

Golding decided to try again. He set up the scenario and waited for the report. He was not pleased with the results.

"They sent the wrong guy," he was told. "And he . . . "

"Don't tell me," said Golding.

They tried a third time, and then a fourth. Each time the dispatchers sent the wrong patrolman. And what was more disturbing was that each time, the wrong patrolman kept the cash.

The sting operation was called to a halt.

"What else could I do?" Golding later asked an Internal Affairs consultant. "It was either call it quits or fire the whole department!"[1]

The above story is a fictionalized account of an actual undercover operation conducted in 1988. The police chief had reason to suspect that one of his officers had been stealing money from suspects, and he did in fact set up a sting operation in which this officer would be sent to pick up a bag of cash. However, the dispatchers somehow got mixed up

---

[1]"Internal Affairs Sting Worked—Too Well," *The Los Angeles Times;* Jan. 26, 1992, p.j6.

and over the course of several weeks, sent four other officers to fetch the bag. Just as in the story, these four officers ended up keeping the cash—and losing their jobs. The sting operation came to an ignominious conclusion.

As far as undercover investigations go, this is not exactly a stellar example. However, it is a good example of how things can go wrong if you are not adequately prepared and informed before embarking upon such an investigation. So, to make sure that any undercover assignments you are given during your career as a private investigator do not end so ingloriously, it is important that you have a complete understanding of the objectives and proper procedures for undercover work.

DEFINITION OF UNDERCOVER

Of course, we all have some idea of what undercover work looks like; we have all seen movies and read books. We know about slouch hats and trench coats, fake names, and elaborate strategies of deception. We know about prying through desk drawers, sneaking through dark and sinister mansions, and knocking a few heads together when our true identity is discovered. However, in actual point of fact, the majority of undercover assignments are work-related. That is, they are conducted in common, ordinary working environments where people spend more time punching time clocks than each other. Simply put, undercover work is a form of investigation where you assume an identity to gather answers that can't be gathered by direct investigation. It is most effective when you as the agent win the confidence of the subject, and is very useful in solving crimes and problems that have organization. Some examples of this type of crime include fraud, drugs, stolen merchandise, and employee theft, because it usually takes two or more people working together to substantially bamboozle an employer. I'm not talking about a few packages of staples or that unused legal pad your boss left sitting out on the corner of his desk. The kinds of crimes in which undercover work is most often needed are those in which the magnitude and scope of theft and corruption are quite large.

The objective of going undercover are quite straightforward. The first and most obvious is to obtain information. You want to find out what's going on, plain and simple. Second, you want to obtain any evidence that might support or invalidate your client's belief that anything of a devious nature is going on in his or her company. You also want to conduct fixed surveillance—you want to be able to watch people without arousing their suspicion. Next, you want to check loyalty, like Chief Golding in the fictionalized sting operation. Another objective is to perform security checks. And, finally, undercover investigations are a preliminary to searches and interviews: they provide the necessary foundation for the interviewers during their confrontations with the implicated parties.

PERSONAL ATTRIBUTES OF A PRIVATE INVESTIGATOR

Before we get too much farther into the whys and wherefores of undercover investigation, this might be a good opportunity to explore just what kind of personality you need to succeed in this field, because undercover work is not something to which all people are vocationally called. While some individuals might take offense at the notion that they would not necessarily make the world's next Alan Pinkerton, these same people would have no trouble recognizing that not everyone is meant to be, let's say, a child care worker, or an optometrist, or a chef at a fancy restaurant. People have different skills and personalities that are perfectly suited for particular professions and perfectly ill-suited for others. The same is true for the field of private investigations, especially when you consider the particular skills you must have to successfully operate undercover.

Temperament

First and foremost, the private investigator should have a calm and steady temperament. Undercover work is nothing if not unpredictable, and if you are highly susceptible to frustration or impatience, you will most likely not last very long as an operative. You should be self-confident—you will be largely on your own while you are undercover, so you will have to be able to function comfortably with a high level of independence—and resourceful. The environment will not always be one with which you are familiar and you will have to learn how to make the most of whatever situation you find yourself in, which means that you will often have to think very fast on your feet. For example, if you are investigating drug use on the job and one of the employees wants you to smoke a joint with him and some other guys in the break room, what will you say? "Uh, no thanks, but I'm a private investigator and it's against my code of ethics to ingest unlawful substances?"

Inasmuch as it is possible, you should be agreeable and likable, although, of course, you cannot expect everyone to be your best friend. As stated in the definition of undercover work, the best way to obtain results is to gain the confidence of your subject. Spend time with him on your lunch breaks; ask him about his kids; let him borrow fifty cents from you so he can buy a soda out of the machine. Build up rapport with your subject, and you will likely have an easier time getting the information you want.

Of course, this practice raises issues of trust and ethics. In a recent undercover investigation conducted for Kmart Corporation by Confidential Investigative Consultants, an investigations firm in Chicago, several of the employees who were involved in the investigation are suing Kmart on the grounds that their rights of privacy were violated. One of the employees, Lewis Hubble, has a particular grievance against a Confidential Investigative Consultants' operative named Albert Posego, who posed as a Kmart warehouse employee. Posego was there ostensibly to investigate the possibility of a theft ring in the warehouse. During the course of the investigation, Posego apparently befriended Hubble, offering to go out with him for a beer after work, visiting him in his apartment, and even volunteering to help him and his family move into a new home. Hubble contended that he was deceived by Posego and that his right to privacy was intruded upon by the operative.

Kmart Corporation, however, remains convinced that undercover investigations are a viable and legitimate way of ascertaining employee loyalty and ferreting out theft. Employee theft, according to the National Retail Foundation, accounted for an estimated $11 billion in shortages for United States retailers in 1992.[2] While undercover investigation does yield results, as a solution it is often costly on more than one level. Investigation firms charge their clients thousands of dollars each month per operative and, on a more personal level, employees lose trust in their employer, which could result in lowered morale and reduced productivity. That is why Doug Hempen, chairman of the investigations committee of the American Society for Industrial Security, says he advocates the use of undercover agents only when all other options have failed. Instead, he insists that instilling in employees a sense of teamwork, and providing assistance for drug or emotional problems, can prove very effective in the deterrence of theft and substance abuse.[3]

---

[2]"Spying Raises Issues of Trust, Ethics." *Press Enterprise*, Jan. 24, 1994.
[3]Ibid.

Background

To successfully conduct undercover operations, it is vital that you have the requisite technical skills, education and experience. Just as a pilot for a major airline doesn't slide behind the controls without first having undergone extensive training both in the classroom and in flight simulators, so too can you not slide into a tricky undercover situation without the necessary knowledge and hope your investigation will fly.

One of the skills you really should have is acting ability. Now, before you roll your eyes and dismiss this as irrelevant, consider this: according to Police Commissioner Raymond Kelly of New York City, a city-wide "casting call" for actors and actresses was contemplated as the Internal Affairs Bureau searched for ways to uncover dirty cops. The idea was that these aspiring thespians, many of whom are so in need of work that they would not be too particular about the type of assignment they received, would masquerade as police officer, and by mingling with the rank and file, manage to procure any information about illicit activity that was going on among the officers. Keith Hutt, a twenty-five-year-old, would-be actor from Manhattan, did express some reservations to this plan: "Suppose a cop finds out who you are. His life, career and family are in jeopardy. Who knows what he'll do?"[4]

While you may not be called upon to assume the identity of a police officer—in fact, in California it is a felony for anyone who is not a peace officer to fraudulently represent him or herself as one (see California Penal Code 538d)—you will certainly be put into situations in which you will need to "fit in" with the people around you. If you are placed as an undercover operative in an assembly line, for example, you will need to be able to converse with your fellow employees *on their terms,* which often means adopting a totally different mode of discourse from your own. As William T. Patterson, director of Universal Detectives, wrote in his book, *Private Investigation Training Manual,* "practically all trades have a lingo or jargon (phraseology) all their own."[5] For example, in the printing industry you will encounter people whose job description is "stripper." This does not mean that these people do nothing all day long but take their clothes off to sultry music! What it does mean is that their job is making materials ready to be brought to press, or "stripping them up." Obviously, however, if you were sent to a printing company to investi-

---

[4]"Like to Act? Police May Have a Role for you," *The Daily Bulletin, c/o The New York Times,* 1992.

[5]Patterson, William T. *Private Investigator's Training Manual.*

gate drug abuse, you would be expected to know what a stripper is; and what a film miser is, and what the difference is between a sheet-fed press and a web press, etc.

Also, when you go into undercover assignments, you are given an entirely new identity: new background, new ambitions, and maybe even a new name. You must convincingly play your part and become that new person or people will not accept you as one of them and your chances of gleaning information from them may suffer.

Acting skills alone will not necessarily ensure success, however, and that is where education and experience come in. For example, you may be doing a bang-up job convincing people that you have never in your life been anything but a forklift driver, and have made all kinds of new friends and in-roads into possible theft rings at your warehouse. But if you don't know about entrapment, you might think it perfectly acceptable and even expedient to suggest to your new friends that they steal some merchandise from the warehouse, so that you can catch them in the act and have a nice bit of malfeasance to report to your client. Or if you were unfamiliar with the Wagner Act, you might think it was okay to report the perfectly legal plans for a strike over wage discrepancies discussed by the union at its last meeting, because even though your client certainly might appreciate such information, it is certainly illegal for you to provide it to him. And, most importantly, if you do not know how to write professional and detailed daily reports on the activity you observe while undercover, the caliber of your investigative work will not be very high in quality. Training and education are essential ingredients for success in undercover work: you must know what to look for, how to look for it without arousing suspicion, and what to do with it once you find it.

Intellect

When working undercover, it is very important that you keep a clear mind, stay rational and remain unbiased. You are not there to pass judgment or form opinions; you are there to gather the facts and report on them objectively and honestly. Keep the objectives for which you were placed undercover as your first priority. In other words, don't allow yourself to get sidetracked or distracted from the original purpose for which you were hired.

While on your assignment, you will need to be making keen and detailed observations of the activity going on around you at all times.

However, it will not be practical for you to be carrying around a note-book in which to record the observations as you make them—you can hardly hope to be inconspicuous if you are always asking people to repeat what they said so you can make sure you wrote it down correctly! And you can only excuse yourself to the restroom a few times a day at the most without arousing suspicion, or even concern, so you can forget the idea of using the bathroom stalls as your professional office space. Therefore, you must develop a good memory, as well as excellent observation skills. An eye for detail is essential.

Along with a good eye for detail, use sound judgment and common sense. Don't let emotions dictate your actions—your whole undercover assignment could be blown by one impulsive move on your part, and then not only would your client have lost a large amount of money, but you might have seriously damaged your chances of procuring future work as an investigator.

An incident that actually happened with one of my former students is a perfect example of how to successfully destroy an undercover operation. This student was on assignment in a warehouse and he had a dispute with his client about his pay schedule. Apparently he felt his services were not being adequately compensated for, and his client did not share his assessment. So he marched himself into the warehouse where he had been working as an operative, climbed up on a pallet and issued his proclamation: "I'm an undercover investigator, and I'm here to bust all of you people for the narcotics you've been doing on the job." You can imagine how the investigation turned out. And I'm sure you can also imagine how many other companies were anxious to hire him afterward!

D.D.T./H.P.

Perhaps the most important and comprehensive thing to remember about your function as an undercover operative is this: *You are the eyes and ears of the company.* Report on everything you possibly—and legally—can, even if it seems insignificant to you. Any information you can bring to your client will be important to him or her, and the more you can provide, the more complete his or her picture will be of the working environment within his or her company. Often, upper management knows very little about what really goes on in the lower echelons, and you can become a valuable link between the two strata, opening up possible channels of communication and pointing out areas that could be changed. Remember that you were hired as an undercover agent because the client knew or strongly believed that there was something amiss in his or her organization, and usually the client is willing to implement changes in order to rectify the existing situation.

Two acronyms I like to give my students are D.D.T. and H.P. D.D.T. stands for *Details, Diligence, and Thoroughness.* Details means that you report item by item, leaving nothing out. Diligence means that you do your job carefully, thoughtfully, and with precision. And thoroughness means that you do it completely, following through to the very end. Another former student of mine failed to grasp this lesson, and on her first undercover assignment she decided she really didn't like it as much as she thought she would, so she quit midway through. A second company hired her and gave her a different undercover assignment, but something about *this* placement wasn't right either, so she quit again. The third company to hire her didn't fare any better. Third time is the charm, as they say, and as a result of her inability to finish what she started, this student was "blackballed" and no one wanted to hire her. So she moved to another state, and we can only hope.

H.P. stands for *Humility and Patience.* Even though the movies often portray private investigators as flashy, arrogant individuals who have all the answers and can produce miracles at will, "real life" investigators are people who know their limitations and function within them. Patience is also a must, as anyone who has sat for long hours in a surveillance van will tell you. Undercover work does not always coincide nicely with the nine-to-five, five-day work week schedule, and investigations can last for months at a time. The old maxim is "good things come to those who wait," and wait and wait . . .

TYPES OF ASSIGNMENTS

There are three general types of investigations you might be asked to perform: neighborhood assignments, social assignments, and work assignments. In a neighborhood assignment, you will need to be able to fit into your surroundings and the surroundings of your subject. Remember that you are on the "home turf" of your subject and your job will be to make it appear as though you belong there just as much as your subject does. If the neighborhood is an upper-middle class, white-collar one, for example, it would behoove you to dress and behave as one who is of upper-middle class, white-collar background. Slouching around in overalls and grease-stained caps would draw undue attention to yourself and would clearly demarcate you as an outsider.

In social assignments, you need to be able to follow your subject into such social settings as bars, clubs, or parties and blend into the milieu. So, if you are following your subject into a sports bar, casual attire is appropriate. If you are following your subject into a posh Italian restaurant where young college students park your car and head waiters anxiously make sure that you are decked out in coat and tie, then it would certainly make sense for you to be decked out in coat and tie. Again, common sense goes a long way in such situations. If your subject goes into an establishment for which you are not suitably dressed, perhaps it would be best not to follow him inside and risk blowing your cover.

Work assignments are the most common types of undercover assignments you will receive. As already discussed the important thing to remember about work assignments is that you will need to convincingly assume the role of an employee.

UNDERCOVER INVESTIGATIONS IN THE WORKPLACE

Since the majority of undercover investigations take place in the working environment, you will need to know the overall purpose of such investigations, the general procedures and qualifications for them, and the proper way in which you should prepare your report, as well as some broad categories upon which you will be reporting.

Purposes for Undercover Investigations in the Workplace

In addition to the general objectives for undercover work discussed in the beginning of this chapter, there are three very specific considerations which relate exclusively to investigations in the workplace. First of all, an agent is there to determine the sources of losses, i.e., theft, production, time, etc. Since theft is a big issue with both large and small businesses, you as the operative need to be especially concerned with those losses that are a result of stealing. Finally, you should also report on the overall efficiency of the workers and their attitudes toward management, since as previously mentioned, there is usually a substantial communication breakdown between workers and those who supervise them. Worker's attitudes toward management can contribute to decreased productivity and a diffidence toward blatant wrong-doing by other employees. For example, if the general attitude toward management is disdainful and disrespectful, workers will be more inclined to turn a blind eye to theft and/or drug use by their coworkers, somehow reasoning that management "deserves it."

General Considerations

Once you are installed in the workplace, it is important that you develop common habits and interactions with your fellow employees. If they eat their lunches together in the downstairs break room, don't make a social hermit of yourself and eat alone in the upstairs break room. If they have football pools or coffee funds, it might be advantageous for you to contribute, even if you think football is a barbaric sport and can't stand the taste of coffee. Never give the impression that you are better than anyone else. Make every effort to blend in and develop feelings of friendship and trust.

When you discover information that is useful, cultivate it; see where it leads you. But remember that you cannot bring something up unless you have already heard it from someone in the workplace. What this means is that you cannot mention anything about a theft or drug ring to any of your fellow employees before they have told you about it, even if you already know everything about it because of the information your client gave you. Besides the obvious reasons for this, you must also consider that your client may have a hidden agenda that you know nothing about, and when he gives you "information" about an employee, he may actually be serving his own interests. There may be an employee with whom your client has had problems in the past, and so the client may fabricate or exaggerate wrongdoings of that employee in the hopes that it will result in that employee's termination. For example, when I was a director of physical security for a large company, my supervisor told me that he wanted to get rid of a female employee because he did not like the way she laughed. In all seriousness, image and deportment were very high priorities with the executives of the company—it was not uncommon for all of upper management to come to work dressed essentially identical to one another. Apparently this woman's laugh did not fall within my supervisor's guidelines of acceptable ways to express amusement. However, what my supervisor wanted to do about it did not fall within the *government's* guidelines of acceptable employment practices. After a lawsuit, this individual ended up at a desk in some obscure corner of the company, shuffling papers and reminiscing about his days in managerial power.

Above all, avoid entrapment at all costs. Do not entice or induce any person to commit a wrongful or illegal act, or you too will end up the recipient of a lawsuit. Subjects of undercover investigation are quick to drum up allegations of entrapment and invasion of privacy, so you must take great precautions to make sure you do not give them legitimate grounds on which to sue. One way to prevent entrapment charges is to carefully document the activities you observe. When writing your daily reports, make extensive use of the Investigator's Code: who, what, when, where, why, and how. Every incident that you report should answer all of those questions. Also, be sure to write down incidents at your earliest possible convenience. The more time that passes, the less your memory retains.

Never fabricate evidence to make your case seem stronger. While this may seem self-obvious, there are cases in which the operative has felt such pressure to "produce" for his client that he has actually manufactured evidence in order to implicate an employee. In one somewhat extreme example, an operative reported on the daily thefts of an employee and even went so far as to place stolen goods beneath the driver's seat of this employee's car. The agent then reported the theft to security. However, the truth eventually emerged, and it was not pretty. Apparently the agent was on the insecure side and had taken an avid dislike to the employee he framed, simply because that employee was good-looking and well-liked by his coworkers.[6] One helpful hint: if you are interested in making friends, then you probably should not make a habit of trying to get them fired for stealing.

When you are on an undercover assignment, your client might attempt to contact you, either to provide you with a "helpful hint" about a particular employee, or just to try and find out how the investigation is going. It is not uncommon, too, for clients to simply have a lot of curiosity about what you do. After all, they have seen the same movies and read the same books about private investigators that everyone else has, and you may be the first bona fide P.I. they have ever seen. Whatever the reason for the contact, it is important that you refer the client to your investigation supervisor. Remember that you are trying to appear inconspicuous, and if the "boss" is constantly coming up to you and taking you aside to whisper confidentially into your ear while the employees are watching, you will certainly have a harder time of it. If it

---

[6]Sennewald, Charles A. *The Process of Investigation.* Boston: Butterworth-Heineman, 1981, p. 54.

is ever necessary for you to contact your client, do not do so during working hours unless otherwise instructed, and never use the company phone.

Finally, do not carry any identification that may give you away were it to fall into the wrong hands. Do not take *anyone* into your confidence—even if it is someone with whom you have developed a close friendship or even a romantic attachment. The person you take into your confidence might have loyalties to other employees that go deeper than their infatuation with you, and if you divulge your secrets to them you might succeed in jeopardizing your entire investigation.

Report Writing

The only proper arena in which you may divulge the information you learn while undercover is in your reports. As already mentioned, these reports are to be written daily, for every shift you work. For those days in which you did not report to work, you must still submit a report giving the date that you missed, the date you expect to return to work, and the fact that the client's company and your supervisor were notified as to your absence.

The reports are generally written on letter-sized paper, unless prior arrangements have been made, and you must always double space, write only on one side of the paper and use third-person. Write legibly in upper-case block letters, and use plain, easily comprehensible language.

Reports are the work-product of the private investigator. The quality of your work will be judged by the quality of your reports, so it is important that they be professional, concise, and detailed. Incidents should be recorded in the order in which they occurred—*chronologically*. Remember that nothing is too small of insignificant to report on: the more information you supply, the harder your client believes you to be working and the happier he is about spending the money to keep you in your assignment.

All people you discuss in your report should be identified by name or, if the name is not known, by portrait parle (if you have forgotten what elements go into a portrait parle, refer to Chapter 1). Use full names wherever possible, although in some instances you may not know a person's last name. In most companies there are people who are known by nicknames only, especially if they have the same first name. For example, in the printing company where a former student of mine worked, there was a man named Al who ran the bindery and another Al who operated the Didde press; and in an effort to distinguish between them, all the employees called the bindery Al "Big Al" and the Didde press Al "Crazy Al." No one had any idea what their real last names were.

When writing your reports, always give the source of your information and never use abbreviations, because even though your shortcuts might make perfect sense to you or your client, an attorney might see them as a great way to cast doubt on the accuracy of your reporting. And since it is vital that your reports contain accurate information, you should not do anything that would allow for ambiguity of any sort. Report fact as fact and hearsay as hearsay. If you overhear something, *state* that it was overheard and give the name of the person who said it. If the information came to you through a conversation with another employee, say who that employee was. And, most importantly, if you were the only one to witness an act or hear a statement, make this clear in your report so that your supervisor will know that the information is restricted and will act accordingly.

Do not put your name on the report, for obvious reasons. Instead, use the operative number that was assigned to you by your supervisor. Remember the reason for the assignment and tailor your reports accordingly: you are there to solve the client's problem, and your reports should address those areas that were of concern to your client.

Basically, the report can be divided into five sections, based upon the five sections of the shift that you worked. The events that you report on in each section will then be listed in the proper order and time sequence.

An example of how to organize your report could go something like this:

1. Start of Shift Activities
2. Morning Activities or Period Before Lunch Activities
3. Noon or Lunch Break Activities
4. Lunch Break to End of Shift Activities
5. End of Shift Activities

The final report you submit is called a "summary report," for reasons which should be fairly obvious. It is turned in to your client at the conclusion of the operation and presents in brief, concise, and comprehensive terms the important points of your investigation. Also included, significantly, are any recommendations you might have for your client.

At the conclusion of your undercover assignment, your supervisor will give you the complete file on the operation for your review. Contained in the file are all the reports you made during the course of the investigation; this file is not to be taken from the office but is to be examined for those matters which have a direct relationship to the client's problem. Also of importance are those items which affect the operation of the client's business.

The most effective way to gather this information is to first set up the subject's titles of items you are interested in reporting on. For example:

Thefts
Supervision
Employee Morale and Activity
Etc.

If the client has a guard department, you would be expected to report on the performance of their duties and the overall effectiveness of the department. You may add to the list as you like, and your supervisor will assist you on choosing the subject headings.

Under the titles you have listed, you should write down the incidents that directly relate to the subject. For example, if you saw a supervisor curl up on the floor beneath his desk for a long nap while he was supposed to be monitoring the activities of his employees, that would be a good incident to record under the "SUPERVISION" heading.

In the section for your recommendations, you should concern yourself with how the client could rectify the undesirable conditions currently existing in the client's company. Try to be specific, offering concrete steps for the remedying of the situation. Also, offer suggestions and possible ways the client could ensure that such situations do not recur.

The summary report is one of the most crucial reports you will write, so you should take your time in preparing it and make sure it is done carefully. Your supervisor should review it with you after you have completed it, and may add any of his recommendations to yours.

General Areas for Reporting

We will cover the areas on which you should report in greater detail later in this chapter, but some more general topics you can refer to are: employee activity, production, theft and pilferage, supervision, security, fire and safety, and store activity (in the event that you are assigned to a retail store).

Some of the things to watch for when reporting on employee activity include gambling (see California Penal Code 337a), bookmaking or betting, and spending above income. Obviously, if someone is making $5.50 an hour as a typist and they have no other means of income, it would be some cause for suspicion if that employee comes to work in a different designer outfit every day and drives a car with gold-plated wheels and Italian leather seats!

Other items to report on are whether employees work rapidly and efficiently, or lethargically and carelessly. If there is any irregularity regarding time clock activity, put that into your report. Unreliability, laziness, and dishonesty in employees are also things employers appreciate knowing about, as are unexcused absences while on company time, loitering in unauthorized areas, and any drinking or drug abuse while at work. Violation of company rules and sabotage of equipment are two additional items of interest to employers, for obvious reasons.

When reporting on production and productivity, watch for any improper filing or mistakes in paperwork. These kinds of mistakes, while seemingly minor or innocuous, can actually translate into substantial losses for companies, as can the damage, waste, or improper use of merchandise or equipment.

You should also look for those individuals who have any suggestions about possible time-saving methods and record not only what they say, but who is doing the suggesting. Just as employers want to know who isn't working up to their full potential, they also want to know about those workers with exemplary drive and initiative. As an undercover operative, you will have unique opportunities to observe both, and should look for chances to commend as well as reprimand.

Theft and pilferage are the most obvious sources of loss for businesses, so you should be sure to report on any employees who secretly or openly take property, and detail what methods were used in the theft. Report on any rumors of theft, giving both the source and implicated parties. Now, in almost every company you are going to come across individuals who will pilfer from their employers, which means they will take home a box of Bic™ pens for their kids, or a roll of masking tape for wrapping their Christmas presents. Some people think of such activity as a kind of "perk" of employment; and, indeed, it is very easy to rationalize such thefts, saying that they're too small to really be considered stealing, and that "everybody does it." However, those Bic pens and rolls of masking tape add up to a sizable sum of money on which the employer will see no return — unless, of course, one of those Christmas presents is for him!

Rampant pilferage could be an indication that supervision is lax and the managers are not particularly well-respected. In your coverage of a company's supervisory techniques, indicate whether or not supervisors are too lenient or too strict, if they are liked or disliked, and whether or not they show favoritism to certain employees.

Fire and safety are two other important elements to include in your reports. You should certainly point out any obvious safety violations and fire hazards, the conditions and expiration dates on fire fighting equipment, and if safety regulations are observed. In one company, there was a policy in effect that after every earthquake the employees were supposed to evacuate the building until the managers on shift declared the building safe to reenter. However, the employees in this company complained that evacuation was too big of a hassle for them and interfered too greatly with their work to be practical. I wonder how greatly the building's collapse upon them would interfere with their work?

Most, if not all, companies have some kind of security system, and part of your job is to report on the effectiveness of that system. If the company employs security officers, you should report on the activity of those officers. Are they attentive to their duties? Are they respected by the company's employees? If the company has lockers, do the officers check them? And if they do check them, are the proper procedures followed?

Finally, if you are assigned an undercover position in a retail store, you can watch for how the cashiers and salespeople treat customers; if the clerks ring up all the items or attempt to defraud the company; if the store detectives are sharp and alert; and if there is any shoplifting activity.

INTERNAL SURVEY INVESTIGATION GUIDE

Now that you have a general knowledge of what to look for while working undercover, we can turn to how you should best get yourself into position to use that knowledge. Placement in undercover assignments involves three phases: the initial assignment, given to you by your supervisor; the process in which you actually "apply" for the job at your client's company; and the assignment itself.

Assignment by the Supervisor

Preparation is essential to success in undercover work. When your supervisor tells you about an assignment, make sure you get all the facts available about the case. You must fully understand before agreeing to take the assignment just what is and will be expected of you.

The first thing to determine is, of course, the nature of the problem the client has, and if you believe yourself capable of solving it. Remember H.P.—humility? Know your limitations. For example, if you are 6′2″, 230 pounds and male, then perhaps you might not be the *best* choice for a client who is concerned about several of his top male executives' alleged sexual harassment of female employees.

If you and your supervisor both decide that you are indeed suited for the task at hand, the next step is to define exactly what the job is for which you will be applying, and the time and place you should apply for the position. There are two ways to go about this: "cold," in which you would go into the personnel office and fill out the application like everyone else, go through an interview like everyone else, and hope you get the job (like everyone else). The other way is by "controlled" application, in which the job is assured to you from the outset and the application process is merely a formality. A very dangerous example of a controlled application is where the client tells the person who will be interviewing you that you are "the son/daughter of a friend," and he is doing you a favor by giving you this job. While this might make your chances of getting the job very secure, it may also set you apart from other employees, who might want to keep their distance from any "friend" of management. And remember that you are trying to gain their confidence, not their mistrust!

Controlled applications don't always guarantee that the interviewer knows you are a private investigator, as the above example indicates. The client could well be suspicious of the hiring personnel, for example, the client would be very anxious to make sure your identity remains unknown to that individual. Therefore, it is imperative that you ascertain before your interview whether or not your interviewer will be informed as to your true identity and purpose. You must also find out if the client's employment office will check your background. If there will be a check, work out an acceptable background with your handling official and memorize it—make sure it and you will stand up to scrutiny. Background would include business, personal references, and education.

How you dress for the interview should be established beforehand. Not every interview mandates a suit and tie. How many warehouse employers care if their workers wear pinstripes and paisleys? All they want to know is if that person can lift sixty pounds and make sense out of invoices. However, if you go apply at a bank in shorts and a tank-top, don't expect to be taken very seriously! The point here is that the way you dress for the interview should be in keeping with the job for which you are applying. Determine if special clothing or equipment will be needed. If you are applying as a plumber or a craftsman of some kind, will tools be needed?

An ever-important question that should be settled before the interview is pay schedule. Pay schedule includes both what you will be getting paid by your client and from your own company. For example, if your company pays you an hourly rate of $15 and the client's firm in which you will be operating undercover typically pays its employees $7 an hour, will you actually be making a gross of $22 an hour, or will there be some sort of adjustment so that your salary will remain $15 an hour? And if you should incur any type of expenses while working undercover, how will they be compensated for? What kind of expenses are authorized? Remember that expenses include the time and any money you spend cultivating employees outside of working hours.

Final considerations before actually going in and applying for the job should include the manner in which you will contact your handling official during both day and evening hours. As mentioned earlier, undercover work requires a great deal of independent functioning, yet it is imperative that you maintain a level of accountability with your supervisor. You need to know how and when you can reach this person, who you should call if your supervisor is not available, and how frequently contact should be made. You should also determine if your own car should be used, or if you will need to be provided with another. If you drive a new purple Camaro, for instance, and you are applying for a job as a warehouse worker whose salary cannot ever hope to top $7 an hour, perhaps you would be better off in an older Ford pickup with a dented grill and a few rusted out patches on the body. Along these same lines, you will need to know if your own private resident address may be used or if you should adopt a fake one. Turn over all identification that might link you to your private investigations company and make sure that the identification you do have will not conflict with the identity you have assumed for the assignment.

Applying for the Job

Now you are ready to go in and actually apply for the position. It is a good idea to arrive at the client's firm fifteen minutes early for your scheduled appointment. However, if you are unable to make it so early, at least make sure that you are there on time. Nothing makes a worse first impression than tardiness.

Once at the client's firm, go ahead and ask for the job in the way previously discussed with your handling official. If the receptionist tells you that they are not hiring, ask to fill out an employment application anyway and once you have filled it out, immediately call your handling official and apprise him of the situation. At no time should you abandon your pretext. That is, don't insist on having your interview by blustering to the receptionist that *you* are a private investigator and that the receptionist "by-golly better step aside" or you'll report this incident to this person's boss.

When filling out the application, be sure to do so carefully and completely, giving your correct name and Social Security number. Use the employment, personal references, and education background discussed with your supervisor, making sure that you stay true to the pretext that you have adopted for this assignment. You should avoid signing up for any insurance plans, especially Blue Cross or Blue Shield, because insurance companies perform extensive background checks on all applicants and as a result, your pretext would easily be revealed. In most companies you are allowed a certain amount of time to decide upon which insurance carrier you want, generally two to three months, and since most investigations do not last that long, you can usually manage to avoid that potential pitfall. Similarly, if it is necessary for you to apply for credit of any kind, be sure to speak first with your handling official. Credit companies also conduct background investigations of their own, so you will need to be very careful in handling situations of this type.

If the person interviewing you already knows all about who you are and why you are there, they may well be either surly and withdrawn or openly curious and inquisitive. They may ask you all kinds of questions: how long have you been a private investigator, what kinds of cases have you had, do you carry a gun, and where's your trench coat? They could press you to divulge the reason for your investigation into their company, asking for names or specifics. Their curiosity is only natural. However, you should discourage further probing as tactfully as possible by stating that the company regulations forbid your discussion of such matters, which they do. You are not allowed to discuss company matters with them, no matter how much you might like the ego boost of this individual's attention. Answer only those questions which relate to your pretext in applying for the job. Be courteous, but do not volunteer any additional information. Make sure that you agree upon the date and time you should report for work, and what your schedule and salary will be.

If there is an accompanying physical examination, you should be sure to answer all questions about disease history negatively. You have no history of high blood pressure or breast cancer or diabetes in your family; you have never been hospitalized, operated upon, or experienced adverse reactions to medication. The reason for such sweeping good health is that you don't want to give anyone any avenue for investigating you and discovering your true identity. If, for example, you indicate that as a child you received an injury to your spleen and pancreas and had to have both removed, it would be possible for someone to search your medical records and discover that you aren't quite who you profess yourself to be. Should you for any reason fail to pass the physical exam administered by your client's medical examiner, don't reveal your true identity to the physician and thereby try to secure a passing grade. Instead, accept the physician's decision and call your handling supervisor for instructions from an outside telephone as soon as possible.

On the Assignment

Now that you have made it through the interview, you are ready to start work. Again, you should arrive early and be among the last to leave. Not only does this make you look like a dedicated and hard-working employee, it also gives you ample opportunity to observe what goes on in the company. However, you must be careful not to appear *too* eager and conscientious, or you will alienate yourself from your fellow employees. No one likes a "teacher's pet." Do your regular job, and do it as well as everyone else does theirs: no better and no worse. Perfectionism and overachievement call just as much attention to a person as laziness and underachievement do. So don't skip lunches and breaks to try and make yourself look like a model employee. Instead, take the same amount of time everyone else does. If everyone goes out for a smoke at 10:30 am every morning, you should be out there with them; if you don't smoke, use the time to chat with people, get to know them, and remind them about lung cancer. In other words, distinguish yourself not in extraordinariness but in your very *ordinariness*. Remember, you can be fired by your client's foremen or managers just like any other employee.

Cultivate relationships with employees both on and off the job. Do not pick favorites—all employees are potentially valuable sources of information. Be careful to maintain your pretext identity at all times and remember: *under no circumstances are you to suggest to a client's employee that he/she commit a wrong.* This, again, is called entrapment, and besides being highly unethical, it is also illegal.

While on the job, you should try not to miss any days of work. The old rule is that the only day you miss will be the day "Joe Suspect" makes off with hundreds of dollars worth of the client's merchandise after two and a half weeks of perfectly exemplary behavior. However, if you are unavoidably unable to work, you should follow your client's established regulations regarding absences. Promptly call your immediate supervisor at your client's plant, inform the supervisor when you will be returning to work. You must also notify your investigation supervisor at once.

INFORMATION TO BE REPORTED

As soon as you walk into that interviewer's office, everything you see and hear is possible information that you can include in your report. Your job as an investigator begins with that initial contact with your client's employee and does not end until you turn in your final summary report.

The following information is provided to you as a guideline and is not by any means complete. Hopefully, though, after reading and studying the possible areas for reporting given here, you will be better prepared and equipped when you go into your undercover assignment and will know some of the things for which you should watch.

Applying for the Job

You should report on the interview you were given by the client's representative. Describe your general impressions of the personnel department: their level of professionalism, courtesy, effectiveness, etc. What kind of reception were you given? What kind of tests were given, and how were they administered? What were the results? If a physical examination was given, report on the thoroughness of the person examining you and any results that were obtained.

First Week of the Assignment

For the first week of your assignment, you will be primarily concerned with orienting yourself to the client's company and to your fellow employees. You should acquaint yourself with the physical layout of the plant as soon as possible, but without attracting undue attention to yourself. If, as a new employee, you are restricted to a particular area and are under close supervision, don't feel pressured. Stay where you are supposed to, be friendly and diligent, and you will soon have opportunity to move about more freely.

When writing about employees in your reports, you should use their names if they are known and their portrait parle if you do not know their names. The first week is a good time for you to be familiarizing yourself with the names and faces of the people you will be working with, as well as their work habits and abilities. Don't crowd people in the beginning; let them gradually warm up to you. Always keep in mind why you are there, but don't let any perceived urgency or pressure from your client override the necessity to work diligently and efficiently.

For the first week, you should report on the instructions and training you received for your duties. Tell who trained you and how thoroughly you were taught. Also describe the conditions of your work area; if it is clean, disorganized, free of fire and safety hazards or a virtual disaster waiting to happen? Say how you were received by the client's employees, and how efficient the supervisors you encountered seem to be. Your initial observation of employees' attitudes toward supervision are also important and should be included. If you see any blatant breach of regulations, like gambling or drinking or playing volleyball in the executive conference room, report on them. Describe your daily routine thus far: where you eat, who you eat with, how many breaks you take and for how long, etc.

By the end of the first week, you should have reported on as much of the plant as you have been able to observe, describing the layout, any exits or entrances, fences, and the like. Tell where employees park their cars and how they enter and exit the building. Identify by name those employees previously unnamed in your report, because by now you should have managed to learn their first names. Include a synopsis of how you were received by employees and supervisors after a week of work, and whether or not they seem to be accepting you.

The Second Week

By now you should be able to move freely about the plant or establishment. Your reports should become more focused and concrete as you begin to cultivate employees for information. Joining with workers in after-hours activities, like parties or picnics or bungee-cord jumping, will make it easier for you and will speed up your acceptance or "initiation" process. Remember that details are what interest clients, so make every effort to prepare systematic, factual reports on incidents that related directly to the specific purpose at hand.

Theft

As already discussed, virtually every company suffers from some kind of theft, whether that be pilferage or well-organized and endemic theft rings in which massive quantities of product are stolen. If you see any employees taking the client's merchandise out of the plant during working hours, say so in your reports. Any conversations you overhear regarding theft of any kind should obviously be reported, as should any rumors that are circulating about theft or shifts other than yours. Take note if it is possible for the client's property to be concealed in the trash, and check to see if this is indeed done. A common technique of theft is to place the desired items in a trash bag, load the bag in with the actual trash to be removed, and then drive by after the trash has been taken out to the curb or the dumpster and retrieve the bag full of stolen merchandise.

You should check to see if employees are concealing any of the client's product in their lockers for later removal from the plant. They could also be carrying it out in lunch bags, pocketbooks or purses, especially if packages and personal belongings are not checked. Your reports should note whether or not such checks occur, and if they happen only at quitting time, so that a worker may feasibly leave with a package during his shift and not be subject to search. If the client's merchandise is frequently left near exits, indicate that in your reports and watch to see if anyone comes along later and surreptitiously walks away with it. Observe if a particular employee goes out to their car during their shift for any reason, and ascertain whether or not they are carting off materials in their lunch box or on their person. Make note if employees are free to come and go as they please during their shift, and if they are taking your client's merchandise out through unauthorized exits as they do so.

Regarding relations between employees themselves, you should determine if there is any kind of undue friendliness between guards and employees, or between truck drivers and workers. Such relationships may indicate collusion: security officers turning a blind eye to theft by plant workers because they receive part of the "take;" truck drivers working with employees to haul off unauthorized shipments and pocket the proceeds. Determine how employees handle the receiving of your client's merchandise. Do they check the load? Are they careful? If trucks are loaded with product and left overnight, you should find out if the doors are properly locked and sealed, or if they are left open and thereby more susceptible to theft. Find out if all goods that are received are taken into the warehouse, or if some are left out overnight.

There are a number of other things you can watch for, such as whether or not employees have their friends come to visit them at the plant, if former employees are allowed to visit, or if certain employees arrive early and/or stay late, and why they do so. Basically, you should be alert and aware at all times of what is going on around you, and report any suspicious or unusual activity.

Supervision

Your client's supervisors are responsible for the controls within the plant. It is their responsibility to make sure that proper production is maintained, that the quality of the product is satisfactory, and that the employees they supervise obey the rules and regulations established by the client. When supervisors are lax in their duties, employee morale breaks down, controls cease to function and problems go undetected until inventory time. Remember that major thefts develop through small pilferage, and poor supervision is often the culprit for allowing pilfering to take place.

Each supervisor should be reported upon individually. Somethings you can cover when reporting on this topic include whether or not the supervisor shows favoritism, tolerates inefficiency, and demands proper performance and work output from those that the supervisor oversees. You should make note of whether or not the supervisor is liked and respected by the employees, and if they work well under this individual's supervision.

An important consideration is whether or not the supervisor knows his or her job. Even though one would like to believe that all managers are in position because of some merit or proven expertise on their part, such is not always the case, as my own personal experience shows. When I got out of the Navy, in my early twenties, I interviewed at a company for the position of production manager, even though I wasn't even sure what exactly a production manager did. I spoke glowingly and vaguely of all my "production managing" experience while in the Navy and managed to convince my interviewer that I was eminently qualified for the position. So he hired me and I showed up for work without the foggiest clue of what exactly I had been hired to do. People kept popping into my office to shake my hand and rave about how excited they were that I had come to straighten things out, so that the first few days passed in a sort of euphoric haze of inactivity. However, I knew that sooner or later I was going to have to produce something or I would lose my job. So, on my lunch hour I walked down the block a ways to a company that was similar to my own, went in and asked to speak with the production manager. Fortunately for me, she was a very nice woman and when I explained my situation, she graciously offered to teach me how to do my job. With lunch hours covered, I only had to worry about the other seven hours. This actually proved to be less of a problem than I first thought, thanks to a fellow at the plant who had been there many years. This man spent the greater part of his day walking about the plant with a clipboard in his hands, making notes and looking incredibly official. Everyone assumed that he was on some legitimate company business. I soon learned, however, that he really wasn't doing anything at all except doodling and looking important, and getting away with it—and *had been* getting away with it for quite a while. He was close to retiring when I came into the company. When he left, he gave me his clipboard, and I learned an invaluable lesson of corporate success: all you have to do to be important and busy is to *look* important and busy.

Employee Morale

The morale and attitude of employees directly influence work production. Dissatisfaction can lead to sabotage and thefts. Your reports should deal with the morale of your client's employees and answer these questions:

1. Does the employee consider the job a good one, and is the employee satisfied with it?
2. Is the employee satisfied with pay and overtime?
3. What does the employee think of their immediate supervisor and of top management?
4. Is the employee satisfied with working conditions, and does the employee offer any suggestions for improvement?

It is crucial to remember here that you are forbidden by federal law to report on any lawful union activities, either verbally or in writing. The Wagner Act makes it illegal for you to report on union members, meetings, or the sentiments of employees toward the union, whether they are prop or con union. You may not even report on individuals who are in the process of organizing a union.

It may be necessary for you to join a union after a certain period of time in your undercover employment to maintain your pretext. This is entirely permissible, but does not give you the right even as an ostensible union member to report on any of the union activities. Even though such information might be appreciated by your client and shed a great deal of light on the level or morale in his or her company, you are legally bound not to divulge it.

Employee Activity

On your assignment, you should develop all the facts concerning matters in the client's establishment. Of course the specific problem for which you were initially hired is of primary importance, but you should investigate all other matters that appear to be relevant. Reporting on the activities of employees is of great significance to the client in operating the client's business. Do not assume the client is aware of any irregularities just because they seem to be common knowledge among the employees with whom you work, or because the supervisors are aware of them and do nothing to remedy them.

Some areas of employee activity on which you can report are any carelessness on the part of employees in the performance of their duties, overstaying lunches or breaks, and any breakage or imperfect work. Note the employee's attention to duties: does this individual know the job and is he a good worker? Sometimes employees will work fast in order to leave early, or slowly so as to get overtime; these are things the client would like to know. The client is also interested, of course, in knowing who is doing a particularly exemplary job or is trying to better themselves, either through schooling or community service.

If there are any time clock irregularities, note them in your reports. In most companies, people know just how many minutes they get before or after the hour until they are credited as being tardy or overtime, and often will leave just that many minutes early or stay late enough to earn fifteen minutes of overtime. They may also take overly long lunches and then fill out time clock adjustment forms claiming a mispunch or an erroneous reading on the part of the time clock.

Report on employees who hold other jobs, and if the other job is interfering with their present employment. Individuals who "moonlight" are often extremely tired and less attentive to their duties, resulting in carelessness and reduced quality. If employees are complaining constantly or not doing their jobs, let your client know in your reports. Any arguments, fights, or animosity that interfere with production should also be included. Remember that you are not to suggest to any employee that they commit an illegal or wrongful act (entrapment) or report on any activity that is in conjunction with lawful union activities (Wagner Act).

Safety

The greatest majority of injuries occur when employees violate safety rules. People slip and fall because of spills that haven't been cleaned up; they hurt their backs lifting when proper lifting techniques are not observed; they twist or break ankles racing each other down the stairs to the time clock at the end of their shifts. The cost to the client in terms of production delays and overtime is considerable, because it is the client who pays for the disregard of safety rules in the loss of revenue to the company, and sometimes in the permanent injuries of employees. Therefore, the benefit to the client and employees that you report any safety violations or dangers is immense.

Obviously, you should report any unsafe equipment use, or on equipment that is being handled in an unsafe manner. If the forklift drivers in your warehouse are having drag races around the pallets, perhaps the client should know about it. If there are pipes or objects protruding from walls or lying about underfoot, report them. Grease or water on the floors invite tumbles and lawsuits; report it. Cluttered aisles and working space, poor or inadequate lighting, and the condition of electrical equipment, exits and elevators are also important things to note in your reports, as are the general cleanliness of the plant, the presence and use of safety guards on equipment, and the safety of stairs, railings and the like.

Along with safety hazards, potential fire hazards need to be recorded for your client. Fire in an industrial plant can result in destruction of equipment, material, and lives. The potential cost to the client could be enormous, particularly if the plant is totally decimated by fire. Therefore, you should be sure to investigate fire extinguishers, hoses, and sprinkler heads to make sure they are in good operating condition. Find out if there are fire drills and if fire regulations are observed. Locate the first aid stations, if there are any, and determine the condition of the equipment.

Report any observed fire hazards, such as exposed electrical wiring or volatile chemicals carelessly stored.

Shipping and Receiving

One of the major areas where theft can occur is in the shipping and receiving department of your client's plant. If you are assigned to this area, or are in a position to observe and cultivate these employees, you should report on how the client's product is checked in and if the checkers are performing their jobs correctly. Any carelessness in the handling of freight, excessive breakage, and misdirection of freight should be reported, as well as by whom and how often such incidents occur. The handling of "valuable" or special freight and how it is stored is also a possible area for reporting.

Watch how trucks are loaded. Is it done carefully and properly? Are trucks overloaded? Are partial loads that are left overnight locked and sealed, and rechecked in the morning? Determine whether or not the client has the area checked during the evening hours, and if all merchandise is taken inside the plant at night or if any is left outside or near exits during the day. Any obvious collusion between truck drivers and employees should be reported.

Unauthorized absences from the area should be indicated to your client. Relay any discussions you overhear regarding dissatisfaction with the company. Note if the foreman or dock supervisor overlooks misconduct, breakage, or idleness, and if there is any talk or evidence of stealing. Find out if employees park their cars near the loading dock area; if they leave early, stay late or overstay their lunch breaks; and if unnecessary and preventable overtime is incurred.

Guard Department

The guard is intended to enforce company regulations. Checking badges or identification, controlling or monitoring packages, escorting visitors, and making inspection tours after dark are all part and parcel of a security officer's duties. The security guard's primary purpose is fire, safety, and theft control. If a client has a good, well-trained guard department, then the client has a useful tool to assist in the operation of the business. However, if the guard force is not functioning correctly, the potential for great harm is immense. A guard who stands by the exit gates being a "good guy" while employees march through with the client's product is hardly a "good guy" to the client. A guard who overlooks misconduct, does not see unauthorized exit doors standing open, or who actively cooperates in theft, is a client's gravest nightmare. In one investigation of a company's security force, it was discovered that the security officers on the night shift—two women—were actively soliciting and engaging in sexual acts with the employees. The snack truck would drive up, peddling sandwiches, sodas and junk food, and then the security car would show up and park right behind it. Thirty dollars bought dinner and a little something extra.

Ideally, it is the security force's responsibility to protect the plant. Your responsibility is to make sure their job is being done. If there is undue familiarity between guards and employees, point that out in your reports. Find out if and how the guards check packages or bundles that employees carry in or out. Do they even inspect the locker rooms or make inspections throughout the plant, outside of the regular rounds? Have you overheard employees talking about how they have timed the guards' rounds?

Ascertain whether or not employees respect the security personnel, and if guards are considered "company men/women" by employees. If employees talk amongst themselves about stealing by guards or their participation in theft, report it. Any gambling, reading, or smoking done by guards while on duty should be noted, as should any sleeping or drinking. Determine whether or not the guard is physically suited to his job; i.e., is the guard overweight, underweight, etc. If the guard allows unauthorized people to enter the plant, accepts gifts from employees, or borrows or lends money to them, let your client know. Any departures from the plant while the officer is supposed to be on duty should also be noted.

Store Investigations

Although many of the preceding guidelines and hints will apply to investigations you conduct in retail stores, there are certain other factors unique to such assignments that you will need to know. Besides employee theft, retail stores are highly susceptible to shoplifters, whether professional or amateur, male or female, child or adult. The apprehension of shoplifters is the job of the store security department, not you. However, you *are* expected to report on the efficiency of the security department.

Your client will want to know if store detectives are alert and active. Most important, your client will be interested in determining the extent of shoplifting activity. Treatment of customers and the accuracy of sales register transactions are also important.

Any drinking or gambling by employees should be reported. If employees wear the client's clothing out of the store (without paying for it, of course), your client will appreciate knowing about it. Find out if salespeople purposefully damage goods to obtain markdowns, if extra goods are mailed out and if credit charge plates are properly handled. If goods are improperly marked down, as in a shoe salesman tagging a box of Italian leather shoes $25 instead of $125 because his potential customer is a very attractive woman with whom he hopes to form some kind of meaningful romantic relationship, report it to your client.

MAJOR HEADINGS FOR UNDERCOVER REPORTS

There is an almost endless number of areas on which you may report while working undercover, as the preceding guidelines indicate. To help you organize your thoughts and prepare you for categorizing large quantities of information, we have provided you with an outline of major headings, each of which is broken down into a number of possible areas on which you may report.

Remember that this is provided as a guide only. You can supply your own headings or modify these as the need arises and you become more adept at recognizing potential areas on which to report. Ideally, your daily report should contain information from at least six of the major headings, and five subheadings for each major heading. For example, you should report on five subheadings for Employee Misconduct, such as any rumors of gossip, fighting/horseplay, profanity, favoritism, and flirting. Such information can be either positive—meaning that you actually *saw* one employee tip another one headfirst into a bucket of hazardous refuse—or negative, which means that you did not see any incidents of such activity. Simply put, for each observed incident, state Who, What, Where, When, Why and How, and if you don't know, say so! It is just as valid for an employer to know who *isn't* stealing as well as who is.

Heading I: Dishonesty

1. Possibility of theft
2. Observed theft
3. Talk of theft

4. Admitted past theft
5. Methods of theft
6. Collusive theft
7. Fraudulent exchanges
8. Fraudulent refunds
9. Kickbacks
10. Padded expenditures
11. Price alterations
12. Theft of merchandise/cash
13. Unauthorized discounts
14. Unauthorized substitutions
15. Shortage from vendors
16. Shortage to customers
17. Give-aways
18. Postage theft
19. Unauthorized Xeroxing
20. Unauthorized phone use
21. Time cheating
22. Record falsification
23. Personal work
24. Espionage
25. Suspicious activities/behavior
26. Insurance fraud
27. Talk of police/security, undercover activities
28. False work application

Heading II: Employee Misconduct

1. Tardiness
2. Absenteeism
3. Break stretching
4. Early departure
5. False time records
6. Smoking in unauthorized areas
7. Eating in unauthorized areas
8. Drinking in unauthorized areas
9. Talk of hard drugs
10. Possession of hard drugs
11. Sale of hard drugs
12. Purchase of hard drugs

13. Use of hard drugs
14. Talk, possession, sale, purchase or use of marijuana
15. Drinking (beer, wine and alcohol) on company time and property, during lunch/breaks
16. Working under the influence of drugs or alcohol
17. Driving under the influence of drugs or alcohol
18. Gambling
19. Loansharking
20. Possession of a weapon
21. Profanity, obscenity
22. Rumors/gossip
23. Fighting/horseplay
24. Insubordination
25. Failure to follow procedures
26. Failure to follow instructions
27. Failure to wear safety equipment
28. Careless handling of property
29. Misuse of company vehicles/property
30. Favoritism
31. Fraternization
32. Flirting
33. Poor customer service
34. Personal hygiene/poor appearance
35. Sabotage
36. Work pacing
37. Sexual harassment
38. Discrimination
39. Markdowns
40. Employee discount abuse

Heading III: Physical Security

1. Door security
2. Unsecured windows
3. Gates and fence
4. Lock-up procedures
5. Defective alarms/locks
6. Key control management
7. Roof/skylight security employee
8. Blocked closed circuit T.V.

9. Blocked fire exits
10. Computer access
11. Telephone access (outside lines)
12. Employee badge control
13. Cash security (coffee can)
14. Tool/equipment control
15. Fire hazards
16. Careless shipping/receiving
17. Exit security
18. Employee respect for security
19. Guard systems
20. Guard fraternization
21. Persons in unauthorized areas
    a. Employees/ex-employees/friends
    b. Customers
    c. Vendors
    d. Contractors/temps
22. Information security
23. Night security
24. Adequate lighting
25. Vehicular security
26. System for merchandise removal
27. Activities/injuries
28. Safety hazards
29. Fire extinguishers
30. Parking lot access
31. Files access
32. Unsafe storage
33. Toxic waste

Heading IV: Supervision

1. Nepotism
2. Favoritism
3. Fraternizing
4. Sexual harassment
5. Discrimination
6. Employee respect for management
7. Unnecessary procedures
8. Unnecessary overtime

9. Padded overtime
10. Lack of planning
11. Duplication of effort
12. Weakness in control
13. Faulty scheduling
14. Poor judgment
15. Overstaffing
16. Leaving early
17. Poor production control
18. Poor quality control
19. Condoning violations
20. Waste of labor
21. Waste of material
22. Lack of supervision
23. Poor training/orientation
24. Poor or no records
25. Poor housekeeping
26. Knowledge of company policy
27. Dissemination of policies to employees

Heading V: Employer/Employee Relations

1. Lack of communication
2. OSHA compliance
3. Promotions
4. Overtime
5. Rumors
6. Hiring practices
7. Attitude toward management
8. Awareness of employee rights
9. Discrimination
10. Suggestion system
11. Safety committee: is it active or just used for venting concerns
12. Employees' job attitudes
13. Benefits
14. Probation period
15. Handling of complaints
16. Customers' opinion of client, facility or employees
17. Customer complaints
18. Handling of customer complaints

19. Hiring procedure
20. Firing procedure
21. Screening procedure
22. Training procedure
23. Employee assistance programs
24. Posting of employee rights

Heading VI: Evaluation of Employees

1. Abilities
2. Ambitions
3. Attendance records
4. Character
5. Conscientiousness
6. Courtesy
7. Friendliness
8. Integrity
9. Morals
10. Vices
11. Drinking (type, quantity)
12. Education
13. Family
14. Friends
15. Hobbies
16. Honesty
17. Illnesses
18. Leadership
19. Past criminal record
20. Past employment
21. Personal appearance
22. Personality traits
23. Physical characteristics
24. Possessions
25. Potential
26. Special interests
27. Talents
28. Value to the company
29. Work habits
30. Willingness to train others
31. General attitude of the work force

Heading VII: New Systems and Procedures

Repeat accordingly

Heading VIII: Lunch/Breaks/Parties

Report with one of the preceding section

Remember: Reports are to be made on a daily basis. There are no exceptions, even if you miss work because of a terrible cold and are absolutely too wretched to stir from your bed. If you are sick, or business is closed, you must still submit a negative report, which means you must report the fact that you did not work for that date and give the reason.

SHOPLIFTING

A very specific form of undercover investigation, as already mentioned, involves the detection and prevention of shoplifting. Because most retail stores operate on a razor-thin profit margin, the losses incurred through shoplifting add up to a significant total cost to the company. Clearly, the need for safeguards against such activity is great; however, it is not practical to expect that such safeguards would consist of catching each and every individual who surreptitiously slips a pack of gum into their pocketbook. The key to preventing shoplifting lies in your ability to identify potential shoplifters as they come into the store, an ability dependent upon your familiarity with the typical profiles of such persons, the methods they employ and the mannerisms they display.

Types of Shoplifters

The first type of shoplifter is the amateur. Usually, amateur shoplifters steal on a whim, or a dare. They are not habitual criminals and generally do not take items of great expense or items that would require a certain finesse and cunning in removing them from the store. The professional shoplifters, or "booster," as they are known, are much more adept at removing merchandise, often employing devices specifically. tailored to expedite shoplifting. Then there is the kleptomaniac, an individual who steals out of a compulsive desire to obtain sexual gratification. Again, like the amateur, the kleptomaniac generally does not make large or frequent thefts. Vagrants steal out of need, having no other recourse at their disposal whereby they may obtain food or money for food. Finally, drug addicts account for seventy-five percent of all shoplifters, a figure that really should not be too surprising. They may steal items to sell later, or they may actually steal food, since they may be spending all their money to finance their drug habit and as such have nothing left over with which to buy basic necessities.

Modus Operandi

There are several methods shoplifters employ, the use of which depends upon the individual and the item to be stolen. In clothing stores, for example, there are two primary ways that shoplifters steal merchandise. In a fitting room they either wear merchandise beneath their own clothing or leave their clothing in the fitting room, walking out with the client's merchandise. If fitting room personnel are not vigilant, this kind of activity can go on very easily.

Tag switches involve taking two items of disparate price and attaching the less expensive price tag to the more expensive item. For example, a shoplifter may take a silk blouse that costs $59.99 and a cotton tank top that has been red-tagged to only $8, into the fitting room and put the $8 price tag on the $59.99 blouse.

Anyone who has ever worked retail at Christmas time is familiar with this next method of shoplifting: exchanging stolen goods. Usually stores require some kind of receipt before they will issue a cash refund, but most have a policy in which they will give the individual a credit voucher good toward the purchase of any item of the same value within the store. This works particularly well in shoe stores, where individuals may abscond with boxes of shoes that unwitting salespeople have left unattended, and later "return" the shoe, claiming that they were given the wrong size or style.

Professional shoplifters often use certain specialized equipment to aid them in their "craft," as mentioned above. Such equipment includes the "booster box," which is a container of some kind with an easily opened false bottom or compartment into which merchandise may be quickly deposited and secreted away. Booster clothing operates on the same principle of concealment: usually there will be some kind of hidden pocket or pouch sewn into the lining where the professional shoplifter can easily and unobtrusively deposit stolen items. And, finally, the "sling-under," used predominantly by women, is a method of shoplifting in which an elastic strap or "sling" is worn around the leg and used to support stolen merchandise as the thief exits the store. The way it works is that the shoplifter "drops" something to the ground, steps over it and hooks it up into the strap on their legs. Women, obviously, are more successful at concealing this activity because they can wear long skirts or dresses. Of course, men can wear long flowing garments as well, but in our culture such attire on a man is much more likely to draw attention.

How to Detect Shoplifters

Because they offer lots of convenient hiding places, baggy clothes are often worn by would-be shoplifters. Of course, since the fashion among young teenagers today is to dress in clothes that are at least fifteen sizes too large for them, baggy clothes in and of themselves are not sufficient evidence that the wearer is a booster. Other things to watch for, then, include customers who walk behind sales counters, people who exhibit quick and abrupt movements, and individuals who appear nervous and unduly sweaty. People who keep one hand in their pocket could be hiding merchandise and should be watched carefully.

Prevention

Some ways that shoplifting can be prevented include installing closed circuit television cameras, convex mirrors, and good lighting. Display shelves that are stacked too high provide good cover for shoplifters; thus, making sure that shelves are not too high to preclude easy visibility over their tops would be another way to make stealing more difficult. Make sure that merchandise is kept in its proper containers; otherwise fraud may take place. For example, at a well-known sporting goods store, there was a sale on basketballs underway and the salespeople had allowed customers to take balls out of their respective boxes and leave them cluttering the display. A man who did not speak or read English came in with his young son to buy a basketball for the boy's birthday. The son picked out a ball he wanted from among the abundant loose balls, and his father, reasoning that all basketballs were the same, grabbed a box, put the ball into it and went to the counter to pay. The cashier recognized that the basketball in the box did not match the ball pictured on the outside of the box, determined that the father had intentionally placed a more expensive ball into a box with a lower price tag, and called the store security. The father was handcuffed and dragged into the back; the boy was in tears; the police were called in. Ultimately it was discovered that no intention existed on the part of the man to defraud the company. And, incidentally, the man got himself a good lawyer and won a nice settlement for being wrongfully accused and subjected to emotional distress.

First of all, the necessary components of shoplifting are: item, intent, and opportunity. In order for shoplifting to occur, you must first have, obviously, something to steal. Second, you must have the intent to prematurely deprive—it is not shoplifting to pick up something, fully intending to pay for it at the counter, and walk out of the store with it in your hands because you honestly forgot to stop at the counter to pay. Absentmindedness is not a crime. A nuisance, maybe, but not a crime.

And, to complete this formulated shoplifting triangle of item and intent, you need to have the *opportunity* to steal. You can have every intention in the world of stealing a box of soda crackers from your local market, but if there is a 6'7" security guard with a big shiny gun and a bad attitude standing watch right in front of that cracker display, your chances of stealing a box are slim and none.

Shoplifting prevention, then, depends upon removing the opportunity. You can't force people to stop formulating the intention to commit theft. You can't take away the items to steal, because then free enterprise would come to a screeching halt and shopping malls would become extinct.

RETURN TO THE SCENE OF THE CRIME

Remember that in undercover work, it is essential that you are a keen observer and are able to remember accurately what you observe. You should never lose sight of the fact that a person's career could be riding on the results of an investigation you conduct in his or her workplace. So, take care, take your time, and take my advice: be *detailed, diligent, and thorough, in all humility and patience,* and you will do just fine.

REVIEW

1. What is the definition of undercover?
2. What are the objectives of going undercover?
3. True or False: It is legal for you to suggest that an employee steal your client's merchandise as long as you are doing so in the context of an investigation.
4. True or False: You may not report any legal union activities in writing, but you may do so orally.
5. What do D.D.T. and H.P. stand for?
6. Name the three general types of undercover investigations.

7. What are the purposes of undercover investigations in the workplace?
8. When may you take people you work with in your undercover assignment into your confidence?
9. True or False: If you do not report for work, you must still submit a report for that day.
10. Why should you avoid the use of abbreviations in your daily reports?
11. What is the summary report?
12. What is pilferage?
13. What do "cold" and "controlled" refer to in the context of undercover work?
14. True or False: While working undercover, you should make every effort to show yourself to be a harder worker than those on your shift.
15. What are the eight general headings for undercover reporting?
16. How many categories should you include for each major heading you report on?
17. What are some things you can report on as regards the shipping and receiving department of your client's company?
18. What are three methods of shoplifting?
19. What three elements make up the shoplifting triangle?
20. Which of the three elements of the triangle do you remove in order to prevent shoplifting?

Chapter 4

SURVEILLANCE TECHNIQUES

Jason Aubrey, sixteen years old, lived in a quiet residential neighborhood not far from the main campus of the University of Miami, Florida. Located behind two shopping centers on Southwest 82nd Avenue near 122nd Street, it was a pretty average neighborhood—even though Miami in 1986 was a center for cocaine and other drug trafficking and had a reputation for being one of the most violent cities in the United States. It was a reputation that the then-popular "Miami Vice" series was built upon and helped perpetuate.

On the morning of April 11, 1986, Jason Aubrey's quiet neighborhood became the scene of one of the worst, bloodiest incidents in FBI history.

For fourteen months prior to April 11, 1986, Miami banks and armored cars had been plagued by a series of armed robberies. The FBI had been conducting an investigation into the robberies but had not had much luck until two of their agents noticed a suspicious black Monte Carlo while they were conducting surveillance. They called in the license plates on the vehicle and discovered that the car, stolen six months ago, was purported to have been used in some of the holdups. The agent requested assistance, keeping the car in sight. Three other cars showed up and the agents, believing themselves sufficiently prepared, ordered the Monte Carlo to pull over.

The two men in the car did not comply quite as expected: they opened fire. By the time the shoot-out was over, the street was strewn with dead and wounded men, cars with obliterated windows, a large assortment of firearms and countless empty shell casings. One of the cars had crashed headfirst into the wall at the back of the shopping centers. Another had careened into a tree, and two others had collided with each other. More than 100 shots had been fired, two FBI agents were killed and two men in the Monte Carlo were dead. Jason Aubrey, hiding behind a bush to watch the shooting, saw "a man in a windbreaker bleeding but still standing and firing at one of the cars."[1] Billie Hollaway, who like Jason lives near the scene of the confrontation, said that "So many shots were fired you could smell the shots."[2]

Duane Parker, twenty-four, said, "I thought it was a Miami Vice episode."[3]

---

[1]Treaster, Joseph B. "Two FBI Agents Killed in Miami." *The New York Times,* Saturday, April 12, 1986, pp. 1, 8.

[2]Ibid., p. 8.

[3]Ibid.

Fortunately for the career private investigator, most surveillance operations do not culminate in the disastrous way the 1986 FBI operation in Miami did. Most subjects will not open fire on you if they suspect you of following or watching them. And most surveillance operations will not resemble highly overdramatized television series—unless, of course, you, like Don Johnson, choose to eschew shaving and wear your shoes without socks!

Surveillance is an important tool whereby the investigator may obtain information that cannot more easily be obtained by using direct means or researching various public and/or private records and documents. Simply put, surveillance involves the direct observation of activity and can be stationary, in which you as the surveillant remain in one place and watch the activity that occurs at that given location; or moving, in which you follow the person, or *subject*, as they are called, about the community. It is also possible to conduct surveillance operations in which both methods are used, depending upon the situation and circumstances.

PURPOSE OF SURVEILLANCE

The purpose of surveillance is to conduct a secretive and continuous observation of persons, places, vehicles or objects in order to obtain information concerning the identity and activity of individuals. It involves waiting, watching, recording, and observing, and therefore it is important that as a private investigator have both good observation skills and power to remember what you observe, as stressed in the preceding chapter. Oftentimes, surveillance operations are conducted only as a last resort, when all other means of gathering information have been tried and proven ineffective, so you need to be aware that the success or failure of your surveillance operation could translate into the success or failure of the entire case.

OBJECTIVES FOR CONDUCTING SURVEILLANCE

Of course, the specific reasons for conducting surveillance depend entirely upon the individual case for which you are doing the surveilling. For example, surveillance is useful both in cases involving runaways and missing persons, and in cases concerned with industrial espionage. Generally, however, the reasons for conducting surveillance include some of the following: to obtain information or develop leads secure evidence that a crime or wrong has indeed been committed and to observe the actual commission of a wrongful act. Determining the identity of a subject or that subject's contacts is another objective of surveillance. Checking the reliability of informants is also a viable reason for conducting surveillance, as is checking on the loyalty of employees. Surveillance is particularly ideal for determining whether a subject is frequenting a particular location. If, for example, you are conducting an investigation for someone who feels her husband is being unfaithful to her, observing that husband parked five nights out of seven in the driveway of a woman might well prove useful to your client.

Surveillance also gives you the opportunity to observe the subject's habits, meetings, and transactions. You can obtain photographs that would implicate the subject for involvement in illicit activities, such as in receiving stolen property, selling or buying drugs, or playing Twister without any clothes on with an individual not his or her spouse.

For criminal surveillance operations, you are looking to detect and prevent crime. If there has been any property stolen, a possible objective of surveillance could be the location and recovery of that property. Any evidence you can obtain that would be sufficient cause for making an arrest should be sought out while you are conducting surveillance. In addition, you want to locate and apprehend suspects or wanted persons: the surveillance of one subject might lead you to the whereabouts of another.

In civil cases, surveillance is used to locate witnesses for subpoena, find missing persons in divorce proceedings, and to verify information supplied by undercover operatives. Any other information that is to be used in civil matters may also be obtained by surveillance. Finally, surveillance can be used to detect insurance fraud, such as the classic example of an individual claiming a back injury in a workman's comp case but whom you observe doing Jane Fonda's aerobics video in their living room.

D.D.T.

Remember in the last chapter when we discussed the three elements necessary for success in undercover operations? In case the answer to this question is "no," let me take this opportunity to refresh your memory. When conducting surveillance operations, you must be sure to be *detailed,* focusing on every possible item that could pertain to the matter being investigated. Item by item, making sure that nothing is missed—this is the first *D* of DDT.

The second *D* refers to diligence. Be careful. Be complete. Be persevering and industrious. Don't fall asleep while you are sitting in your van; don't give up and go home just because you've spent thirty minutes outside your subject's residence and haven't seen anything more exciting than a cat doing its business in the rose bed. Remember that surveillance entails waiting, watching, recording, and observing, and as such requires that you be patient, observant, and intelligent.

And, finally, be thorough. Stay with your case to the very end, and carry it out completely. The outcome of your case depends entirely on your ability—a big responsibility. So be thorough.

As mentioned in the preceding chapter, it might be a good idea for you to test your attention to detail by giving yourself frequent "quizzes." Walk into a room, look around for thirty seconds, walk out of the room and write down everything that you remember, testing yourself for accuracy by checking your list once you are back inside the room. You might be surprised to "discover" details about rooms in which you habitually spend a great deal of time, simply because you have never made the effort to fully acquaint yourself with the contents of those rooms. Learn to recognize and remember important features and characteristics that you might otherwise overlook, but that could prove important to your investigation at a later date.

You can do a similar kind of thing while driving. Simply look at the license plate in front of you and read it out phonetically. For example, the plate "HOT4U" would be read out Henry Ocean Tom Four Union. You can also look at vehicles as you drive and not their identifying characteristics: license plate number, make, model, color, year, etc. So, in the example given above, you could note the license plate (HOT4U), the make (Porsche), model (Slantnose), color (Fire Engine Red), and the year (1974). But remember—never close your eyes while you are driving— not even to test your recall.

PROPER DESCRIPTION

Before we send you out on your first surveillance, we need to make sure that you go out knowing what you are looking for and how to go about preparing proper descriptions of what you see. Some of this will be review from Chapter 1, namely portrait parle of a person and of a vehicle, but some of this we have not yet covered and applied directly to the subject of surveillance.

Residence and Neighborhood of Subject

When you go into a subject's neighborhood, you need to observe the demographics of the area. Ascertain the typical ethnic group and the general income of the residents, as well as the apparent population density of the area. What is the typical layout of the neighborhood—is it a fairly upscale stretch of custom homes and four-car garages, or is it a low-income housing project? Also, what is the condition of the neighborhood? Is it well-kept or has it been allowed to deteriorate into disrepair? Look at the spacing of the buildings. In much of San Francisco, for example, there is no spacing between houses, whereas in most suburbs the houses are further apart, with more spacious yards and varied landscaping.

As for the actual house of the subject whom you are surveilling, you should note the color of it, how many stories it has, and what its construction is (i.e., brick, stucco, frame, etc.). If there are any sheds or garages, swimming pools or tennis courts within the subject's property lines, describe them. Also observe the land around the subject's house and describe it: whether it is wooded, flat, hilly, littered with trash or impeccably groomed.

Description of Vehicles

As discussed in Chapter 1, there are a number of components that go into the identification of a vehicle. Vehicle identification numbers provide the most positive identification of a vehicle, but they are less readily apparent than are other characteristics. License plate numbers, the make of the vehicle, model, and color are the other four characteristics you learned about in Chapter 1 that go into a vehicle's portrait parle. For purposes of surveillance, all five of these identifying traits apply, with the addition of two more: the year of the vehicle and any identifying marks, such as a dented left fender or a bumper sticker that reads "I may be slow, but I'm ahead of you!"

Description of the Subject

Since it is obviously of the utmost importance that your description of the subject be as accurate and detailed as humanly possible, you should know exactly how to render a complete portrait of your subject. As given in Chapter 1, this description should include the following, in this order: gender, ethnicity, hair color, eye color, age, height, and weight. However, just as we added two more to the vehicle portrait parle for the purposes of surveillance, so too have we added on a few more to the portrait parle of an individual: build, clothing, jewelry, and tattoos. Thus, a very complete and workable description of a person might go something like this: female, Caucasian, blond, brown eyes, twenty-four, 5'2", 200 lbs., stocky, dressed in army fatigues and silver brocade shoes, with four earrings in her left ear, and a large tattoo shaped like a pitbull on the back of her neck. The margin of error in identifying such an individual after you are armed with as complete a definition as that is really very small.

Subject's Activity

In your surveillance report, you will be giving descriptions of what your subject is doing while you watch him or her. Such descriptions need to be as detailed as possible. "He worked in the yard and then made dinner" is not nearly complete enough. Describe *what* he did in the yard—pulling weeds, trimming hedges, mowing the lawn—and *how* he did it—kneeling to pull weeds, reaching over his head with the shears to trim the hedges, pushing an archaic, dull-bladed lawn mower across the grass, etc. How long did he work, and how much did he get done? And when he made dinner, what did he make? How did he make it? Was it a meal that required much preparation, or was it a microwave pizza that only required removal from the box and the pressing of a few buttons? These are the types of questions—*details*—that you should be watching for when you conduct your surveillance operations. Such details round out your report and provide a complete picture of what went on. Basically, you want to describe each move so that the reader may easily visualize it.

In case you think such attention to detail is a waste of time, consider this: you have been sent to surveil an individual who is claiming a back injury and has filed a suit for $200,000 in damages. Your client wants to determine if this individual really does have an injury of the magnitude he or she assets in the claim. In your report, you write that the client "bent over to pick up a piece of paper." Now, what is wrong with that?

Plenty.

Individuals with back pain move in a particular way. Every move is studied so as not to exacerbate the pain they are experiencing. Thus, persons with genuine back pain will not likely execute a bend from the waist, but from the knees, lowering themselves carefully toward whatever object they need to retrieve. That, or find someone else to pick up the object for them! In other words, they move in a way indicative of injury. The statement that an individual "bent over to pick up the piece of paper" tells the client nothing about the manner in which that individual executed the move. Now "he bent slowly from the knees and leaned slightly to his left side, his right hand on his lower back" is a much more detailed description and reveals a great deal more about the actual action.

Description of Individuals Other Than the Subject

As with the subject, you should provide a portrait parle of other individuals. In addition, describe any distinguishing uniform or clothing worn by these persons—if the individual wears a U.S. Postal Carrier uniform, for example, it might be safe to presume that this person works for the U.S. Postal Service!

PRETEXT

Funk and Wagnall define pretext as "A fictitious reason or motive advanced to conceal a real one." During the course of your surveillance operations, it will often be necessary for you to come up with various pretexts as to why you are spending time parked in strange neighborhoods or following a certain individual around. Ideally, the questions will not come from the person you are following, but may well come from suspicious neighbors. For example, if you are conducting a stakeout in a neighborhood where the neighbors are very tightly knit and have formed all kinds of neighborhood watch committees, you might very well be approached by someone inquiring what exactly you are doing. Thus, it is important that you learn to develop plausible pretexts and an ability to answer logical questions about them.

Basically, a pretext is a skillful plan whose objective is to obtain a specific piece of information. One example of a very simple pretest is to go to the door of your subject with a pizza and "pretend" that you are merely a Pizza Hut™ delivery man with an extra large pepperoni-with-anchovies for a Mr. Joe Blow. This pretext allows you to determine two very important things: first, if Mr. Joe Blow truly resides at the home of which you intend to set up a surveillance, and second, if Mr. Joe Blow is at home. Of course, to operate this pretext you will need a pizza and maybe a cap or t-shirt of some kind with the name of your ostensible pizzeria on it. Don't come to the door with a Domino's™ pizza if you are wearing a Tower of Pizza hat!

It is important that your misdirection appear harmless. Your pretext should not be malicious or calculated to incriminate your subject.

POSITIVE IDENTIFICATION OF SUBJECT

I like to show my classes a videotape of an actual surveillance conducted by two private investigators as an example of how *not* to do a surveillance. In the tape, we see a group of young men playing soccer in a grassy park. The men taking the video talk constantly in the background, often using vulgarity and an impressive assortment of profanities and racial slurs as they watch the soccer game going on roughly two hundred feet away from them. Some of the topics of discussion include the feelings of one man about rap music and the fear that the battery on the camera might be low. As we watch this soccer game, trying not to be too distracted by the stimulating and relevant discussions going on in the background, we see that one player in particular is being singled out and we naturally conclude that this is the individual on whom the surveillance operation is being conducted. However, after about twenty minutes of tape, one of the men wonders aloud if they really have the right guy. They talk about this briefly and decide to resolve their dilemma by filming some of the other young men as well, "just to make sure."

Hopefully, the mistakes in this scenario are readily apparent to you, but I will take the liberty to point them out anyway. First of all, remember that anything you do in the course of an investigation could be subject to subpoena: your notes, your reports, and certainly your surveillance videos or pictures, if there are any. How credible do you think a judge and jury would find your videotape if, as they play it in a court of law, all they can hear is you in the background talking about that damn rap music and how Evander Holyfield needs to retire?

Second, and most important, *they were not even positive they had the right subject.* How happy do you think a client would be if the client paid two investigators for four hours of work and it turned out those four hours were spent spying on the wrong guy?

Therefore, it is crucial that you make a positive identification of your subject before you sink hours into a surveillance that could prove an utter waste of time and money. There are a number of ways to make a positive identification, one of which is to make sure that the physical description of the person you are watching matches the portrait parle you were given before the investigation. Second, make sure the address you are given for the subject is indeed where that individual lives. You can do this in a number of ways, including the pizza delivery pretext mentioned above. Similarly, ascertain that the vehicle used by the person you are watching matches the vehicle portrait parle of your intended subject. Finally, if the subject you are supposed to surveil has any physical impairments, make sure that the person you *believe* to be the subject exhibits those same impairments.

Because it is so important to make sure that the person you are surveilling is indeed the person you are *supposed* to be surveilling, in order to make a positive identification, you must have two of the above characteristics. For example, even if the person's physical description matches the portrait parle, you must still either verify the address, verify the vehicle or make sure they have the physical impairments your subject would have. Only when you have made sure of two of these conditions should you proceed with the surveillance.

PRESURVEILLANCE CHECK

Before beginning any surveillance, no matter how routine or simple it may well seem, you should be sure to conduct a presurveillance check of the area in which you will be working. This will familiarize you with the area, alert you of any potential hazards, and acquaint you with the possible routes of escape a subject might pursue.

To impress upon you the importance of such a check, I'll tell you the story of Curtis Watton, a young investigator's assistant who worked for Fra-Mar Investigations in Orange County, California. Curtis was shot and killed on February 8, 1991, while he was conducting a stakeout for an insurance fraud case in Los Angeles. Sitting in his 1989 Isuzu Trooper, legally parked in front of a residence in the 5400 block of Smiley Drive, Watton was confronted by an irate resident who said he did not want Watton's car parked on his street. The resident became angry, punched out a window on Watton's vehicle and dragged the 24-year-old out of the car. Watton managed to wrestle free and tried to run away, but the resident pulled out a 9mm pistol and shot Watton in the back of his neck. He died in the street.

Police said the Smiley Drive had a reputation for violent crimes, including gang and narcotic-related incidents. Robert Frasco, then president of the California Association of Private Investigators, said that stakeouts in such neighborhoods "can be dangerous because people often mistake an investigator sitting in his car for a drug dealer or police officer."[4] He also stressed that investigators need to inform the local police department that a stakeout is being conducted.

It is not known whether Watton conducted a presurveillance check, but if he had, surely he would have discovered the particular volatility of the neighborhood. He might have discerned that 1989 Isuzu Troopers were out of place; he might have realized that young white men sitting idly in 1989 Isuzu Troopers were *particularly* out of place. In other words, if adequate preparation prior to the actual stakeout had been made, perhaps the death of a young private investigator could have been avoided.

BACKGROUND CHECK

Because you can never have too much information, it is generally a good idea to conduct a background check on the individual you will be watching. Check the city directories at the local library to confirm address and telephone numbers; you can usually obtain addresses and signatures at the Voter's Registration office. Then you can go to the post office to confirm if the individual still receives mail at the address you have obtained for him or her. Any prior surveillance reports should also be obtained and studied carefully. Check marriage, civil and criminal records to determine marital status; whether or not they were sued by anyone, the outcome and jurisdiction of the case; and any prior criminal activity. If possible, you should get the subject's traffic records as well, to determine if they were involved in any traffic accidents, received speeding tickets or "fix-it" tickets, etc. Due to changes in legislation, it is now more difficult to obtain such information from the DMV, and it is illegal for a police officer to provide you with it as well. Only licensed private investigators with authorized computer requester codes may obtain information on license number and driving records.

---

[4]Chow, Robert. "Private Eye's Stakeout Ends in Death." *The Orange County Register,* Wednesday, February 13, 1991.

NECESSARY EQUIPMENT FOR SURVEILLANCE

Charles Sennewald, in his book *The Process of Security Investigation,*
declares:

> Whenever practical and possible, surveillances should be conducted by the
> human eye, without the use of any devise of hardware, save binoculars. There
> is no substitute for the total comprehension afforded the observer—in terms of
> clarity, detail, color and dimension (depth of field)—when he or she person-
> ally views the scene of an unfolding event.... In addition, there is the
> interpretive value of the human mind where the observer directly witnesses an
> act or event. Most surveillance films cannot stand on their own. They require
> some interpretation.[5]

However, Sennewald does acknowledge the value of surveillance equipment when it is impossible to conceal the investigator, and when the
investigator is desirous of recording the scene they witness. What we
recommend for surveillance operations is that you carry out with you a
duffel bag containing a camcorder with a minimum 20mm lens; the
brand we most strongly recommend is Sony™, but others may be just as
high-quality and less expensive. Comparison shop before actually making your purchase.

In addition to a camcorder, you should take with you extra batteries
and tapes/film. For shooting still photos or prints, use a 35mm camera
with a 200mm zoom lens. You should also have a voice-activated tape
recorder, 7×35 binoculars (or, for viewing a wider area, 10×50), and an
infrared scope for night viewing, although depth perception is mini-
mized with such a scope. In addition, a parabolic receiver, which is a
highly sensitive listening device, may also prove useful.

Along with the recommendations for equipment come warnings and
restrictions upon their use. These restrictions are enumerated in California Penal Code 630 and 635a.

CPC 630

This code deals with legislative intent concerning the use of listening
devices and techniques by law enforcement in the course of criminal
investigations:

> The Legislature hereby declares that advances in science and technology
> have led to the development of new devices and techniques for the purpose of

---

[5]Sennewald, Charles A. *The Process of Investigation: Concepts and Strategies for the Security Professional.*
Boston: Butterworth-Heinemann, 1981.

eavesdropping upon private communications and that the invasion of privacy resulting from the continual and increasing use of such devices and techniques has created a serious threat to the free exercise of personal liberties and cannot be tolerated in a free and civilized society.

The Legislature by this chapter intends to protect the right of privacy of the people of this state.

The Legislature recognizes that law enforcement agencies have a legitimate need to employ modern listening devices and techniques in the investigation of criminal conduct and the apprehension of lawbreakers. Therefore, it is not the intent of the Legislature to place greater restrictions on the use of listening devices and techniques by law enforcement agencies than existed prior to the effective date of this chapter.

This code was added in 1967.

CPC 635(a)

This code deals with the manufacture or selling of devices intended for eavesdropping or interception of radio telephone communications.

(a) Every person who manufactures, assembles, sells, offers for sale, advertises for sale, possesses, transports, imports, or furnishes to another any device which is primarily or exclusively designed or intended for eavesdropping upon the communication of another, of any device which is primarily or exclusively designed or intended for the unauthorized interception or reception of communications between cellular radio telephones or between a cellular radio telephone and a landline telephone in violation of Sec. 632.5, or communications between cordless telephones or between a cordless telephone and a landline telephone in violation of Sec. 632.6, shall be punished by a fine not exceeding two thousand five hundred dollars ($2,500), by imprisonment in the county jail not exceeding one year or in the state prison, or by both that fine and imprisonment. If the person has previously been convicted of this section, the person shall be punished by a fine not exceeding ten thousand dollars ($10,000), by imprisonment in the county jail not exceeding one year, or in the state prison, or by both that fine and imprisonment.

CAMERA USE

Because the use of a 35mm camera can be such a vital part of surveillance work, it is very important that you know how to operate one comfortably. Many people are "camera shy" in a different sense than not wanting to have their picture taken—they simply are a little afraid of cameras and do not know how to use them. Once you get the basics of 35mm camera operation, however, there really isn't anything to be leery of. This section is not intended to serve as the definitive manual on how to take perfect photos. It is provided as a guideline only, so that you will be better equipped when you go out into the field to take pictures that will best support and assist your investigation. Underexposed, over-exposed, and grainy, out-of-focus pictures will not do anyone any good and may even prove detrimental to your case.

The first thing you need to remember is that cameras don't take pictures, people do. Despite all the "point and shoot" simplicity adver-tised by most modern camera manufacturers, no camera in the world can decide what shot to take, where to stand when taking it, what film to put into the camera, etc. For all intents and purposes, cameras today are essentially the same: Minoltas™, Nikons™, Pentax™, etc.

I have often found that an understanding of how cameras work takes away a certain element of the mysteriousness that surrounds cameras and allows people to approach them more comfortably. Because of the great increases in technology, cameras have become more complex and can therefore seem quite intimidating. Really, though, modern SLR, or single lens reflex, cameras operate on the same basic principle as the early "pinhole" cameras. Light enters through a small hole at one end, is organized or focused by the lens, and exposes or creates an image on the film. The lens is just a metal barrel in which several glass components are arranged in groups. A certain advantage of SLR's is that the image you see in your viewfinder is the same as the image in your lens.

When light enters the lens, it is reflected by a mirror upward through a prism and out to your eye. The image you see in your viewfinder, besides being identical to the one "seen" by the lens, is always at the widest possible aperture or opening of the lens. Thus, the image you see is always as bright as it possibly can be.

Pressing the shutter release button first causes the aperture to close down to the f-stop you have selected. Second, the mirror swings out of the way so light can reach the film, temporarily blocking your view through the viewfinder. Then the shutter opens for the amount of time you have selected through your shutter speed control, allowing the film to be exposed. Adjust the mirror to its widest possible opening, and you are ready for your next shot. Sounds simple enough, right?

Loading the Film

Now, before we deal with such questions as "What's an f-stop?", I would like to start from the very beginning—putting film into the camera. Most point-'n-shoot cameras come with an auto load, which means you just drop the film into the back and push a button, and it whirs into place for you. This is all very well and good when things are working perfectly. However, should a malfunction occur and you need to load the film yourself, or should you be one of the purists who remains staunchly loyal to your manual operation camera, you will need to know the proper technique and procedure for loading film.

You start by holding the camera with the lens pointing down. Open the back of camera and push the tongue of the film into the groove of the take-up spool, pulling the film cassette across the back of the camera and dropping it into the take-up chamber. Advance the film one time, making sure the teeth on the take-up spool are lodged in the perforations along the edge of the film. Turn the rewind lever to take up the slack, advance the film and press the shutter release button. Advance the film and fire a few more times before closing the back. Advance until the number one shows in the window where the number of exposures is displayed. If the rewind lever is turning in the opposite direction of the rewind arrow, your film is loaded and ready to go.

F-stops and Shutter Speeds

The whole concept of f-stops and shutter speeds is a deceptively simple one. All that an f-stop refers to is the size of the hole through which the light is allowed to pass. Shutter speeds refer to the amount of time the light is allowed to pass. Shutter speeds refer to the amount of time the light is allowed to expose the film. Shutter speeds and f-stops work together to control the amount of light that reaches the film. It is important that you keep in mind the fact that these two controls work *together* and are integrally related to one another. What you do to one affects what happens to the other, etc. They do the same thing—controlling the light that touches the film—but they do it in very different ways.

Obviously, larger apertures or holes will admit more light. Smaller holes admit less light. Wide open lens apertures allow the greatest amount of light to touch the film, which is why I said earlier that when the image you see in your viewfinder is the brightest possible, your lens aperture is at its *widest* possible.

So far so good.

The confusion comes in when we say that f-stop numbers get smaller as the hole size gets larger. For example f4 is actually a larger lens aperture than f8, f8 is larger than f16 and so on. Really, though, it doesn't have to be confusing when you realize that f-stops are expressed in *fractions:* in f4, the 4 is really the denominator in the fraction ¼; f8, ⅛; and f16, 1/16. In other words, at an f-stop of 16, the lens aperture is 1/16 of an inch wide, whereas at f8 it is ⅛ of an inch wide. Remember: the smaller the hole, the bigger the number. The bigger the number, the smaller the hole. The more you repeat this, the sooner it will make sense. The smaller the hole. . . .

Moving on to shutter speeds, you will find that fractions are also the preferred mode of expression. Shutter speeds are expressed in terms of fractions of seconds: 15 is actually 1/15 of a second, 30 is 1/30 of a second, etc. So, the bigger the number, the faster the shutter speed.

Shutters themselves are nothing more than curtains positioned in front of the film, and when they open, light reaches the film. At slower shutter speeds, more light is allowed to expose the film; at faster speeds, less light gets through.

The relationship between f-stops and shutter speeds is one of reciprocity. If you make your lens aperture very small, you have to compensate for it by using a slower shutter speed. If you have a very fast shutter speed, you will want your lens aperture as wide as possible. For example, if you start at f-4 with a shutter speed of 500 and you stop up to f-5.6, you will need to decrease your shutter speed to 250 in order to get the same exposure. If you stop down one, you need to increase your shutter speed to the next fastest increment. If you stop up two, you need to decrease shutter speed by two.

Exposure

All modern SLR's have Through The Lens light meters, or TTL's, to help you in making decisions about exposure. A photoelectric cell measures the amount of light emanating from a scene, converts that into an optimal f-stop and shutter speed reading, and displays the information in your viewfinder. Most of the time your TTL will be accurate, but in scenes where you have a lot of shadow or one large white reflective area, the reading may be a little off and you will have to compensate for it. It is a good idea to bracket your shots, which means to take one picture at the f-stop and shutter speed you think right, and then to take one at a higher f-stop and another at a lower one. This way you are almost sure that at least one picture of your client's husband playing naked Twister with Fifi the buxom will come out acceptably.

Depth of Field

Depth of field is another term that creates confusion. Simply stated, it refers to the amount of sharpness in your finished picture. In all shots there is a plane of sharp focus, which means that all objects along this plane will be perfectly sharp in the finished photo. However, there is also a zone of acceptable focus that begins at a point between the camera and the focal plane and extends to a point beyond the focal plane. Objects in this area will appear to be sharp in the actual picture. This zone of acceptable focus is called "depth of field."

When your lens is at wide apertures, the depth of field is not very large; in other words, only your intended subject will come out in focus and the foreground and background will appear slightly blurry. When your lens is at smaller apertures, your depth of field is greater.

Film

Film speed refers to that film's sensitivity to light. The higher the number, the more sensitive it is. The most common ASA/ISO numbers for color film are:

25	slow
64	medium
100	medium
200	fast
400	fast

At film speeds below 50, you get the best grain for reproduction or for making large prints; however, working with such slow speed film translates into working with low shutter speeds, in which case a tripod is usually needed. For most normal shooting, 64–100 speed film is adequate, whereas 200–400 is strictly for low-light situations.

Another consideration with film is whether to buy daylight-balanced film, which is balanced to the light of the sun and intended for outdoor shots, or tungsten film, which is balanced to most common indoor light settings. Using the wrong type of film could result in off-color shots.

Lenses

Most SLR's come with a 50mm normal lens, which in effect "sees" like the human eye. It is not as good as a wide-angle lens for showing all the detail in a scene, and it is not as good as a telephoto for isolating single details, as in a portraiture. For the purposes of surveillance, the most functional lens is the 75–200mm zoom lens, because it takes the place of an 85, 100, 105, 135 and 200mm lens.

VIDEO CAMERA USE

Video cameras are perfect for "catching people in the act." They can be an invaluable means of recording activity that might otherwise be lost if only a 35mm camera were used. Since the basic mechanics of a video camera are similar to those of 35mm cameras, we won't spend a great deal of time on them. Instead, we will look at some important tips you should keep in mind while operating your video camera that will allow you to make cleaner, more precise videos for your client.

First of all, keep your shots simple. Don't try to get thematic or cinematic; you are not making a movie; you are conducting a surveillance.

Remember, that just as with 35mm cameras, shutter speeds affect video. Faster shutter speeds freeze action, whereas low shutter speed improve performance in low light condition. High speed shutters give added stability to your image, but when you use low speeds you can get a chattery, artificial motion that can be very distracting.

The lens aperture on a video camera, called the iris, affects exposure. Small apertures give good depth of field, particularly when shooting outdoors. Focusing, therefore, is not too critical. Indoor shooting, however, necessitates a larger iris, resulting in shallow depth of field and critical focusing. So, when filming indoors, prefocus to ensure a sharp image. This is accomplished by focusing in on one point and then moving away from it slowly, so that as much as possible remains in focus.

Depth of field is related to focal length. Wide angle shots give leeway in focusing. Conversely, the more telescopic your lens, the more critical focusing becomes. Zoom or focal length affects how the subject appears. The more your lens is consolidated, the more compressed is your depth of field.

Finally, it is important to realize that what you see in your viewfinder isn't always what comes out in your finished video. In other words, objects that you think are fully contained in your shot may actually come out cropped, which could translate into decapitated subjects for your surveillance videos. Therefore, you must become familiar with your viewfinder and the actual range it has. Allow some leeway in your shots, so that if some cropping occurs it won't be too critical. Also, conduct tests to determine the calibration and accuracy of your viewfinder. Take some videos of your dog or your kids or your neighbor's dog and kids, and measure the actual footage against what you thought you were shooting.

SURVEILLANCE

Now that I have given you an overview on the purpose of surveillance, how to formulate a proper description, the importance of presurveillance checks and basic operating techniques, we can now learn the methods. There are basically two types of surveillance: fixed, where you stay in one place and observe the activity that goes on in a specific location, and moving, where you follow the subject from place to place. Moving surveillance can be done while in a vehicle or while on foot. In many surveillance operations, a combination of fixed and moving surveillance techniques are used. For example, suppose you are parked across from a subject's house when all of a sudden that subject comes storming out of the house, jumps onto his Harley Davidson Springier Softail motorcycle and guns away down the street. Do you continue to keep watch outside of a house you now know to be empty? Or do you start up your 1979 Honda Civic Hatchback and hightail after him?

Fixed Surveillance

Fixed surveillance operations are particularly useful in observing and detecting low-level criminal activities. Stake-outs are ideal for observing payoffs on extortion cases and kidnapping, for identifying context and movements of subjects in narcotics cases, and for detecting and apprehending criminal suspects where advanced information is received concerning robbery and burglary. Also, where incidents of mugging, molestation of women and/or children, purse snatching, or confidence operations have been going on, stake-outs can lead to detection and apprehension of the responsible parties. Garages and auto repair shops that are suspected of being used for automobile theft rings can be ferreted-out through stake-outs, as can receivers of stolen property.

As already mentioned, in fixed surveillance operations you are assigned to one particular spot. Presurveillance checks allow for you to determine the best possible vantage point from which you may see without being seen. Particularly when the surveillance is expected to last a long time, such selection of a vantage point should be done very carefully.

Other preparatory and precautionary steps to take include assessing modes of transportation available to the subject. Find out if your subject drives only one car or if he also has a motorcycle, moped, roller blades, etc. You will need to know what kinds of vehicles to watch for as you conduct your surveillance: it would not be wise for you to be exclusively on the alert for a blue Hyundai Excel and so miss those times when your subject pulls up to the residence in a flaming red Mazda Miata. Along the same lines, look to see what kinds of escape routes are open to the subject so that, in the event that he may make a rapid or sudden departure, you will not be left without recourse to follow.

Donald Rush, in his book *Fundamentals of Civil and Private Investigation,* cautions that "automobiles are a means of transportation, a means by which people travel from one location to another. Once at the desired location, people do not generally sit in their vehicle but rather get out and walk away."[6] Because it is rather conspicuous to sit in your car and concentrate on a particular dwelling, Rush suggests a number of ways in which such suspicious conduct could be mitigated. One thing he suggests is to park among other parked vehicles in such a way that visibility is maintained but a certain degree of cover is provided. Also, he stresses that in residential assignments, parking on the next block is a good way to avoid detection by the actual person under surveillance. Even if the people on the block where you decide to park become a little suspicious, your intended subject is less likely to notice you. This is another good reason to inform the local police—using discretion, of course—of your intended surveillance. That way, if people do become suspicious and approach you with questions, you can direct them to inquire with the police department. Never park directly across the street from a subject's location.

Other ways to make fixed surveillance from automobiles less obvious is to position the vehicle in the opposite direction so that observation of the subject is done through the rear view mirror. While this is certainly a more awkward and less direct means of observing activity, when it comes to a choice between discomfort and discovery by the subject, discomfort is a much more attractive option.

Covert Stationary Vehicle

This surveillance technique requires the use of two investigators and two vehicles. Here's how it works. You and Magnum Peeyie are private

---

[6]Rush, Donald A. and Siljander, Raymond P. *Fundamentals of Civil and Private Investigation.* Springfield: Charles C Thomas, 1984, p. 30.

investigators working for a firm that has been hired to investigate a man suspected of stealing from his company. You have been assigned to do a surveillance of this man at his house. So, on the day the surveillance is to start, Magnum and you drive up in separate cars and park two blocks away. You get out of your car, toss the keys to your good friend Magnum, and get into the back seat of his car. Magnum then drives you to a location closer to the subject's home, a location from which you will be able to observe very nicely all the comings and goings of your subject. He parks his car, pockets his keys and yours, and walks the two blocks back to where you left your vehicle, leaving you comfortably in place in the rear seat of his car. Once at your car, Magnum slides behind the wheel and drives away, to return for you at a later date. Of course, the idea is that you try and be as inconspicuous as possible in the back seat of Magnum's car, so that any neighbor or passerby would believe that the driver of the vehicle had simply gone off and left an empty car.

Broken Down Vehicle Ploy

This pretext is fairly self-explanatory. You are a poor unfortunate motorist who happened to stall-out right in front of the person upon whom you are conducting a surveillance. Put up the hood, look frustrated and tell anyone who asks or stops to help that the automobile club is on its way to rescue you. While you are tinkering with hoses and valves, you can also be keeping a very close eye on whatever occurs at the location you are supposed to be surveilling.

Loose Fixed Surveillance

Sometimes, the layout of the neighborhood or the absence of other parked cars along the sides of streets will make stationary vehicular surveillance impractical. In such cases, loose fixed surveillance may be used in which two investigators circle the location under observation so that one investigator is always able to view the subject. Before the investigator can draw attention to themselves by lingering too long in one location, he moves on and the second investigator swings into place. This can be done in a number of ways, including hesitating at stop signs and watching the subject in the rear view mirror until a car pulls up behind you or until a neighbor seems to get a little suspicious. Two cars diffuse the attention that one car attracts to itself and make sure that at no time is the subject not under observation.

Telephone Repair Ploy

All you need for this pretext is a hard hat, a few tools, a saggy pair of blue jeans and written permission from the telephone company, and you have yourself one very effective means of keeping an eye on a person or place. Who ever asks the guy they see clinging to their telephone pole and tinkering away with a large metal tool of some kind, what the heck is he doing? People generally like to think they *know* what the guy is doing.

The important thing to remember when utilizing this ploy is that you need to have with you written permission from the telephone company to be up their pole. As an example, the California Penal Code 653b states that:

> Every person who shall, without permission of the owner, lessee, or person or corporation operating any electrical transmission line, distributing line or system, climb upon any pole, tower or other structure which is a part of such line or system and is supporting or is designed to support a wire or wires, cable or cables, for the transmission or distribution of electric energy, shall be deemed guilty of a misdemeanor; provided, that nothing herein shall apply to employs of either privately or publicly owned public utilities engaged in the performance of their duties.

Thus, even while you certainly want to appear to be an employee of the telephone company, you are not in all honesty a telephone repair technician and therefore you need to have written permission to be hanging from the wires and *acting* like a telephone repair technician.

Power Company Line Ploy

This ploy works about the same as the telephone repair ploy. If you have a tool that people will cheerfully accept as viable for power line repair work, an aura of being exactly where you are supposed to be and doing what you are supposed to be doing, for the most part you will be left alone and will be able to conduct surveillance successfully.

Traffic Counter

We've all seen them. Sitting in folding lawn chairs, a can of diet cola on the sidewalk beside them and a floppy wide-brimmed hat to shield them from the sun, they plant themselves on corners and count the number of cars that go by. Sometimes they have a hand-held counter, similar to the one used by umpires in intramural softball games to count the number of balls and strikes thrown. And sometimes they have clipboards and some "Traffic Volume Survey" forms. It's a good job for retired people. And it's a good pretext for private investigators who are conducting surreptitious observation of a particular location.

Street Repair Ploy

This is a bit more complicated and could require the cooperation and collaboration of several people. But the street repair ploy allows you to "set up shop" directly in front of your subject and remain for as long as needed. Of course, you will need to procure the requisite equipment and garb to pass as a bona fide street repair crew. And if the street that you suddenly determine needs repairing was just mended and repaved a few weeks earlier, people might become suspicious. Generally, simpler pretexts work better.

In addition to the various technical difficulties posed by street repair ploys, there is a legal one as well. For example, California Penal Code 647c mandates that:

> Every person who willfully and maliciously obstructs the free movement of any person on any street, sidewalk or other public place or on or in any place open to the public is guilty of a misdemeanor.
>
> Nothing in this section affects the power of a county or a city to regulate conduct upon a street, sidewalk or other public place or on or in any place open to the public.

If you decide that a street repair ploy is the best possible method at your disposal for the conducting of your surveillance, it would behoove you to contact the local police department and let them know what you are doing. This way, should a high-speed chase occur through the area you have blockaded off with cones and set up as your observation post, the police will not be totally taken off guard and left with no readily available detour.

Road Survey Crew

Even though most people don't know what exactly they're looking for when they press their squinting faces up to those all-weather cameras and examine the road, most people do not question the right of these people to be doing what they're doing. So, if you can procure an all-weather camera, a sturdy tripod and maybe a hard-hat or a protractor or something, the road survey ploy is highly useful for surveillance purposes. It is also an unobtrusive and ideal opportunity for you to bring out a camera and record on film whatever activities you observe.

Alternatives

If none of the above sound practical for you, don't be afraid to be creative and come up with plans of your own. Maybe you could offer to paint people's house numbers on the curb for them like so many starving college students do. Maybe you could offer your services as a gardener for the people across the street from your subject, and while you are trimming the azaleas you find that you are in perfect position to observe the illicit activity going on at your subject's place of residence. Remember that simpler pretexts work best because they are easier to remember and answer any questions about. If you don't think you could convincingly pass as a telephone repair worker, then don't climb up on a pole and hope no one expects you to look like you know what you're doing. Be sure that you are very familiar with the area in which you will be conducting surveillance, so that you will know what kinds of pretext will work and what will not. For very temporary surveillance operations, pretext may not be needed. Be sensitive to the particular needs and considerations of each assignment, and use the method that will garner you the best possible results.

Vehicular Surveillance

When your subject leaves his home or office, gets into a car and drives away, if you wish to continue observing that person you will need to get into a car and follow him. We have all seen movies where the person who is doing the tailing oh-so-slyly pulls away from the curb just as the investigator's subject drives away, and follows along behind without even so much as one car length in-between the subject and the investigator. The subject, usually inadvertently, glances into the rear view mirror, catches sight of the glowering and determined person in the car behind him, and becomes hysterical, crashing over sidewalks, careening through alleys, and causing all kinds of traffic accidents in an attempt to evade the pursuer. This makes for exciting movies. However, it poses a real problem for private investigators who are trying to conduct surveillance.

Often, people who follow other people in the movies do so in flashy cars. In the television series "Stingray," for example, the hero drove a very lovely and very conspicuous black Stingray. When conducting vehicular surveillance, it is a good idea to use a fairly nondescript vehicle, of a make or model that would not draw attention. For example, Fords or Hondas or other common cars usually do not call undue attention to themselves unless, of course, they are painted bright fuchsia and have been lowered to the point of causing severe damage to the undercarriage whenever they go over speed bumps. Use discretion when selecting a vehicle for tailing someone.

The Progressive Surveillance

It happens to the best of investigators. You were following your subject through heavy traffic and somehow they made a turn before you could get to the intersection, and by the time the light changes he is gone. Does this mean that your entire surveillance operation has been rendered ineffective? Not at all. It simply means that at a later time you will pick up where you left off. On another day, at another time, find your subject and resume tailing him.

Sandwich Tail

In heavy traffic, you should really only use one vehicle; however, in moderate to light traffic, the sandwich tail can be a good way to keep a close watch on your subject. This method of surveillance requires two investigators and two vehicles equipped with radio communication devices. For simplicity's sake, we'll say you are the first investigator and your old colleague Magnum Peeyie is the second. Like the name implies, the sandwich tail involves your vehicle driving in front of the subject's car and Magnum's vehicle driving behind. Magnum is supposed to remain out of sight of the subject. It is your job, watching through the rear view mirror, to keep tabs on the subject.

If the subject makes a turn after you have passed through the intersection, you simply radio this information to Magnum, who then works his way into position as the lead vehicle. You fall into place as the second vehicle, keeping out of sight of your subject, and the surveillance proceeds smoothly.

Paralleling

If it is just you and the subject, one possible way to maintain surveillance is to keep to the right rear of the subject's vehicle. Keeping somewhat in the blind spot means that you will not as easily be seen, although it could make you an easy target for sideswiping. Remain alert and responsive to sudden changes in the subject's driving pattern and you should not have too much difficulty keeping up with your subject.

Leap Frog

This method requires three or more cars and incorporates both the sandwich tail technique and paralleling. Because of the potential for complication and detection of such a technique, this method is usually used only in those instances in which losing a subject would be particularly detrimental to the case. For example, if it is known that your subject has a car full of stolen merchandise and is heading for a one-time only meeting with their buyer, then it is imperative that you maintain continual surveillance.

Foot Surveillance

Because you are much more susceptible to detection when you follow someone on foot—especially if you are following a woman, since women are trained from the cradle to be constantly on the lookout for potential rapists, muggers, and purse snatchers—foot surveillance should only be used as a last resort. It is very easy to lose sight of your subject when the both of you are on foot; and if your subject should happen to get into a car after you have been following for some distance, you will be left stranded with no readily available means of following your subject.

When you are following someone on foot, try to avoid direct eye contact with that person. Don't slink from place to place, thinking that will make you less conspicuous. Walk normally, casually, as if you have every right to be in the area just like anyone else. Don't give the impression that you think the person knows you are following them. Peeking around corners or through holes in fences is a sure way to attract unwanted attention, as is loitering around schools. Always have a pretext ready in case the subject confronts you with the suspicion that you have been following them.

If the subject goes into a restaurant and you follow, you should be sure to pay in advance so that in the event the subject leaves suddenly, you won't have to waste time settling the bill with the waiter. On buses, you should try to sit behind the subject; if your subject buys a ticket to go somewhere, try to buy a ticket for the seat next to them. On elevators, you can avoid suspicion by pressing the number of the floor directly above theirs. For every person the subject encounters, you should get a portrait parle or, if possible, take a picture. Remember, use discretion. If it is not possible for you to maintain close surveillance of the individual without attracting attention, discontinue for that day and resume some other, more convenient time.

IDENTIFYING SUBJECTS WHO ARE SUSPICIOUS

You've done everything perfectly. You did a presurveillance check of the area where you would be working, and even arranged to borrow a friend's gray Honda so you wouldn't attract too much attention. You didn't park your car directly in front of your subject's house, just like you were supposed to. When you had to follow your subject in your car, you allowed enough distance between you so that no suspicion would be aroused.

However, on the day the big theft occurred, you wanted to make sure that you kept a particularly close watch. You followed when the client left the house for the office, you waited while he was inside the building, and you followed your subject out of the office parking lot into the city streets. You notice that your subject has been adjusting their rear view mirror a lot, and that at stop signs and red lights, they check the mirrors constantly. And all of a sudden your subject begins driving at very high speeds, changing lanes in an unsafe manner. At the next intersection they make an unexpected U-turn, and when your subject drives past you they give a certain gesture with their left hand that has been widely accepted to mean something terribly unflattering.

You, my friend, have been what is called "burned."

How to Detect Suspicion in Vehicular Tailing

People test to see if they are being followed in a variety of ways, but some of the more common ones that you should be aware of include driving at high speeds, making unexpected U-turns, stopping and parking frequently to watch who drives past them, and driving in and out of cul de sacs. Sometimes the subject will start to go somewhere and will suddenly turn around and go back to where they started from without actually going anywhere.

A good rule of thumb is that you are not "burned," or discovered, until you get three good looks from the subject, two of which are accompanied by evasive maneuvers. Some examples of typical evasive maneuvers include driving through congested areas, pulling into parking lots and immediately exiting, and committing traffic violations, such as running red lights or making left-hand turns from the wrong lane. The use of decoys and traps is also common.

How to Detect Suspicion in Foot Surveillance

If the person you are following stops and looks around, or even looks casually behind him while still walking, you should be very careful. If he reverses the course of his progress and starts coming toward you, just keep walking calmly past, avoiding eye contact. Use discretion about whether or not to continue following him.

Getting on buses and then at the last minute disembarking is a fairly well-known ploy to throw people off track. Entering buildings and leaving through a different exit accomplishes the same thing. Alternately walking fast and slow could be an effort to determine if someone is following a little too closely. Riding short distances in taxis or even circling the block in a taxi before getting out are methods of checking for surveillance as well. A very clichéd way of ferreting out a tail is to stop and tie one's shoes—particularly conspicuous if the individual is wearing sandals. Checking reflections in shop windows and mirrors, stopping and turning around after going round a corner, and having a friend trail along behind (called a convoy) to watch for possible followers, are all methods people use to find out if they are being watched.

The important thing to remember is if you get "burned," or if your subject becomes cognizant of the fact that you are surveilling him, discontinue the surveillance. The gig is up.

SURVEILLANCE REPORT

Just in case you thought you would get to the end of a chapter without being informed about another report, Figure 4.1 shows an example of the type of report that you should prepare when you conduct a surveillance. Basically, it is a chronological report without headings—the time increments and date serve as your headings. Each entry should answer the six essential questions: who, what, where, when, why, and how. If you don't have anything to report, say so. Remember that *not* seeing any wrongdoing says as much as *seeing* it does.

REVIEW

1. Define surveillance.
2. Name two types of cases in which surveillance is useful.
3. What are some reasons for conducting surveillance?
4. Give the eleven things you need for a portrait parle of a person for surveillance purposes.
5. What are two things to observe in the residence and neighborhood of the subject?
6. True or False: A complete portrait parle of a vehicle for purposes of surveillance has five characteristics.
7. What is pretext?
8. True or False: It is acceptable to use misdirection as long as it is not malicious.
9. Name two ways to make a positive identification of a subject.
10. Why is a presurveillance check necessary?
11. Where are some places to look for information when conducting a background check?
12. What is CPC 630?
13. What is CPC 635a?
14. What is the difference between f-stops and shutter speeds?
15. Give two examples of stationary surveillance techniques.
16. Give two examples of moving surveillance techniques.
17. What is CPC 647C?
18. What are some ways to tell if a person suspects they are being followed?
19. What is a convoy?

Chapter 5

GENERAL INVESTIGATIONS

General investigations is one of the most common forms of investigations used today because it is not limited to one particular area. The investigator can readily use the direct investigative approach which allows the investigator to obtain information through the process of research, interviews, and the use of public records. Some of the most common types of general investigations would include background, divorce, and missing person searches. Other types of general investigations include prenuptial, perspective business partners, child custody, infidelity, and asset investigations.

Anthony M. Golec writes from his expertise on sources of information:

> Perhaps the greatest asset of the investigator is his knowledge of *sources,* that he knows where to go for the information an attorney is seeking, whether it to be a particular government agency, private party, or private industry.
>
> The investigator must know what in the way of public information is available to him and then exhaust every possibility in checking out this information.[1]

Information from Public Records and Documents

The first thing that must be done in any type of search, is to compile as much information on your subject as possible. Information obtained from records and documents, such as the public library, is a great place to begin. Telephone directories are the most common and easiest way to begin your search. Here you may be able to locate your subject's address, telephone number, and the area code in which that person lives. You may then want to go to city hall to look up the blue prints of city streets to obtain a more accurate location of your subject's residence. If your subject owns a business, it would be fairly easy to obtain a copy of that subject's business license, giving you another location of where that subject could be found.

---

[1]Golec, Anthony M. *Techniques of Legal Investigation,* 2nd Ed. Springfield: Charles C Thomas, 1985.

Assessors Office

It is important to remember the information obtained from public records and documents is the most accurate and precise way to help you obtain the necessary tools in gathering as much information on your subject as possible. For example, the county tax office of land assessment may help you verify your subject's address or may also tell you if your subject is living elsewhere. With today's economy, housing has become affordable to many individuals. Many people find themselves buying property as investments because many homes are being sold below market value. If your subject owns any property there will be a tax record on file. With the record, you will find the location of the property as well as the address of where the tax bill is being sent. It is possible for the addresses to be different because the subject may be renting out that particular property. However, you are now in possession of the subject's current mailing address. With this in hand, you can always refer back to the local telephone book.

County Recorders Office

Continuous searches of public records and documents can also be located at the county courthouse. In the county recorders office, you can easily obtain any birth or death certificates you may require. Birth records will usually contain the ages of both parents, occupations at the time of birth, the address and birth place of the parents, and the mother's maiden name. This will be of importance because this may be one of the only records you will be able to retrieve to access the mother's maiden name. All of this information may be crucial to your case, especially when your trying to locate a missing person. Death records are also of value because they too, like birth certificates, provide quite a bit of information. Death records provide the following information: a person's complete name, date of death, date of birth, social security number, place of birth, place of death, occupation, name of mother and father, mother's maiden name, name of physician who certified cause of death, and the name and address of the cemetery or crematory. With the death record, you now have several different avenues to explore or you may be able to directly contact individuals who knew your subject. Like the birth certificates, death records contain crucial information that may be helpful to your search.

County Clerk's Office

The county clerk's office is an excellent place to obtain information such as marriage certificates, divorce papers and fictitious business names. Marriage certificates will not only provide you with the names of the couple, but will also provide you with the number of previous marriages. You will also find the date of birth, place of birth, names of witnesses, and the signatures of both the bride and groom. Marriage certificates can be the best way to locate the changes in a female name so you don't waste your time researching the false last name. Divorce records can be useful in obtaining hard to find information. This record will contain the names and ages of the subject's children, a list of the couple's vehicles, including the vehicle identification number (VIN), and all property owned by the subject. When searching through the subject's property records, you may also want to conduct a thorough tax and asset search. The information provided in the divorce record may redirect your search to a more successful conclusion in a less time-consuming manner. You may have found that one of the properties owned by your subject is a business. The county clerk's office also contains records of fictitious business names that may be of help to you in your search. The application on file will provide you with home and business addresses. This may be the simplest way to obtain this type of information because your subject may not have wanted to incorporate his small business.

State Records

State sources of information can be very useful in your search. The Department of Motor Vehicles (DMV) has a person's driving record, driver's license number, date of birth, current home address, and a list of all vehicles owned. You will find many possibilities for new information regarding the location of your subject from this simple method of inquiry. However, all government agencies, including a DMV, are constantly changing their policies as to what access to records and files will be left open to the public. Today most DMV's require you to fill out a form to determine why the information you are requesting is necessary. In California this recent change was due to the murder of actress Rebecca Schaffer. Her killer obtained her home address through DMV records. When a search at the DMV proves to be unhelpful, it would be wise to try the Worker's Compensation Bureau. Those individuals who receive Worker's Compensation benefits have suffered some type of injury caused during the performance of their job. This file will contain information including addresses, names of dependents, telephone number, and previous employers.

Federal Records

As you have read, there are many places to obtain sources of information. Along with the state sources you may also want to refer to the federal sources of information. The post office is also a good place to obtain a person's change of address; however, it is important to note the post office limits their information to process servers only. You may also want to try the Immigration and Naturalization Service, the U.S. Armed Forces, the FBI, IRS, and Social Security Administration.

Private Organization and Agencies

There are several options available to you when trying to locate a particular person. You can always contact private organizations and agencies. They include the telephone company, insurance reporting services, credit reporting services such as TRW, public utility companies, real estate agencies, the personnel departments of private agencies, and so on. All of these private agencies can be very useful in your search despite the small fee for the information you will have obtained. The purpose of the investigation is to find someone. Always compile as much information on your subject as soon as possible and know where to locate the sources of information.

As an investigator, two primary sources of information can also be obtained from professional organizations. In California, for example, these are the California Association for Licensed Investigators (CALI) and the California Institute for Professional Investigators (CIPI).

Other sources of information include physical evidence and information from scientific examination. Physical evidence is tangible items found at the scene of an incident, crime, or event. It would include finger prints, clothing, personal effects, photographs, tire marks, identification cards, licenses, weapons, or anything else tangible that can lead to more investigations. Information from scientific examination is that which cannot be seen by the naked eye. The most common type of scientific examination is usually done on: blood, bullets, laser finger prints, and DNA samples. Both physical and scientific evidence are crucial sources of information in any type of investigation.

If you find your subject is from out of state, you may wonder how to begin your search. You do not have to travel around the country to obtain sources of information. Instead, you can easily obtain the necessary information simply by writing a request. The U.S. Department of Health and Human Services has provided a booklet titled "Where to Write for Vital Records" (see Appendix). This booklet contains information on how to write the appropriate office to have your request filled.

Background Investigations

The background check has proven to be one of the most foundational elements an investigator can build on. Charles A. Sennewald wrote the following regarding the background check:

> No investigative function serves the best interests of the corporate organization more than the employee screening process—the background investigation. Cases demanding investigative expertise come and go, day in and day out. Even truly exciting and significant cases involving large monetary risks or losses come and go, though with less frequency. But despite the importance or magnitude of any given case, the humble background investigation remains pre-eminent in its overall importance.[2]

The successful investigation of background checks depends in great measure upon the effective verification of information on the subject's application. In any type of background investigation, always start with a basic check of the application. Look it over and see if you notice anything unusual such as a mailing address that differs from the subject's home address. It is important for the investigator to verify and confirm all information given by the subject. Many employers today, such as the state and federal employment agencies, require a thorough background investigation on all prospective employees.

Preemployment Check

When beginning your investigation, you will always want to include a thorough and in-depth check of your subject's background. You may want to begin by confirming your subject's address. An excellent place to start would be voter registration. Voter registration is available to you upon written request. This card will list the subject's address, the last time your subject voted, previous addresses, the date of your subject's initial voter's registration, date of birth, and signature. With the former addresses of your subject, you may want to confirm addresses by speak-

---

[2]Sennewald, Charles A. *The Process Investigation.* Butterworth-Heinemann, 1981.

ing to former neighbors or landlords. The information you can obtain at voter registration makes this one of the best searching techniques.

Always verify your subject's social security number. Make sure your subject is not using another person's social security number, like their spouse, for example. Find out if someone else is using your subject's social security number and if the subject is aware of this. It is important to be aware of all transactions your subject is involved in. Your subject may have misleading information on their application and it is up to you to find all the discrepancies.

If the employment position requires driving, you must verify your subject's driving record. Check the Department of Motor Vehicles (DMV) and find out what your subject's driving record contains. You will want to research the past seven years of the subject's record to determine if he has had any previous offenses, such as driving under the influence. Such information is vital to your client because the subject could be applying for a position as a school bus driver. Search for speeding tickets, traffic violations, or suspensions. Check on the subject's criminal history. Determine if the subject has been prosecuted for any driving-related incidents. You can obtain this information through the courthouse. When conducting this type of search do not overlook the magistrate's office. Here you will find all the lesser crimes, whereas the county courthouse keeps only records of the more serious offenses. Arrest records can give you detailed information regarding the offense. You will find the subject's portrait parle, social security number, date of birth, address at the time of incident, vehicles, and anything else that may have pertained to the incident. It is important to remember that DMV and criminal records are vital pieces of information when determining a subject's eligibility for a certain type of job.

Many corporate and upper management positions require a certain level of education to be considered for employment. When conducting a subject's background investigation, never assume that their diplomas are legitimate. Always verify your subject's education. A diploma can be easily obtained from any campus bookstore. Always verify the subject's transcripts. Contact the college or university the subject listed and request a copy of his transcripts. You will need a signed statement from the subject giving the school permission to release their student transcripts to you. If the subject is a recent graduate, you may want to interview the subject's instructors. Get their opinion on the subject and find out what kind of student he was. Verify the subject's previous employers. Verify the start date, end date, pay rate, position, and title. Check to make sure everything coincides with what the subject has provided on the application.

Personal Source of Information

A good investigator will always verify the subject's references. Many individuals do not give careful consideration of whom they list as references, and many employers today will not hire an individual without credible references. There are two ways you can verify a subject's references. One way is by telephone and the other way is by a personal interview. Remember, you don't just need to verify the references which your subject has listed. It would be more thorough for you to contact references the subject did not list on his application. This may give your client a more accurate insight to the personality and capabilities of their prospective employee. You will want to contact the following former and current groups of people: neighbors, employers, co-workers, spouses, and business associates. It may be difficult to find people who are willing to speak freely about the subject, so be prepared to develop some sort of pretext. Be friendly, courteous, and considerate to people. This interview is an informal questioning to learn facts about the subject.

Credit Check

A subject's credit record is a very important factor when conducting a background investigation. With written permission from the subject, you will be able to run their credit history. Check with TRW, Transunion, or Equifax. When conducting this type of search try to answer some of the following questions:

- Does this person pay their bills on time?
- Do they pay out more than they take in?
- Do they have a spouse who contributes?
- How many dependents do they have?
- Does the subject own or rent a home?
- Does the subject have medical expenses not covered by insurance?
- How long has the subject been employed at his job?
- Does the subject jump from job to job?

All of these questions answered will be valuable information to your client. This may give your client a clearer picture of who and what the subject is all about. It will help the client decide if the subject is right for the job. It takes more than qualifications to make a good employee and many employers use this type of investigation to help them determine if the subject is the best choice for the job.

Asset Checks

In any background investigation you may be called upon to do an asset check. Find out what the subject is worth. Conduct a thorough net asset check. See what the subject is worth after expenses. There are several options available to you. Check the county recorders office, Grantee-Granter Index, divorce records, bank accounts, credit applications, rental application, and probate records. An asset check can provide vital information to a client who may be involved in a civil suit with the subject. Always be thorough when conducting an asset search and check for all available resources.

Prenuptial Checks and Business Partners

A prenuptial and business partner investigation is very personal and private; therefore, never conduct a personal interview. Your job, as an investigator, is to provide as much information to the client as possible. Begin your search by checking for previous marriages. Verify the subject's income and employment. Always check for a criminal record. Conduct a search on the subject's civil history, driving record, and credit report. For a business partner search, check for fictitious businesses and corporation records. The key to this type of investigation is to make sure the subject is who he says he is. It is important for the client to know that the person they are contracting with is a legitimate individual.

In any background investigation you will always need to refer to several sources of information. You may need to check state records to look up a subject's DMV record or check the Worker's Compensation Bureau to see if your subject has made any recent claims. You may want to continue your search by checking the subject's insurance background, medical and civil history. Always be precise and thorough in your background checks. Gather as much information as possible and try to give specific details in your reports. Do not leave out any vital information, even if it may not appear significant to you. Let your client decide what is important. As an investigator, your job is to thoroughly investigate the subject and present all information obtained to your client for their review.

Divorce Investigation

California, as an example, is classified as a no fault state, meaning a couple does not need a reason to divorce. It may sound simple, quick, and easy, but on the contrary, divorce is a very complex situation. After a divorce has been initiated, the dispute usually begins when it comes time to divide up the couple's assets. Investigators become involved within the divorce realm when a private party sees it necessary to prove that the other spouse is unfit. Many divorce cases involve major issues such as the following: drug and alcohol abuse, cruelty, financial disputes, child custody, bigamy, abandonment, and infidelity.

Divorce Surveillance Techniques

In any type of surveillance, always conduct a presurveillance of the surroundings before you begin. Conduct an interview with your client and get a list of all activities pertaining to your subject. Ask your client for a photograph of the subject or get a thorough portrait parle. Make sure you have a list of names and addresses of the subject's friends. Obtain a photograph or description of the subject's vehicle. Make sure you check stake-out positions before you begin.

When you begin the actual surveillance, make sure you conduct a fixed observation. Bring all appropriate supplies so you don't have to leave your post. If you are tailing your subject by vehicle, make sure you are paralleling the subject's vehicle while using the sandwich technique. Always stay focused on your subject and avoid a burnt subject. Here are a few tips you should look for to determine if the subject knows you are following them: subject keeps adjusting the rear view mirror, turns to look at you when at stop signs, drives around in circles, parks and stays in the vehicle, and leaves and returns without going anywhere.

When updating your client on the status of the investigation, never give the photographs you have taken of the subject to the client until the investigation has been completed.

Drugs and Alcohol Checks

In any type of investigation it is important for the investigator to acquire as much information from the client as possible. When conducting a search involving drugs and alcohol you will want to begin your search at the criminal courthouse for the subject's criminal history. If the accusation has been made that your subject is a strong abuser of alcohol and drugs, chances are they may have a criminal record. Always interview friends, neighbors, and relatives of the subject. If your subject does not drink at home you may want to set up a surveillance where the subject does go to drink. You will need to check the subject's DMV record.

Cruelty Checks

One of your main sources of information will come from interviews. Have an in-depth interview with your client to obtain witnesses to the cruelty. Friends and family make excellent witnesses when trying to prove cruelty. If the subject has a violent temper and is being accused of any type of abuse or cruelty, chances are you will be able to obtain quite a bit of information from people who witnessed the act. Take witness statements and be as accurate and detailed as possible. You will want to obtain police reports to determine if the subject has a history of being abusive. It is important for the investigator to obtain his own credible witnesses, from places the couple frequents together, to gather a more objective perspective.

Asset Investigations

A major issue involved in divorce cases is assets. An investigator may be called upon to search for hidden assets that their client feels the subject is withholding. It is important to have your client provide as much financial information on the subject as possible. Search county courthouse records or the county tax office to see if the subject owns any additional property that the client is unaware of. Search the subject's trash for clues. Prepare a surveillance or subrosa to check hidden business dealings. Be thorough and check all possibilities. Don't leave any of the client's questions unanswered.

Child Custody

Child custody also plays a major role in the divorce battle. It is important not to become personally involved in this type of case. Your job is to investigate and report all information obtained to your client. Begin a checklist and determine the subject's daily schedule. Set up a surveillance to obtain photographic evidence in an attempt to prove fitness of the child's custodian. Ultimately, this is the best way to obtain physical evidence for this type of case.

Bigamy Checks

Bigamy is a serious offense and constitutes grounds for a divorce. When conducting a bigamy investigation, you will begin searching for the subject's marriage records. You will also want to consider a surveillance if you think the subject is cohabitating with someone else. Conduct a thorough background check and always investigate the subject's previous addresses.

Abandonment and Desertion Checks

When conducting an abandonment check, you may first want to check for possible acts of bigamy. Interview employer, friends, neighbors, relatives and coworkers for evidence of cohabitation. Be sure to use a pretext when conducting an interview so your investigation will be complete and thorough.

Infidelity Checks

If the subject has been accused of infidelity you will need to prove intent through surveillance. Try to gather as much film evidence as possible and always follow-up with interviews. You will need to interview the hotel or motel managers of where the subject stayed. Examine the subject's telephone bills and document patterns of schedule changes obtained from the hotel managers, acquaintances, and even the client. Document unexplained card charges and gifts. It is important to remember that you as the investigator may not entice the subject to commit an illegal act. For example, do not hire a prostitute so you can gather great film evidence. Entrapment is an immoral act and is against the law. If the subject is being unfaithful to his or her spouse, you will have plenty of opportunities to gather physical evidence.

Divorce Statistics

It is important to remember there are many issues involved in a divorce investigation and it is up to you, as the investigator, to determine how to conduct the investigation. Every case is unique and should be handled accordingly. Here are some divorce statistics that may prove useful:

- 33 percent of divorces occurs within five years of marriage
- 30 percent of divorces occurs within 6–10 years of marriage
- from 11–15 years of marriage the divorce rate drops to 8 percent

- from 16–20 years of marriage the divorce rate is 10 percent
- from 21–25 years of marriage the divorce rate is 18 percent
- 40 percent of divorces occur for reasons of cruelty, mental or physical abuse
- 33 percent of divorces are caused by abandonment
- 3 and ½ percent of divorces are a result of infidelity
- 2 percent of divorces are a result of alcohol or drug abuse
- majority of police calls involve domestic issues
- twice as many men petition for divorce than women
- the larger the population, the higher the divorce rate
- the highest divorce rate is among travelers such as pilots or actors
- the lowest divorce rate is among ministers, farmers, and teachers
- two-thirds of couples without children end up in divorce

Missing Persons Investigations

In any missing person case always start with an initial interview. Try to keep the client calm. Obtain as complete a story as possible and don't judge your client. People are usually missing because they want to leave a bad situation.

Start your search with an initial investigation. You will always want to check the bad news first. Make sure the subject is not dead by contacting local mortuaries for recent activity. You will then need to check the local hospitals and jails. With the client you will then want to check all of your subject's personal belongings. Look carefully through items such as a wallet, purse, diary, under the mattress, and check the calendar for written clues that may help determine the subject's location. Never open unlocked personal items. You will need a search warrant to open locked personal belongings. However, ask the client to open the locked item. It is the easiest and quickest way around a search warrant.

Missing Juveniles and Runaways

A profile of a missing juvenile usually ranges between the ages of 14–16 years old. In many cases the juvenile girl tends to be slightly older than the juvenile boy when she decides to leave home. However, the average runaway usually returns home within one week.

Most of the juvenile runaways are likely to be hostile and defiant. They are extremely impulsive and have no definite long-term plans. Most juveniles will have mood swings and will sometimes be unable to distinguish the difference between right and wrong. When locating a runaway, the juvenile must be convinced that it was he or she who decided to return home. This theory may temporarily deter the juvenile from running away again.

Motives

The most common motives for juvenile runaways include poor home conditions, alcohol, drug abuse within the home, constant arguing and fighting with parents or siblings, and a lack of attention or affection. Some juveniles choose to run away to avoid over strict punishment, criticism, and the relocation of the family to another city or state. Many female juveniles engage in marriages and elopements to males who are of legal age. Unfortunately, statutory rape also plays a major role in juvenile runaways.

Begin the investigation on the juvenile's home situation. Find out if there is any hostility between the child and the parents. Determine if the parents are having marital problems. Speak with the other siblings in the home and determine if there is a conflict between them and the runaway. Ask the parents if they have noticed any sudden personality changes within the child or if the child has brought home a sudden change of friends.

Locating a Runaway

When trying to locate a juvenile runaway, it is best to check all locations that are familiar to the runaway. Check their friends' homes, all-night public places, lobbies and basements, abandoned cars, vacant buildings and abandoned homes, campgrounds, parks, beaches, circuses and carnivals, and always check the local shelters. The final determination on where to search for the juvenile is entirely dependent upon the initial investigation and/or information acquired during the search.

When you have located the runaway, call the parents immediately. Determine if the child needs help. Check to make sure the child does not require medical attention. Determine the method of operation. Analyze step by step on how the child ran away and watch for discrepancies in the child's story. It is important to gather as much information as possible so the parents can prevent the child from becoming a runaway in the future.

How to Disappear

As an investigator, be aware of those sources available to individuals who decide to escape their present life style by creating a brand new one. A subject may not only change his or her personal appearance, but will also try to obtain a new identity. There are booklets on the market that will instruct a person on how to create a brand new identity. Those booklets also contain the names and addresses of where a person can obtain a new identification card, awards and certificates, baptismal certificates, marriage certificates, divorce papers, medical cards, military documents, social security cards, diplomas, degrees, and birth certificates.

It is very simple for a person to obtain a new birth certificate. First, obtain the obituaries from a newspaper dated the same year you were born. Search for a name of a deceased infant, preferably one who was born in one state and died in another. This will eliminate any cross-reference check the state may conduct on you while applying for your new birth certificate. Be sure to write down correctly the names of both parents, birth date, and place of birth. Once you have obtained the birth certificate try aging it by soaking it in coffee, then place the certificate in the hot sun to dry. When a person decides to disappear from their own life style, it is not too difficult to do so. However, it may be difficult for you as the investigator to locate such a person. It is always helpful to be aware of the techniques and information that is available to people because any and all tips can prove to be useful in your search.

Chapter 6

INTERVIEW AND INTERROGATION

The successful investigation of any civil or criminal action depends greatly upon the effective questioning of complainants, witnesses, informants, subjects and/or suspects by seasoned, professional investigators. Questioning is divided into two broad classifications: interrogations and interviews. It is important for the investigator to master a variety of questioning techniques as well as being able to detect the body language of the person being questioned. The investigator must not presume a person's guilt during questioning but must be able to obtain a thorough and accurate statement-taking process which can be written or recorded.

In order to expound on this philosophy I have included this extract from Charles A. Sennewald:

> Once a crime, act or incident has occurred, the reconstructive process has but two sources to draw on: (1) the physically observable, i.e., physical evidence, and (2) the written or spoken word of those who witnessed or in one way or another participated in the act or incident.[1]

INTERROGATION

Interrogation is an accusatory questioning in which the person being questioned does not have the freedom to leave. Interrogations are primarily used in criminal investigations. An interrogation is conducted to obtain admission of guilt and to gather more information which can lead the investigator to prove or disprove the truth of an admission or confession. It is important that the investigator use the proper techniques to ensure they can gather an accurate statement of facts. This process is used to obtain accurate information regarding occurrences of a crime and can be useful in obtaining an admission of guilt. Interrogation enables investigators to gather more physical evidence as well as learn-

---

[1]Sennewald, Charles A. *The Process of Investigation: Concepts and Strategies for the Security Professional.* Boston: Butterworth-Heinemann. 1981.

ing the identity of accomplices and details of the crime in which the subject was involved.

Along with having good questioning techniques, it is important for the investigator to be able to read the body language of the person being interrogated. Nonverbal responses are indicative of deception and it is important for the investigator to be aware of them. Nonverbal responses may redirect an investigators approach to questioning depending on the body language of the person being interrogated. Much of the body language, or nonverbal responses, occur when a person is not comfortable with the questions being asked of them. This type of response usually indicates to the investigator the subject is either lying or is feeling the pressure to tell the truth. Here are some nonverbal responses that are indicative of deception:

- Yawning or stretching
- Refusing to respond
- Nervousness
- Blushing
- Pupils dilate when observing a threatening piece of evidence
- Running fingers through their hair
- Rubbing the back of their neck
- Perspiring
- Increase or decrease inhaling, exhalation ratio (breathing)
- Refusing to shift body position even though they are uncomfortable (posing)

When questioning your subject, it is important to not let the subject try to move you away from the issue. The subject may appear verbally aggressive by trying to convince you that they had no knowledge of the crime in question. Make sure you, as the investigator, pay special attention to both the body language and verbal responses of the subject you are questioning. Here are some verbal responses that are indicative of deception:

- How long is this going to take?
- I don't have much time; I have to pick up my children.
- I've got a business to run and I can't spend much time with you.
- Why would I do such a thing?
- Who . . . me?
- I swear to God.
- I swear on my mother's grave.

- I really didn't do it.
- I'm a good mother/father.
- I come from a good church-going family.
- I'm a born again Christian.
- I think I know who did it.
- I guess I'll have to pay for it and then I'll go and find the person that really did it.
- They become irrational and say things that don't pertain to the questioning.
- Repeating the question.
- Stuttering.

The investigator should always familiarize himself with the information gathered from credible witnesses and victims, background data, and physical evidence to obtain a psychological advantage over the subject being interrogated. The subject should be placed in a room where there are no distractions so the investigator can easily observe the subject's verbal and nonverbal responses.

Interrogated-Miranda Rights

It is crucial the investigator explains to the person being interrogated of their rights under the Fifth Amendment to the Constitution of the United States:

> No person shall be held to answer for a capital, or otherwise infamous crime, unless on a presentment or indictment of a Grand Jury, except in cases arising in the land or naval forces, or in the Militia, when in actual service time of war or public danger; nor shall any person be subject for the same offense to be twice put in jeopardy of life or limb; nor shall be compelled in any criminal case to be a witness against himself, nor be deprived of life, liberty, or property, without due process of law; nor shall private property be taken for public use, without just compensation.

Miranda Rights must be given to all subjects before any interrogation is to be conducted. It is important for the investigator not to overlook this concept because the subject is protected under the Fifth Amendment. Any incriminating statements made by the subject will not be admissible in a court of law unless the subject has been advised of his rights. A landmark decision of Escobedo vs. Illinois confirms the importance of implementing the Miranda Rights.

On January 19, 1960, Danny Escobedo was arrested for fatally shooting his brother-in-law. Another suspect, Benedict DiGerlando who was already in police custody, named Escobedo as the one who fired the fatal shots. Escobedo was then taken into police custody without a warrant and was interrogated for several hours. Police had informed Escobedo that the case was pretty tight and he might as well admit to the crime. Escobedo refused to admit to the crime and requested to speak to his attorney. When Escobedo was brought to the police station, he had not been formally charged. When Escobedo's attorney finally arrived at the police station he had been denied, by several chain-in-command officers, to speak with his client. Interrogations of Escobedo continued despite his several requests to speak with his attorney. At one point, an officer told Escobedo his attorney refused to speak with him. Another officer, Montejano, who knew Escobedo's family, told Escobedo if he pointed to DiGerlando as the murderer, he would guarantee Escobedo's freedom and see to it that Escobedo would only be used as a witness in court. Because of this assurance, Escobedo went ahead and accused DiGerando of the murder, not realizing he had just implicated himself as having some knowledge of the crime. Escobedo, along with DiGerando, were sent to trial and convicted.

This was a landmark decision that provided citizens with the Miranda Rights. Miranda Rights results in the individual's awareness of their rights before they make incriminating statements. Even though murder is a very serious crime, the importance of this case centered on determining whether or not Escobedo's constitutional rights had been violated. If the interrogators followed their legal procedures correctly, Escobedo vs. Illinois would not have been overturned.

INTERVIEW

Donald A. Rush writes from his book:

> One of the methods of gathering information most widely used by investigative personnel, regardless of what phase of investigative work they are engaged in, whether it be law enforcement or private investigation, is interviewing people. It is not uncommon for an investigator, perhaps several investigators, to spend days interviewing people in connection with one particular case. The days can, in some cases and not infrequently, extend into weeks and perhaps even months.[2]

An interview is a questioning process to seek information in which the person being questioned has the freedom to leave at any time. An

---

[2]Rush, Donald A. *Fundamentals of Civil and Private Investigation.* Springfield: Charles C Thomas, 1984.

interview is conducted for witnesses of crimes and subjects of civil investigations. The purpose of the interview is for the investigator to gather as much information, from the person being interviewed, that may lead to further investigations or questioning. It is important for the interviewer to gather from the person being interviewed what they have observed through the use of the five senses: sight, hearing, taste, smell, and touch. An investigator should neither accept what a person is saying as the truth or ask a question they do not have the answer to themselves. It is important to never under estimate the person you are questioning.

When writing an interview report, make sure the report is written in the first person. An example of an interview is called statement taking. Always take a written statement and make sure the person being questioned signs the written statement at the interview. Three main elements must be included in a statement report. The Identification Paragraph, Body of Statement, Attestation or Closing Paragraph. It is your choice to conduct a tape recording or video recording of the interview. However, you cannot tape record anyone without that person's knowledge. You must have the person's knowledge, not consent, before you can tape record the interview. Yet, there is one exception, if you are in fear of your job or safety at the time of the interview you may tape record someone without their knowledge, but the proof must be substantiated.

Identification Paragraph

When writing an identification paragraph you must include the following:

- the name of the person
- resident address and telephone number
- employment address and telephone number
- age and date of birth
- marital status
- dependents

Body of the Statement

When writing the body of the statement it may be of any length, however, you must:

- never skip lines
- never use abbreviations

- always make mistakes (at least one per page)
- use the investigator code on every issue
- leave no room for questions
- preferably use legal paper (numbered and lined)
- familiarize yourself thoroughly with the scene or incident
- draw and use incident/scene diagrams
- use vocabulary of person making statement
- never lead the witness: let them say what they want to say the way they saw it
- if they deny knowledge, take a negative statement
- never deny use of phone, drink, food, bathroom or any other need or request
- insure there is no diminished capacity by threat, prejudice, bias, or other outside influence to the best of your ability

Attestation-Closing Paragraph

The attestation is signed at the end of the statement by the person being interviewed.

I have read the preceding statement consisting of _____ complete pages and a page of _____ lines, and consider it to be true and correct to the best of my knowledge. No threats or promises have been made to me to force me to make this statement which I hereby acknowledge has been made of my own free will. This statement has been taken at _____ in the city of _____, County of _____, on this _____ day of _____, 19_____.

It is important to remember that witnesses, subjects, and clients should be interviewed in surrounds unfamiliar to them, which would give you the psychological advantage. If you interview someone in their home or place of business they have the advantage.

All interviews should be conducted immediately following a crime or incident. The investigator should make sure they have complete control over the interview process. The investigator should remain impartial, understanding, and considerate at all times. It is important to make the person being interviewed feel comfortable. When a person feels relaxed he or she will speak honestly and freely. It is vital for the investigator to gather as much information from the person without any conflicts or disruptions. The investigator should use as much time as needed to complete the interview. However, a time-consuming interview may cause the person to feel uncomfortable and tiresome. Here are some reasons why a person might not recall a specific incident:

- Prejudice
- Bias
- Diminished Capacity
  a) liquor
  b) drugs
  c) prescribed medicine
  d) illness
  e) fatigue (mental or physical)
  f) visual impairment
  g) color blindness
  h) illiteracy
  i) threat
  j) latent prejudice—brought out by incident being investigated
  k) personal gain/loss
  l) others

As discussed in interrogations, the interviewer must acknowledge the credibility of the witness by observing and evaluating the person's body language. It is imperative for the investigator to observe the emotional state of the witness. Determine if the witness is telling the truth, or if the witness is just being uncooperative.

It is important to remember an interview should be conducted immediately following a crime or incident. A detailed and accurate statement must be taken and signed, by the person being interviewed, to verify all information gathered during the course of the investigation.

Interview Process

When conducting an investigation in the workplace, it is not uncommon to have interview teams. An interview team consists of two people per team. Depending on the size of the investigation, up to five teams may be required. One member is considered the team coordinator who inadvertently keeps logs of the interview process. It is that person's job to document items, dates, names, and background information of the person being interviewed. The coordinator supplies all documented information to the person conducting the interview. This information updates the interviewer on the course of the investigation and provides him with information regarding other employees who are to be interviewed. The coordinator is also responsible for collecting all interview notes, tape recordings and written statements taken during the interview.

Interview Matrix

Once an investigation has been completed, the interview coordinator must prepare an interview matrix. This is a structured interview format on how the interview will be conducted. It is important for the interviewer to be well informed of all the activities that occurred during the course of the investigation. The coordinator provides the interviewer with vital information on all employees involved in the criminal investigation along with records regarding the implicated employees background check. This information is vital to the interviewer so that they do not elicit false information through improper questioning.

Interview with the Implicated Employee

The interviewers should always conduct themselves in a courteous manner while remaining impartial throughout the entire interview. James F. Broder, C.P.P. wrote, Regardless of the type of interview conducted, it is essential for the interviewer to establish the nature of his or her relationship with the interviewee at the outset.[3] Try to make the employee feel as comfortable as possible. It is important to remember that this is an interview process and not an interrogation. As an investigative interviewer, you should always identify yourself to the employee and explain to the employee that the company has hired the investigative agency to gather information regarding the problems in the company. You may want to explain to the employee that this is an interview process to solve the problems arising in the company.

The purpose of this interview is to induce the implicated employee to disclose what they know about the investigation. Use the background information you received on the employee to your advantage. Try to gain the trust of the employee being interviewed. Engage in general conversation with the employee then redirect the conversation to the investigation. The interviewer must be extremely observant of the employee's body language, determining whether or not the employee is lying or is simply being uncooperative. If the implicated employee is being uncooperative, be careful not to turn the interview process into an

---

[3]Broder, James F., Schur, Peyton B. *Investigation of Substance Abuse in the Workplace.* Boston: Butterworth-Heinemann, 1990.

interrogation. If an interrogation becomes necessary, make sure the employee is aware of their rights.

The Essentials of the Signed Statement

Once an interviewed employee has confessed to any violation of company policy or state law, a written, signed statement is taken. The following elements should be included within the signed statement:

- Acknowledge that he or she has been offered representation (if appropriate).
- Acknowledge that he or she was told that the interviewer was a private investigator, hired by the employer; not a police officer.
- Acknowledge that the statement was given freely and voluntary and was not induced by threats or promises on the part of the interviewer.
- A detailed list of the offenses he or she has verbally admitted to the investigator, how many times those violations were committed and over how long a period, for first and last times the violations occurred on company time and/or property.
- Details on the involvement of other employees who have committed like offenses.
- An account of his or her motivation for engaging in the confessed actions.
- An explanation of why he or she willingly confessed, knowing that the result could be termination, prosecution or both.
- A statement indicating what he or she would consider as appropriate disciplinary action for the offenses admitted.

It is important to determine how the interview of the implicated employees must be conducted. Try to have different groups of implicated employees per interview team. You will want to get these people interviewed before word gets out that an investigation is being conducted. You do not want to alert the entire work force of the investigation. This is to prevent other employees from getting together and discussing what not to say during the course of the interview. You must be discreet when organizing the employees to be interviewed.

Employer Representative

It is important to have an employer representative assigned to the interviewer team. The purpose is for the representative to have an understanding of the interview process and to provide the following:

- They can witness that all employees are treated fairly and with courtesy and dignity by the other members of the interview team.
- They will be present in the room with the employees and the interviewers when the employees read their signed statements aloud, thus ensuring no coercion was used to obtain the confession.
- Employer representatives will ultimately determine what dispositions will be taken regarding the culpable employees and advise them of some. They can also answer any questions the employees may have regarding their future with the company (which should purposely be left unanswered until investigation is concluded).

The employer representative is primarily used to make sure the employee being interviewed is treated fairly, with respect and that no coercion was used. The interviewer has no decision-making role on what happens to the employee. The employer representative makes all the decisions regarding the status of the employee with the company. As an interviewer, you do not want to intimidate the employee in any way. Have the employee sign the written statement, then you may want to tape record the interview. Most employees will not object to a tape recording of the interview after they have signed the statement. Remember, you do not need the employee's consent to tape record their statements. You only need the employee's knowledge. There are some advantages to tape recording the statements of a subject:

- The recording will clearly indicate the voluntary and spontaneous nature of the confession and it's authenticity.
- It will establish the noncoercive atmosphere in the interview room and will help to verify that the interviewer dealt fairly and justly with the interviewee points that may be disputed if only a written confession is obtained.
- It will be evidence of the questions asked and the interviewing techniques used, so that the employee cannot allege that the interview was handled otherwise.
- Much can be inferred about the integrity of the process by listening to the recorded narrative responses and the tones of the participant's voices.

There is no guarantee that a dispute will not surface. However, the interviewer and the employer will have an advantage with the use of the tape recording technique should an employee dispute the way the interview process was conducted.

Chapter 7

LEGAL RESEARCH

In the United States there are three (3) branches of government. The Legislative branch, which makes the law; the Executive branch, which enforces the law; and the Judicial branch, which interprets the law. After the law is enforced, case law, which is the interpretation of the legislative intent, results. Primary authority is that law which is issued by the three (3) branches of government. In mandatory/precedent, law, in general, is divided into authorities. The lower courts only follow rulings of higher courts in jurisdiction. Through persuasive authority the court considers reasoning of another court (i.e., decision by Court of Appeals for 11th Circuit would only be persuasive on another circuit Federal Court of Appeals). In secondary authority, all other written expressions of law in which the court can use as basis for decision will also furnish a basis for argument to change the law.

This foundation is possible due to the Doctrine of State Decisis which states:

1) All courts are bound by their own earlier decisions unless reversed by a higher court or later by themselves.
2) Binding authority comes from higher courts in same jurisdiction.
3) All Federal Courts must follow United States Supreme Court decisions.

The knowledge of case law and legal research are very important to the investigative process. You must determine how the law relates to the facts of the case. You will search for authority that resolved the legal issues in your factual situation.

As an investigator, you could be called upon to conduct an investigation of crime. Crimes and public offenses include felonies, misdemeanors and infractions. A crime is defined as:

A crime or public offense is an act committed or omitted in violation of a law forbidding or commanding it, and to which is annexed, upon conviction, either of the following punishments: death, imprisonment, fine, removal from office; or disqualification to hold and enjoy any office of honor, trust or profit in this state.

When presented with a criminal case of a client who was convicted of Penal Code section 187, homicide, begin by looking up the code at the law library. You may also acquire the name of the case by searching through the annotated codes. Annotated codes contain several aids to legal research. In addition to printing the word of the statute, they contain a legislative history for each code section and references to other statutes, case decisions and articles in legal journals. Remember, you are searching for the name of one case dealing with the point of law that will be helpful to your client's case. Once you have located the name of the case, you will also find a list of other relevant cases and articles. You will want to locate these other cases through *Shepard's Citations.*

It is important for you, as the investigator, to become familiar with all the reference sources of legal information. Remember, your objective in legal research is to locate case decision and/or statute which answer the questions created by a specific legal problem. All legal research begins with knowledge of the law. Therefore, it is vital for you to develop the necessary research skills so when presented with such a case, you'll know where to begin your search without any delays.

Case citations are broken down into three segments. For example: 168 Cal. App 3d 631; 168 is the volume number of the book. Cal App 3d is an abbreviation for California Appellate Cases Third Edition. 631 refers to the page number within the 168th volume of the California Appellate Cases in the Third Edition.

People vs. Callahan

168 Cal. App. 3d 631; 214 Cal. Rptr. 294 (May 18/985).

Summary

A highway patrolman arrested defendant for interfering with the performance of his duty (Penal Code, Sec. 148), as the officer was investigating a traffic accident in front of defendant's home. A jury found defendant not guilty of violating Sec. 148, but guilty of uttering offensive words in public which were inherently likely to provoke immediate violent reactions (Penal Code, Sec. 415, subd. 3), a lesser related offense. (Municipal Court for the North County Judicial District of San Diego County, Nos. Ca 70005, B 92179, Zalman J. Scherer, Judge.)

The Court of Appeal reversed, holding as a matter of law the facts did not support the conviction, noting under the circumstances the language used by the defendant was not inherently likely to provoke an immediate violent reaction. The record showed the officer was neither offended by the language nor provoked to react violently, his only concern being not to be interrupted in performing his duty. (Opinion by Brown (Gerald), P.J., with Staniforth and Butler, JJ., concurring.)

In any criminal case the prosecutor must prove that a crime has occurred. In order to do so, the prosecutor must show both the act and intent. In People vs. Callahan, the prosecution believed that Callahan's act was the "use of profane language" toward the officer while the intent was to provoke an "immediate violent reaction."

When conducting a legal research on any type of criminal case, it is important for you to remember, as the investigator, that if you take away one of the elements of a crime you will have no crime. For example, the Court of Appeals reversed, "holding as a matter of law the facts did not support the conviction." In other words, the prosecution could not prove that Callahan's use of profane language would positively provoke the immediate violent reaction. The officer stated that he was not offended by Mr. Callahan's profane language. Usually a person will somehow feel threatened by an individual's use of profanity sensing that a physical confrontation may occur, however, the officer had testified Callahan's language did not provoke a violent reaction.

This nation prides itself as unsurpassed in upholding the freedom of its people to express themselves as they see fit without fear, subject only to certain reasonable conditions prescribed by the law.

A land as diverse as ours must expect and tolerate an infinite variety of expression. What is vulgar to one may be lyric to another (Cohen vs. California (1971) 403 U.S. 15, 25 (29L.Ed. 2d 284, 293–294, 91 S. Ct. 1780). Some people spew four-letter words as their common speech such as to devalue its currency, their repetition dulls the sense; Billingsgate thus becomes commonplace. Not everyone can be a Daniel Webster, a William Jennings Bryan or a Joseph A. Ball.

When conducting a legal research on a specific case, such as People vs. Callahan, you must locate all other cases that may be similar to this one and determine how the law in those cases relates to the facts of your case. The Doctrine of Stare Decisis states a court must follow precedent cases until ruled differently by the same level court or a higher level court.

People vs. Woody

Defendants were convicted before the Superior Court, San Bernardino County, Carl B. Hilliard, J., of illegal possession of peyote, and they appealed. The Supreme Court, Tobriner, J., held that California could not constitutionally apply statute proscribing use of peyote so as to prevent Indian tribe from using peyote as sacramental symbol similar to bread and wine used in Christian churches.

Judgement reversed.

Opinion, 35 Cal. Rptr. 708, vacated.

Constitutional Law 274:

Constitutional amendment providing that Congress shall make no law respecting establishment of religion or prohibiting free exercise thereof is operative upon states by means of the Fourteenth Amendment. U.S. C.A. Const. Amends. 1, 14.

Constitutional Law 274
Poison 27

Statute proscribing use of peyote imposed burden on free exercise of religion observed by Navajo Indians who used peyote as sacramental symbol similar to bread and wine used in Christian churches. Est's Ann. Health & Safety Code, Sec. 11500; S.S.C.A. Const. Amend. 1.

Constitutional Law 84

Although judicial examination of truth or validity of religious beliefs is foreclosed by First Amendment, courts of necessity must ask whether claimant holds their belief honestly and in good faith or whether the claimant seeks to wear mantle of religious immunity merely as cloak for illegal activities.

Constitutional Law 274
Poisons 2

California could not constitutionally apply statute proscribing use of peyote so as to prevent Indian tribe from using peyote as sacramental symbol similar to bread and wine used in Christian churches. West's Ann. Health & Safety Code, Sec., 11500 U.S.C.A. Const. Amend. 1.

In People vs. Woody, you will find many annotated codes that will enable you to further research in other cases regarding the law in question. In this particular case, the law in question may appear to be the use and possession of peyote; however, while analyzing this case, you will learn that the freedom of religion is what is being disputed. Every culture has its own religious beliefs and ceremonies and it is the Constitution that allows these cultures to practice their beliefs without the interference of the law. However, the Constitution does state, "Although judicial examination of truth or validity of religious beliefs is foreclosed by First Amendment, courts of necessity must ask whether claimant holds their belief honestly and in good faith or whether the claimant is seeking to wear mantle of religious immunity merely as cloak for illegal activities."

In People vs. Woody, the court continues to state, "Although the prohibition against infringement of religious belief is absolute, the immunity afforded religious practices by the First Amendment is not so rigid (Sherbert vs. Verner (1963) 374 U.S. 398, 403, 83 S. Ct. 1790, 10 L.Ed. 2d 965; In re-Jenison (1963) 375 U.S. 14, 84 S.Ct. 63, 11 L.Ed. 2d 39; West Virginia State Board of Education vs. Barnette (1942) 319 U.S. 624, 63 S.Ct. 1178, 87 L.Ed. 1628, 147 A.L.R. 674; Braunfeld vs. Brown (1960) 366 U.S. 599, 81 S.Ct. 1144, 6 L.Ed. 2d 563; Cantwell vs. Connecticut, supra, 310 U.S. 296, 60 S.Ct. 900, 84 L.Ed. 1213, 128 A.L.R. 1352; Reynolds vs. United States (1878) 98 U.S. 145, 25 L.Ed. 244). But the state may abridge religious practices only upon a demonstration that some compelling state interest outweighs the defendant's interests in religious freedom (Sherbert vs. Verner, supra, 374 U.S. 398, 406, 83 S.Ct. 1790, 10 L.Ed. 2d 965; In re-Jenison, supra, 375 U.S. 14, 84 S.Ct. 63, 11 L.Ed. 2d 39; Braunfeld vs. Brown, supra, 366 U.S. 599, 613–614, 81 S.Ct. 1144, 6 L.Ed. 2d 563; Cantwell vs. Connecticut, supra, 310 U.S. 296, 311, 60 S.Ct. 900, 84 L.Ed. 1213, 128 A.L.R. 1352; West Virginia State Board of Education vs. Barnette, supra 319 U.S. 624, 643–644, 63 S.Ct. 1178, 87 L.Ed. 1628, 147 A.L.R. 674).

The annotated codes within this case will enable you to further investigate and research several other cases which may help you to determine if the case you are handling is similar to those you have researched. You are looking for case precedent. Do not look for similarities such as the type of crime that was committed. Rather, you are searching for case law. Search further by determining how the law relates to the facts of the case. Many issues are raised with the interpretation of the law. Another example of this is the case of "Taylor vs. Taintor." This case is concerned with the issue of bounty hunting in 1873. Bounty hunting in 1873 or today is not a licensed activity. Today this case remains precedent.

Chapter 8

A.O.E./C.O.E. WORKER'S
COMPENSATION INVESTIGATION

When conducting a Worker's Compensation Sub Rosa investigation, you will want to use various techniques such as surveillance, undercover, activity checks, interviews, and report writing. It is important to be accurate, detailed, and precise in your reports, using the correct names and dates pertaining to your subject. Based upon the information gathered by your client, decide what type of investigation should be conducted. For instance, if the information you have is no more than a medical evaluation, you should, perhaps, start with a neighborhood canvass or activity check. This can usually be done without alerting the claimant. If the claimant is never home when you call, or if you have specific information as to suspected work or recreational activity, do not risk alerting the subject with an activities check. Conduct a surveillance. Then, if they are not active, do a neighborhood investigation to determine why.

If you are an accident investigator, whether P.I. (personal injury), A.O.E. (arising out of employment), or C.O.E. (course of employment), etc., you should have a 35mm camera with a changeable lens. If you are a surveillance investigator, you should have an 8mm video camera camcorder with a c-mounted (removable) lens, and a reliable automobile of a nondescript make and color.

Worker's compensation investigations require the investigator to be experienced and to have some knowledge in this type of investigation. As the investigator, you must be familiar with the following laws and case law decisions which pertain to worker's compensation investigations. They are: Noble vs. Sears, 632 (a) California Penal Code, 7539(a) of the Business and Profession Code and 7561.3 of the Business and Profession Code. It is important for both the investigator and operative to understand the potential civil liability if any investigations are mishandled.

632(A) EAVESDROPPING ON OR RECORDING CONFIDENTIAL COMMUNICATIONS

Every person who, intentionally and without the consent of all parties

to a confidential communication, by means of any electronic amplifying or recording device, eavesdrops upon or records the confidential communication, whether the communication is carried on among the parties in the presence of one another or by means of a telegraph, telephone or other device, except a radio, shall be punished by a fine not exceeding two thousand five hundred dollars ($2,500), or imprisonment in the county jail not exceeding one year, or in the state prison, or by both that fine and imprisonment. If the person has previously been convicted of a violation of this section or Sec. 631, 632.5, 632.7, or 636, the person shall be punished by a fine not exceeding ten thousand dollars ($10,000), by imprisonment in the county jail not exceeding one year, or in the state prison, or by both that fine and imprisonment.

7539(A) PROHIBITED ACTS

Any licensee or officer, director, partner, or manager of a licensee may divulge to any law enforcement officer or district attorney, or their representative, any information he or she shall not divulge to any other person, except as he or she may be required by law so to do, any information acquired by him or her except at the direction of the employer or client for whom the information was obtained.

7561.3

The director may suspend or revoke a license issued under this chapter if he or she determines that the licensee or his or her manager, if an individual, or if the licensee is a person other than an individual, that any of its officers, directors, partners, or its manager, has: (a) used any letterhead, advertisement or other printed matter, or in any manner whatever represented that he or she is an instrumentality of the federal government, a state, or any political subdivision thereof. (b) Used a name different from that under which he or she is currently licensed in any advertisement, solicitation, or contract for business.

NOBLE VS. SEARS

Summary

A retail store and its attorneys hired a private detective agency to assist in the defense of a personal injury action. An employee of the detective agency gained admittance into the hospital room where the plaintiff in the action was confined, and secured by deception the address of the person who had accompanied plaintiff on her shopping trip when she was injured. In an action arising out of the investigation, the court sustained demurrers of the retail store and its attorneys to three causes of action charging them with liability for the actions of the detective agency and its employees, and dismissed the action as to the store and its attorneys (Superior Court of Los Angeles County, No. WE C 21930, Laurence J. Rittenband, Judge).

The Court of Appeals affirmed the order of dismissal as the cause of action seeking to predicate liability on the attorney's violation of rule 12 of the Rules of Professional Conduct, prohibiting an attorney from communicating with a party represented by counsel on a subject of controversy in the absence and without the consent of the party's counsel, but reversed the order of dismissal as to the causes of action charging the store and its attorneys with liability for the intentional torts committed by the employee of the private detective agency for either a single investigation or for the protection of property may be liable for the intentional torts of employees of the private detective agency committed in the course of employment (Opinion by Kingsley, J., with Jefferson, Acting P.J., and Dunn, J., concurring).

Guidelines for Sub Rosa Assignment

Red flags to consider when determining to conduct an outside investigation:

Surveillance

1. Did the claimant secure an attorney prior to or immediately following seeking medical attention?
2. Any subjective complaint that exceeds or could potentially exceed $20,000.00.
3. Any subjective complaint that prevents the applicant from returning from his usual and customary employment.
4. Any 100% disability.
5. *Any complaint* when *your* doctor feels the applicant is malingering or exaggerating.
6. Any time the applicant is never home during normal working hours.
7. If the applicant is observed with paint or grease on their hands or shoes when picking up their check, or doctor's appointment.
8. If the applicant has had restricted use of any of their extremities over a period of months and there is no atrophy.
9. If the applicant is seen obviously exaggerating their restrictions.
10. If the applicant or spouse is seen switching hands with their cane.

11. If neither the applicant or spouse is working and their life style indicates otherwise.
12. If the applicant appears trim, fit, tanned, etc.
13. If an activity check indicates an applicant is active or employed.
    • An activity check frequently alerts an applicant, so a period of time should elapse between an activity check and sub rosa.
14. Temporary disability has exceeded six weeks or more.
15. An anonymous tip indicates the subject is working, faking, exaggerating, etc.
16. You have information the subject is about to move.
17. If you receive any information the subject has previously been involved in any sports or other activities, and a major event is upcoming.
18. In reviewing the file or speaking to the applicant, you have a strong feeling that something significant is out of place.
19. If the applicant is banking out of their area.

If the investigation you are conducting can lead to prosecution, here is an outline of what most District Attorney Special Investigation Units (SIU) like to see in your completed investigation:

Organized Claim Files

A case synopsis without too much detail. A brief, concise overview of the *crime* (not the petty stuff), and a short statement of evidence supporting the allegation (i.e., what is (are) the specific misrepresentation(s)? What evidence is available to show that the representation, when made was false? If the true facts had been known, how would it have changed the eligibility for benefits or benefits received (materiality)? What evidence is available to show that the suspect is knowingly responsible for the misrepresentation?) Put DWC1 and employer's first notification in a prominent place. Please do not send multiple copies of medical reports or bills. Separate and clearly mark, label or tab: liens and bills, medical records, investigation, depositions and other witness statements/videos, etc. Do not include internal memoranda and notes to the file; however please include the carrier's attorney correspondence. Please do not send the entire file until it is requested.

Thorough and Complete Investigation

Interview all witnesses (coworkers, neighbors, doctors, etc.). If written statements were taken, include copies of those. If statements are tape-recorded, please include a copy of the cassette along with a transcript of the statement. Please note current whereabouts of the various witnesses. Photographs of "scene" or accidents, if possible. If there is a Sub Rosa video—the tape should be shot over multiple days, preferably over several months time, showing a wide variety of repetitive activity. The video should be shot in conjunction with either a defense or applicant medical examination, so the applicant will give a complete history to some doctor while the concurrent video shows a completely different person. Include all potentially exculpatory evidence as well—even if you believe it is controvertible.

Thorough and Complete Depositions

Build a picket fence around the applicant-deponent. An attorney should ask not only about prior accidents and injuries, but follow up on those answers in some detail, including duration—dates/years. Same with questions about current restrictions and pain. Same with questions regarding activity shown on the sub rosa tape of which the attorney is aware, but not the applicant or applicant's attorney. Ask about any subsequent injuries or accidents or medical conditions. Ask applicant how long he/she was examined by each doctor. Make the applicant clarify every subjective complaint (insomnia, weight loss, inability to stand for a long time, etc.) with specific examples (i.e., cannot get to sleep right away, lost 5 lbs. in one week, waiting in line at post office causes back pain, etc.) so that you can see what the applicant is complaining about is just part of everyone's life. Ask if applicant is so disabled that he/she is unable to work (establish time periods for the answer)—and whether there is some other job applicant who thinks he/she could work. Is he/she employed? Self-employed? Volunteer efforts? Recreational/sports activity?—Since accident? How are you supporting yourself financially these days?

Outline for Worker's Compensation File Review

If you, the investigator, are sent to review a worker's compensation file, here is what you will need to look for:

1. The case number
2. Date of injury
3. Insurance company's name and address
4. Insurance company's file number
5. Brief description of the accident
6. Injuries received and patient's complaint
7. Medical information; all doctors, their names, addresses and dates of treatment. Also, all hospitals, names, addresses and dates of confinements
8. Job title and amount of earnings
9. Date of lost time from work
10. Date subject returned to work (name and address, if new employer).
11. Amount paid in temporary total disability

12. Amount paid in permanent disability, and how paid: by companies and release or findings and awards.
13. Date of settlement
14. Permanent disability rating and was there apportionment?
15. Attorneys for the applicant and for the defendant (names and addresses)
16. Prior medical in file (again, get names, addresses and dates of treatment)
17. Previous resident addresses
18. Previous employers (concealed job skills)
19. Any identification of sub rosa

You Don't Say!?!

The following statements were taken from California State Disability Claim applications:

Describe how your disability occurred:

- I fell from the ceiling at home and I am too nervous to work now.
- It started with a cough and ended with an appendectomy.
- Fractured jaw, hit by a person who must have figured I was someone else.
- Quit to get married for two months.
- Getting on a bus, the driver started before I was all on.
- I was struck by a dog.
- Back injury received from jumping off a ladder to escape being hit by a train.
- I woke up unconscious.
- A hernia, from pulling a cork out of a bottle.
- An airplane hit the house and came in.
- I was up in a tree after a squirrel and a guy shot me.
- I fell or jumped off a bridge and landed on my head on a rock in some water.
- A carrot slipped out of my hand. As I tried to catch it, my hand hit another.
- Sore and painful feet if I do more than a little walking because of muscle problems dating back to father's side.
- Wrestling with a 12-year-old boy on the rug.
- Large chocolate cyst, right ovary with twist.

Cannot work due to sickness or injury because:

- A light case of severe flu.
- Stripped throat.
- I had the flu with a small touch of pneumonia.
- Bad eyes and well feet.
- Traffic pain in my side.
- Fleabites.
- I have athlete's foot on my hands.

EXAMPLE: A.O.E./C.O.E. REPORT

CASE: _____, DANIEL E.

BACKGROUND: This investigation received instructions to interview four (4) employees of the "_____" Drug Store located at _____ Fallbrook Ave., West Hills, Ca. 91307.

The interviews pertained to a worker's compensation case generated by a former drug store employee (claimant), Daniel E./A.K.A. Jose.

SUMMARY: This investigator arrived at the above location, "_____" Drug Store at West Hills, and interviewed Michael B./Asst. General Manager, and a former supervisor, Farhad "Fred" (see attached interviews). Dave, who was to be interviewed, no longer is employed by "_____" Drug Store, was not interviewed. Robert, Store Manager, was not available and could not be interviewed. However, he will be interviewed as soon as his availability permits.

CONCLUSION: Based on the interview conducted with Assistant General Manager, the claimant has extreme difficulties communicating, orally and in writing, in English. As a result of this difficulty, part of claimant's "write-ups" stem from his frustration in communicating effectively with customers, as "_____" store corroborates claimant's difficulty in communicating effectively in English. As a result of claimant's rudeness to customers, management was forced to act in order to correct claimant's "behavioral deficiencies." Claimant distorted management's attempt to correct these deficiencies as discrimination, which was not evidenced, orally or in writing.

The interview with claimant's former supervisor, Farhad, indicates claimant had developed severe domestic problems with his wife, (possible girlfriend), and their year old baby.

Neither _____ nor _____ has ever heard claimant complain of any injuries prior to claimant's first known revelation of domestic problems on or about October of 1991.

CHRONOLOGICAL INVESTIGATIVE REPORT

CLAIMANT: Daniel E. (AKA: Jose Contreras)

0800 HOURS: Departed office, enroute to "_____" Drug Store located at _____ Fallbrook Ave., West Hills, Ca. 91307

0955 HOURS: Arrived at "_____" Drug Store, _____ Fallbrook Ave., West Hills, Ca. Met with Assistant General Manager, Michael B.

1000 HOURS: Interview conducted with Mr. _____.

1105 HOURS: Interview terminated with Mr. _____.

1110 HOURS: Met with claimant's former supervisor, Farhad "Fred" _____ and conducted interview.

1215 HOURS: Concluded interview with Mr. _____.

1220 HOURS: Departed "_____" Drug Store. Enroute to office.

1330 HOURS: Arrived at office. (5½ Hours, 48 miles).

ATTACHMENTS:

1) Chronological investigative report.
2) Statement of Dave non availability.
3) Statement of Michael.
4) Statement of Farhad "Fred".
5) Identification of Jose, AKA: Daniel E. dated 11/6/89.
6) 9/4/90 letter from _____ to _____.
7) 9/21/90 letter from _____ to _____.
8) Inter-office memo from Thompson to General Manager dated 10/15/90.
9) Account closed "check" issued to "_____" Drug Store by Jose.
10) 5/5/91 letter from Jose _____ to _____.
11) 10/9/91 letter from _____ to _____.
12) Unknown dated letter from _____ to _____.
13) 10/12/91 memo of meeting with Fred and Jose.
14) 1/16/92 employee review to _____ by _____.
15) 1/27/92 letter by _____.
16) 1/27/92 letter by _____.
17) 1/30/92 employee review to _____ to _____.
18) 1/30/92 letter of meeting by _____.
19) Undated, unsigned memo of customer complaints.
20) 3/13/92 letter by K.L.
21) 4/9/92 letter to _____ by _____.

GUIDELINES for A.O.E./C.O.E. INVESTIGATIONS

1) Any injury that results or potentially could result in death.
2) Any cardio vascular complaint.
3) Any injury resulting in loss of any extremity.
4) Any injury resulting in loss of hearing.
5) Any injury resulting in blindness.

6) Any continuous trauma or occupational disease (also check for future potential problems that would effect continued insurability).
7) Any off-premise incident resulting in injury (auto, etc.).
8) Any second or third degree burns over 15% of the body.
9) Any injury caused by defect of malfunction of machinery, tools, scaffolding or other equipment.
10) Temporary disability is reasonably anticipated to be in excess of six weeks.
11) Any injury that results in the employee being terminated or quitting.
12) Any injury where there is a question of serious and willful misconduct on the part of the employer or employee.
13) Any injury resulting from illegal conduct.
14) Any injury resulting from the abuse of drugs or alcohol.
15) Any emotional stress or psychological trauma claim.
16) Any claim filed immediately upon or after a lay-off or termination that is apparently unrelated to the claim.

INVESTIGATIONS VOCABULARY

W.C.A.B.:	Worker's Compensation Appeals Board
A.O.E.:	Arising Out of Employment
C.O.E.:	Compensation: used to refer to the WC law, compensation benefits generally or compensation payments.
T.D.:	Temporary disability or temporary compensation: T.D. rate, T.D. period. (He was T.D. T.D. was paid.)
T.C.:	Temporary compensation.
F&A:	Findings and award.
F&O:	Findings and order, usually in connection with a "take nothing" decision against an applicant.
P.D.:	Permanent disability: P.D. compensation rate, P.D. rating, P.D. was paid.
P&S:	Permanent and stationary, to determine when T.D. ceases and P.D. is ratable; his condition became P&S on.
Standard:	P.D. rating before adjustment for age or occupation; the rating was 30% standard; we settled for the standard P.D.
Group:	Occupational group for adjustment of standard P.D. rating: group 1 is high for backs.
New & Further:	New and further disability; he petitioned for new and further (after case has been decided).
Self-Procured:	Medical treatment obtained by applicant for which applicant seeks reimbursement.
Medical-Legal:	Medical-legal costs for medical reports, tests, X-rays, testimony; to be relevant to the legal dynamics of the case.
U.I.:	Unemployment insurance benefits.

U.C.D.:	Unemployment compensation disability benefits; also referred to as D.I.; Disability Insurance.
C&R:	Compromise and release agreement; settlement.
O.T.O.C.:	Order Taking the Matter Off Calendar.
S&W:	Serious and willful misconduct.
I.M.E.:	Independent medical examiner (not used often) appointed by Appeals Board or approved by State at the expense of one of the parties.
A.M.E.:	Medical examiner agreed upon by the parties; appointed as I.M.E. by Judge or Appeals Board at the expense of one of the parties. Usually six months to one year.
SubRosa:	(Undercover) Clandestine worker's compensation investigations.
Recon:	Reconsideration; appeal to Appeals Board. Twenty (20) days plus five (5) days from date it was mailed; extended to next working day if 5th day falls on a weekend or holiday. (Preliminary Appeal)
Writ:	Writ or review; appeal to Appellate Court.
Petition:	Commonly used to indicate an appeal, i.e., for recon or a writ.
P.J.:	Presiding Judge.
W.C.J.:	Worker's Compensation Judge
U.E.F.:	Uninsured Employer's Fund
Q.I.W.:	Qualified Injured Worker
Pro Per:	Propia Persona, act as your own attorney.

Chapter 9

PHYSICAL EVIDENCE

Physical Evidence may be defined as articles and material which are found in connection with an investigation and which aid in establishing the identity of the perpetrator or the circumstances under which the crime was committed or which, in general, assist in the discovery of the facts. In order to realize the full probative value of physical evidence it must be intelligently cared for from the point of view of science and the law. A few simple rules can guide the investigator in the protection of evidence from its initial discovery at the scene of the crime until its final appearance in the court. A violation of these rules may lead to a partial loss of the value of the evidence and, in some instances, to the loss of the case.[1]

Evidence is proof that exists in support of a fact. Four types of evidence will be presented: psychological, blood typing, fingerprinting classification, and DNA (Deoxyribonucleic Acid).

The rules of evidence will be outlined using the California Code of Civil Procedure followed by the Laws of Evidence, what can and cannot be used in a court of law and the weight given to different types of evidence.

Psychological Evidence

Psychological evidence is an issue that has been highly debated within the courts. Psychological behavior is the study of the human mind and the prediction of one's mental state through their past performances. What we have learned through the court system is that if one is to place emphasis on facts only, as the prosecution normally does, you will have a conviction. However, the defense usually focuses on the "why" of a crime. This is where the past performance behavior of an individual is determined. High profile defense teams have used this means as a way to gain the sympathy of a jury.

To predict a person's behavior pattern can be difficult to those who

---

[1]O'Hara, Charles E., O'Hara, Gregory L. *Fundamentals of Criminal Investigation*, Rev. 5th Ed. Springfield: Charles C Thomas, 1988.

believe there should be no basis for this type of defense. However, the science of psychology believes that people are creatures of habit and all behavior can be predicted. If a person cannot control what they have done in the past, chances are they will continue to conduct the same type of behavior in the future. A person who does not have a thought process cannot have intent. Therefore, the person should not be held accountable for chargers of wrongdoing. Despite your personal opinion on this view, this type of conclusion has been accepted by the courts and is part of the judicial system.

History of Fingerprinting

One of the most unique effects in investigations today is the use of fingerprinting. Throughout history, fingerprinting has provided many uses, but today it has proven to be most useful in the field of criminal investigations.

Fingerprinting has been traced back as far as the biblical period by speculative scholars; however, the first scientific observation of fingerprints was made by Marcello Malpighi in 1686. A professor of anatomy, he founded the "elevated ridges" on the hands that are now drawn out into ridges, loops and spirals. In 1823, another professor of anatomy, John Purkinje, published a thesis on the nine classifications of the "elevated ridges."

In 1858, Sir William James Herschel was the first person to use the fingerprint classification on a large scale. He was a Chief of Law Enforcement in his country and he used the fingerprinting method by requiring natives to put their fingerprints on contracts. Sir William James Herschel did not have the ability to identify individual prints; however, the natives believed he did. This proved to be an effective deterrent to dishonesty. Twenty years later, Herschel became more proficient at identifying fingerprints and he requested this system be used on prisoners.

In 1892, Sir Frances Galton, an anthropologist and cousin to Charles Darwin, published a book titled, *Finger-prints.* Sir Frances Galton developed a scientific method of classifying patterns to search and identify fingerprint records in a timely manner.

In 1891, a police investigator in Argentina, named Juan Vucetich, was the first criminal investigator to solve a crime by the use of fingerprints.

In 1903, Bertillon Signalment's use of the fingerprint method prevented a murderer, who was an identical twin, from leaving prison under the pretext of his twin brother. This case proved to the prison officials that fingerprinting was a foolproof method that must be adopted into the prison system.

In 1924, congress enacted the FBI Identification Division. This division began with approximately 80,000 fingerprints and in 1946 had over 100 million on file. Today, that same file contains more than 174 million fingerprint records with approximately 22,000 fingerprints processed daily. Fingerprints today are not only used in criminal investigations, but are also used by the United States military for soldier identification.

Presently, the fingerprinting system has been updated by the use of today's technology. The computerized system has provided its user with a tremendous cost savings in both labor and time. Although today's technology has proven to be a necessity in the fingerprinting realm, the final step of verification must still be done by a fingerprint technician.

Latent Fingerprint

A latent fingerprint is best described as a combination of chemicals which is exuded by the pores on the surface of the skin. These chemicals consist of perspiration, which contains water, oils, amino acids, and salts. The latent print is not visible to the naked eye. When a person's hand comes in contact with another surface, the moisture from the hand is deposited onto the surface leaving a latent print.

As an investigator, you will always want to check the "point of entry" at a crime scene for latent fingerprints. Because these prints are not visible to the naked eye, a scientific method must be conducted to be able to see the print. One method is by dusting with fine powder over the print. The pattern of powder is lifted with transparent tape. Some prints can be made to glow with a laser and then be photographed.

The most common problem you will find at a crime scene, when trying to locate fingerprints, is the crime scene security. Most often family members or bystanders disturb crucial pieces of evidences by touching them. The search for latent fingerprints require both skill and patience. The investigator must think like the criminal and follow the same path as the perpetrator:

1. Always begin your search for the latent fingerprints at the point of entry of a crime scene.
2. Check all items the victim believes have been moved by the perpetrator.

3. Check all surrounding areas of where the victim has kept their valuables.
4. Check the not-so-obvious places such as the refrigerator for visible prints on food.

Documentary Evidence

Documentary evidence is all evidence gathered during the investigation which is recordable. This includes all writings, reports, photographs, papers, and other tangible items which can be examined that are relevant and material to the case.

FORENSIC LABORATORY

DNA

DNA fingerprinting: Polymerase Chain Reaction is a chemically-enduced reaction that allows a person to look at DNA. There are four things that no two people contain alike: DNA, pupils, teethmarks, and fingerprints.

Here's how a laboratory tests for matching DNA:

1. DNA is extracted from blood, hair, semen, or other tissue found at a crime scene and from a sample from a suspect.
2. Chemicals called "restriction enzymes" cut the DNA strand every place they find a sequence of bases. In different people, the fragments vary slightly in length and weight.
3. A drop of sample is put on as tray of gel. An electric current pulls the fragments along the gel. Heavier fragments move a short distance; lighter fragments go farther.
4. Pattern of tracks is stuck to a nylon membrane and treated with radioactive chemicals that bind to the DNA fragments.
5. The membrane is pressed for several days against X-ray film which records the radioactivity.

Blood Typing

Not as precise as a DNA test, although blood typing can be used to eliminate suspects and point to a specific suspect. Besides the four blood types, A, B, AB and O, labs can identify 10 other enzymes and proteins in blood.

Rules of Evidence

The success or failure of a criminal prosecution usually depends upon the evidence presented to the court. It is in the court that the investigator must present the evidence which he has so laboriously collected over a period of months. Will his evidence be admitted? Has he taken precautions to obtain evidence that is admissible? Has he observed the rules which govern admissibility? A failure through ignorance on the part of the investigator may lead to the rejection of a vital piece of evidence by the court with the result that a conviction cannot be sustained. Since the investigator is occupied constantly with the business of evidence, it is an indispensable part of his training to understand the purpose of evidence and the rules that control its admissibility. It is only in this way that he can serve the cause of justice efficiently. The rules of evidence lie at the heart of modern judicial systems, and their understanding is necessary for an intelligent participation in prosecutive procedures.[2]

General definition and division, Sections 1823–1831. Code of Civil Procedures.

CCP 1823. Definitions of Evidence: judicial evidence is the means, sanctioned by law, of ascertaining in a judicial proceeding the truth respecting a question of fact.

CCP 1824. Definition of Proof: proof is the effect of evidence.

CCP 1825: Definition of the Laws of Evidence:

1. For declaring what is to be taken as true without proof. Example: the sun is going to come up every morning. After January 15 comes January 16. The law accepts that as proof.
2. For declaring the presumptions of law both disputable and conclusive.
3. For the production of legal evidence.
4. For the exclusion of whatever is not legal. The Excluding Rule.
5. For determining the value and effect of evidence. Example: "If he did that, then he must have done this."

CCP 1826. The Degree of Certainty Required to Establish Facts: the law does not require absolute certainty. However, moral certainty is required. It produces conviction in an unprejudiced mind.

CCP 1827. Four Kinds of Evidence Specified:
1. Knowledge of the Court.

---

[2]O'Hara, Charles E., O'Hara, Gregory L. *Fundamentals of Criminal Investigation,* Rev. 5th Ed. Springfield: Charles C Thomas, 1988.

     2. Testimony of Witnesses.

     3. Writings

     4. Other material objects presented to the five senses: hearing, taste, touch, smell and sight.

CCP 1828. Degrees of Evidence:

     1. Primary and Secondary

     2. Direct and Indirect

     3. Prima facie, satisfactory and conclusive

Laws of Evidence

Evidence is that which demonstrates, makes clear, or ascertains the truth of the very fact of point in issue, either on one side or the other. It supplies proof. It is important for you, the investigator, to understand what can be legally admitted in a court of law. If you do not understand the fundamental rules of governing the admission and rejection of evidence, you are wasting your time, your client's time and the court's time.

Tests of admissibility are applied to all evidence. There are three principal tests of admissibility that must be met before testimony or physical evidence is allowed into evidence: relevancy, materiality and competency.

RELEVANCY: Concerns the logical relation between the proposed evidence and a fact to be proved.

MATERIALITY: Not only must evidence be related to the case being proved, it must also combine the fact with the issue of the law.

COMPETENCY: Concerns evidence which is qualified, reliable, and suitable for the case in point. Example: Can an idiot comprehend what is said? Does the evidence have the ability to withstand the truth?

Burden of Proof

The burden of proof is the result or effect of evidence. No person in a criminal case can be convicted without the burden of proof. This responsibility lies on the prosecution which must prove three facts in order to convict a person: the act charged was done or omitted, it was done by criminal means, and it was done by the accused. The proof must always be beyond a reasonable doubt.

Direct Evidence

Direct evidence is that means of which tends to show the existence of a fact in question without the intervention of proof of any other fact. Example: "I heard a shot, turned, and saw the defendant running." "Turned and saw the defendant running" is the direct evidence.

Circumstantial Evidence

Circumstantial or indirect evidence tends to establish the issue by proof of various facts. For example, "I heard a shot and saw you standing there sweating." "Standing there sweating" would be considered circumstantial evidence because you did not actually see the individual running which would have caused the person to sweat. The essence of circumstantial evidence is inference, which draws a conclusion from facts or propositions known to be true. Therefore, all circumstantial evidence should be carefully examined.

Real Evidence

Real Evidence is furnished by objects themselves. It requires no explanation, merely identification. Example: "The gun." Evidence that speaks for itself.

Presumptions

A presumption is an inference as to the existence of one fact from the existence of some other fact. There are two major types of legal presumptions: conclusive and rebuttable.

CONCLUSIVE PRESUMPTION: is considered final, unanswerable, not to be overcome by contradictory evidence. Example: children under the age of seven are conclusively presumed to be incapable of committing a crime. A child under the age of seven cannot determine the difference between what is legally right or wrong.
REBUTTABLE PRESUMPTION: May be overcome by proof of its falsity. Presumption of innocence. Can be overcome by use of McNaughton Test. A McNaughton Test is a psychological test given to a child under the age of fourteen to determine if the child understands the difference between right and wrong.

Hearsay Evidence

Hearsay Evidence is based not on a witness's personal knowledge, but on matters told to him by another. It implies the possession of information by the witness but not the knowledge. Generally, hearsay evidence is not admissible in court, but here are some exceptions:

CONFESSIONS EXPRESSED: A confession voluntary in expressed terms made against the interest of the defendant by an accused person. Shows guilt in of itself.

CRIMINAL ADMISSION: Different from a confession in that the evidence heard is rebuttal.

DYING DECLARATION: A dying declaration is made by a person who, at the time of the statement, knew that he was dying and felt that death was inescapable.

RES GESTAE: "The origin of things." The association of time. The person does not have the time to think. A spontaneous statement. Example: Defendant shoots someone and a woman walks into the room hearing the defendant say, "Oh my God, I've killed him." This type of spontaneous admission is admissible in a court of law.

Best Evidence Rule

The Best Evidence Rule provides that one shall present in court the best available evidence of the fact you are seeking to establish. Example:

When the investigator goes into court on a traffic accident, the investigator produces pictures and diagrams of the roadway where the accident occurred. This is admissible because the investigator cannot physically bring the roadway into court.

Chapter 10

CASE PREPARATION

Many attorneys assign private investigators the tasks of investigations. It is important for the investigator to understand the scope of the investigations in detail during their discussion with the attorney. The investigator should always familiarize himself with the facts of the given case. It is also important for the investigator to understand the legal implications so they do not jeopardize or influence the outcome of the case. The investigator should always maintain good communication with the supervising attorney so that they do not waste their own time investigating unnecessary facts.

If the case you are investigating contains an aspect of the law you are unfamiliar with, be sure to spend some time reading a legal encyclopedia so you will have a better understanding of the legal implications that may be involved with the case. Without accurate and detailed knowledge of the law, you will be unable to determine what facts are important to the investigation.

Before you conduct an investigation, be sure to familiarize yourself with the facts of the case by thoroughly reviewing the client's file. Read all documents and interviews in the file. Begin your preparation by making a list of all witnesses that must be interviewed or contacted. Write down questions you may have for these witnesses. Make a list of all documents that need to be obtained. Develop a checklist for the case type. Listing all the information to be investigated, the checklist assures the private investigator and the attorney that every possibility has been investigated.

Sources of Information

As an investigator, you should consider every possible source of information. Information can be obtained from:

- Physical evidence, such as the murder weapon, clothing worn by the client, or other objects.

- Photographic evidence, which includes pictures taken or the scene of the incident, of motor vehicles involved in the accident, or of the client's injuries.
- Documents, such as letters and memos in the case of a breach of contract case, or police reports and medical reports for a car accident case.
- Witnesses, who are any individuals who have first-hand information about the case.
- Other sources, such as tenancy applications, the credit bureau, and the Department of Motor Vehicles.

To begin an investigation, the private investigator must always go to the scene of the case to observe and take measurements along with photographs. This should be done immediately upon receiving the case so you, the investigator, can obtain accurate evidence. According to Anthony M. Golec, the Director of Anthony M. Golec and Associates:

> The general scene of any type of occurrence, whether civil or criminal, should always be adequately photographed so as to show the general conditions which exist at the scene, even if these photos are not intended to be used as evidence in court. They will show greater facts that state an understanding of the situation.[1]

Some attorneys prefer that a professional photographer take photographs of the scene, but if the private investigator is an experienced photographer, the law firm may allow the investigator to do it. When taking photos, show the scene from several angles and include shots of any traffic control signals, such as stop signs, yield signs, speed limit signs, and stop lights.

You may want to sketch the scene you are investigating, but to be admissible as evidence, the sketch must be drawn to scale. To guarantee the drawing is to scale, you will need to measure the distance between objects in the scene with a tape measure. Sketches are becoming increasingly valuable because many details of the scene are too difficult to describe and they do not present well in photographs. Sketches can help a jury see the incident from your client's viewpoint and can also assist witnesses in describing how a particular event has occurred.

It is important to remember that you must always examine and make a list of all physical evidence available in the case. Physical evidence is any

---

[1]Golec, Anthony M. *Techniques of Legal Investigation,* 2nd Ed. Springfield: Charles C Thomas, 1985.

tangible object, such as a gun or clothing, left behind at a crime scene or incident.

Documents and Reports

Reports are valuable sources of information to a private investigator investigating a case. Reports are generated whenever the police investigate a complaint or car accident, a doctor sees a patient, a person is hospitalized, a pathologist examines a dead body, or a person is booked into jail. Since these documents are the source of valuable information to the investigator, the investigator should strive to obtain copies of those that are relevant to his case. For example, suppose you are investigating a murder case in which the defense claims a woman killed her husband because she was a battered wife. As an investigator, you will want to obtain hospital records, police reports, and the records kept by battered women's shelters. These records will help prove or disprove the wife's defense.

Strive to establish a good rapport with members of the law enforcement community. Law enforcement officers are often the first ones on the scenes of car accidents and crimes and are often called as witnesses in trials. Law enforcement officers are valuable sources of information and it is important that these officers and state patrol forces respect you and the law firm you work for.

To obtain copies of police reports or hospital records, you may need to submit an authorization form signed by the clients or patient. In some states, these records are available only with a subpoena duces tecum, which is a court order requiring the agency to release the records.

Once you have obtained these reports and documents, thoroughly review them, taking additional notes if necessary. Only if you have a thorough grasp of the case should you then begin to interview witnesses.

In investigating any case, you should interview all witnesses, plaintiffs, and defendants in the lawsuit, unless that party is represented by an attorney. The rules of ethics prohibit an investigator working for a law firm to speak to a party represented by an attorney unless the attorney consents. If the attorney agrees to allow the investigator to interview a witness, usually the attorney will want to be present.

Credibility of witnesses depends on their appearance, personality, confidence, and ability to remember. This is why it is crucial that you interview witnesses in person to evaluate them (see Appendix for example of a case preparation).

Interviewing Witnesses

As a private investigator, you should interview all witnesses including those who are uncooperative. Try to be friendly to all witnesses, even those who are hostile to the party your firm represents. If some witnesses are reluctant to speak with you, use the following methods of approach to persuade them:

- Tell a reluctant witness that you want to make the process easy for them by just asking a few simple questions. Otherwise, inform the witness they will be forced to take a deposition which is a much longer process, requiring that the witness appear because they now have been served a subpoena.
- Try to appeal to the sympathy of the witness by asking, "If you were in my client's position, wouldn't you want to find out the truth about what happened?" If the witness still refuses to be interviewed, document the refusal because later this refusal can be used against the witness at trial. Likewise, if a witness who should know something claims that they know nothing, then get a statement from that witness to that very effect. Such a statement will prevent the witness from later "remembering" something detrimental to your client's name.

Most witnesses who say they will not talk may eventually answer questions. One way to get a useful statement from a hostile witness is to drop in on the person unexpectedly. Since the witness has had no time to prepare a statement, they may give you useful information. This type of information is considered valuable to your case.

To obtain information from a business, go to the chief executive officer or general manager, since people in these specific positions have the authority to release information. If you must interview an elderly witness or one in poor health, talk to your supervising attorney about the possibility of deposing the witness soon to preserve the testimony in the event of that witness's untimely death.

It is important to become thoroughly familiar with the case before conducting interviews with witnesses. This will help the case move along in an efficient manner without unnecessary delays.

Witness Statements

Lawsuits often take months or even years to resolve. During that time, witnesses may forget what happened, die, move away, or are never to be found again. This is why it is extremely important to take a statement from each witness interviewed. Testimony preserved in a statement can be used later to refresh the witness's memory. The statement also serves the purpose of showing exactly what the witness knows. Statements can also be used to impeach a witness on the witness stand if the witness tries to change their testimony.

There are several types of witness statements. The most common is the handwritten statement. Other types include the tape-recorded statement and the question and answer statement taken by a shorthand reporter.

The Handwritten Witness Statement. The handwritten witness statement is written by hand, by the investigator and then signed by the witness at the time of the witness interview. After the interview, the witness should read the statement. If there are any inaccuracies, the investigator should change the statement and have the witness initial the change. The statement should begin with the preamble that gives the witness's name, address, age, occupation, name of employer, and marital status. The statement should include, in chronological order, the events the witness observed.

Print the entire statement on white 8½ by 11 inch, ruled paper. Avoid using yellow legal pads since they do not copy well. At the end of the statement, always include paragraph and have the witness sign the statement (refer to Chapter 6).

The Tape Recorded Statement. While conducting the investigation, you may take a tape recorded witness statement, which is quicker and easier than the handwritten statement. However, an interview recorded on magnetic tape can easily be altered. If possible, record the interview on plastic tape or on another medium that cannot be altered.

Begin the tape recorded interview by asking the witness background information such as name, address, age, occupation, name of employer, and marital status. Direct the interview with questions and do not allow the witness to ramble. After the interview, let the witness listen to the recording and tape-record the witness making an actual statement that they have just listened to the recording they have given and then allow the witness to add or to correct any part of their statement. Remember, you do not need a witness's permission to tape record their statement, you only need to have their knowledge of the tape recorder.

The Question and Answer Statement. The question and answer witness statement recorded by a shorthand reporter is useful for interviewing an unfriendly or hostile witness. This process appears to be less intimidating to the witness being interviewed. A shorthand reporter is a person who knows shorthand well enough to be able to take verbatim notes of a conversation. From the time you first meet the witness, have the shorthand reporter with you. As you ask the questions, the shorthand reporter should take verbatim notes. The interview should be question and answer — one in which you can obtain information about the witness's background and any other additional information you may need from the witness. After the interview, have a certified copy of the statement transcribed by the reporter.

Use of Expert Witness

In every case, you should consider whether an expert witness can help your client's case. Experts are available for every conceivable specialty, from handwriting analysis, to hair samples, to accident reconstruction. An expert is a person who has special knowledge, skill, experience, training, or education in a particular subject. Often attorneys ask their private investigators to locate and interview experts. Two useful references to use in locating experts are *Lawyer's Desk Reference: Technical Sources for Conducting a Personal Injury Action,* and *The Directory of Expert Witnesses in Technology,* both of which are updated periodically.

Before contacting any expert witness, seek the approval of your supervising attorney since expert witnesses frequently charge dearly for their time. However, the testimony of an expert often makes the difference in the client's case.

The Investigative Reports

Once you have completed your investigation, write an investigative report for your attorney. Include all information in the report no matter how insignificant as well as the copies of all photographs taken; copies of all witness statements; and a list of all possible witnesses with their names, addresses, and phone numbers (see Appendix-Example of Case Preparation of Civil Rights Investigation).

Anthony M. Golec stated in his book on legal investigation:

> The legal investigator should be aware that federal civil rights violations are almost always involved in cases of police abuse, involving the gratuitous use of "official violence." Civil suits brought by the victims in such cases are under the Civil Rights Act of 1871,[7] for conspiracy to deprive a person of his or her civil rights, and the landmark 1964 Civil Rights Acts. The penalties under these acts are monetary damages and injunctive relief.

The legal investigator should also be aware that an unofficial code of silence usually exists among police officers in such cases, and the burden is on the prosecution to prove specific intent on the part of the police officer.[2]

,

---

[2]Golec, Anthony M. *Techniques of Legal Investigation,* 2nd Ed. Springfield: Charles C Thomas, 1985.

Chapter 11

COURTROOM TESTIMONY

Courtroom testimony is very important in the investigative field. As an investigator, you must know all courtroom procedures and tactics. A successful courtroom testimony will make all your hard work worthwhile. It is important to understand how the court system works and the role that is played by the investigator. Remember, it was you who conducted the investigation so no one else knows or understands the case better than you. You must always show confidence in your testimony and answer all the questions as brief and concise as possible.

Courtroom Demeanor

First impressions have a lasting effect. It is important for you not to draw attention to yourself in a negative aspect. The importance of your testimony is to bring successful attention to your case and not to yourself. Be sure you have a confident posture. Sit up attentively with a straight back and keep your hands on your lap. Don't slouch or use hand gestures while speaking. The use of hand gestures suggests a nervous person. Make sure you have direct eye contact with the person to whom you are speaking at all times. Do not allow your eyes to wander around the courtroom. It is important to emphasize self-confidence.

Effective Testimony

Honesty (118P.C.) as stated in California Penal Code.

(a) Every person who, having taken an oath that he or she will testify, declare, depose, or certify truly before any competent tribunal, officer, or person, in any of the cases in which the oath may by law of the State of California be administered, willfully and contrary to such oath, states as true any material matter which he or she knows to be false and every person who testifies, declares, deposes, or certifies under penalty of perjury in any of the cases in which testimony declarations, depositions, or certification is permitted by law of the State of California under penalty of perjury and willfully states as true any material matter which he or she knows to be false, is guilty of perjury. This subdivision is applicable whether the statement, or the testimony, declaration, deposition or certification is made or subscribed within or without the State of California. (b) No person shall be convicted of perjury where proof or falsity rests solely upon contradiction by testimony of a single person other than the defendant. Proof of falsity may be established by direct or indirect evidence.

When testifying in a court of law it is important to be both brief and concise. Never elaborate on your responses unless told to do so. Make sure you clarify your responses and if you do not understand the question asked of you, ask for the question to be repeated. Always remain objective by stating facts without bias or prejudice and never give your opinion unless you are asked to. Never become emotional while testifying. Do not get angry, do not cry or laugh, and most importantly, do not argue. Never come to court unprepared. Always read and know your notes. Study and know it the night before. Review and be prepared for all types of questions. Think of how you are going to respond. Be confident; remember this is your case.

Written Reports

A Private Investigator needs to be aware of the importance of a well-written report. Contrary to beliefs, a report reflects the investigator's character. You must remember that a well-written report should always be neat in appearance and correct in both grammar and spelling. This is important, especially if your report is presented in a courtroom. You will want a neat well-written report to reflect your image as a professional investigator.

Always remember to be precise in your reports by not leaving out any details. Do not take for granted that the individual reading your report will understand what you are trying to say. Do not use flowery words or slang phrases unless you are quoting a person. Never assume that you will be able to elaborate on the missing details of the report once you have been called to testify. The case itself may never get to court if some details are left out. This may be because the opposing counsel may feel that there is not enough evidence to send the case to court.

Details should be explained thoroughly. Use what your training has taught you and be an expert at examining and explaining the details of the case. For example, you may need to explain what "contraband" means. Be detailed and precise when using your expertise by thoroughly explaining its meaning and uses. Details like this will be crucial in a successful case.

With the amount of available information and the number of knowledgeable people who are available to an investigator, the investigator should not be caught with an incomplete report. Case decisions do not always favor investigators, but the investigator should not help the situation by writing an incomplete report.

Courtroom Tactics

A private investigator, when preparing to go to trial on a case that he has made, should always review his report. It is important for the investigator to refresh his memory of the incident along with the details of the report. Some cases take several years before going to court, so it is crucial for the investigator to reread his old notes to familiarize himself with the details of the case. An investigator should only testify to what he knows in his report. Never to speculate or assume, because a sharp attorney will only lead you into a trap that you will not be able to recover from. It is that attorney's goal to make it sound as if you don't have a clue to what is going on. Appear knowledgeable and speak with confidence. Answer questions as briefly and concise as possible.

A private investigator should present a professional image when in court. A private investigator should wear business type apparel. An investigator should know his training record and be able to testify in court in a clear, concise, and correct manner. An investigator, when testifying in court, should look at the person asking the question when answering questions. Looking down at the floor or all around the courtroom will distract the jurors from what you are saying. When answering questions, do not get into a shouting match with the attorneys or try to match wits with them in courtroom tactics. Answer the questions with an even and controlled voice. There will come a time when you do not know the answer to a question. When asked this question, just say that you do not know.

Conduct

It is important to be aware of your conduct at all times when you are in or near a courtroom. When you appear in court for the trial, remember that you are being viewed by many people long before you get to the correct courtroom. Your demeanor and conduct in the parking lot, elevator, restrooms, and hallways can make impressions, both good and bad, which may impact the outcome of the trial. Be professional and courteous at all times in and around the courthouse.

Testimony

When you are called to testify, you will be required to take an oath. This is the first official act you perform in front of the jury. Remember, first impressions count. First impressions are lasting impressions. You never get a second chance to make a good first impression. It is important to take your oath seriously. Cases are won and lost based on the first impression that a juror has of the credibility and professionalism of the involved investigator. This credibility and professionalism start with a professional attitude when taking the oath.

The prosecuting attorney will begin the case by asking you a series of questions; this is called direct examination. Based on your pretrial interview, you should know all of the questions that you will be asked, and the attorney should know the answers you will give to these questions. Keep your answers short and direct. If the attorney asks you to explain an answer, do so by giving more details of exactly what did occur.

Following direct examination, the opposing attorney will conduct cross-examination. In cross-examination, the opposing attorney is allowed to ask "leading" questions, i.e., questions which suggest the answer desired by the opposing attorney. Listen carefully to these questions and do not allow the opposing attorney to put incorrect or inaccurate facts into your testimony. If the opposing attorney inadvertently or intentionally states the evidence incorrectly in his or her question, do not allow it to become part of the record. Politely correct the attorney, and state what the true facts are. If the opposing attorney attempts to cut you off and prevents you from properly answering the question, do not despair. Hopefully, the attorney, whom you are testifying for, will make a note of this and allow you to explain fully on redirect examination.

If you become aware that you have made a mistake in your testimony, make certain that you correct it at the earliest possible opportunity.

Ways to Help Support your Court Case

1. *Walk into court with a professional appearance.*
   Never come into court looking unprofessional. The judge and the jury may not find your testimony credible. Always dress professional. You do not want to draw the jury's attention to your attire rather than your testimony.
2. *If your case has a weak point, tell the attorney.*
   Always tell your attorney in detail what you have written in your

report. This will enable the attorney to prepare their briefs on the weak points the opposing attorney may attempt to attack.

3. *If the claimant/subject pleads not guilty, do not take this personally.*
   Never speak in a courtroom unless asked to do so. Remember, you are there to testify and explain your part in the investigation. Do not take courtroom situations personally or give your opinion on courtroom tactics.

4. *When the opposing counsel wants you to become angry, remain calm and focused.*
   Never show emotions in a courtroom while testifying. Do not get angry, do not cry or laugh, and do not argue with an attorney or judge. Answer all questions in an even and controlled voice.

5. *Be meticulous regarding the facts.*
   Always be clear, concise and brief in your testimony. Always state your facts and never give your opinion. Facts are important to a case, so never allow an opposing attorney to state you incorrectly on what you have said. Politely correct the attorney and state what the true facts are.

6. *If you are positive you do not know . . . be honest.*
   If you do not know the answer to a question asked then simply state that you do not know. It is fairly easy for an intelligent attorney to prove that you are lying. Do not allow the opposing attorney to discredit your credibility.

7. *Take your notes at the time of investigation.*
   Always make notes at the time you are conducting an investigation. Most cases take several years before they go to trial. Taking notes will enable you to refresh your memory when called upon to testify.

8. *Display humility and professionalism.*
   Always present yourself in a professional manner: both in appearance and conduct.

9. *Remain unbiased and objective with the claimant/subject at the time of the investigation.*
   Never do anything to jeopardize a case. Remember, the person you are investigating has rights and is protected by those rights. Follow procedures and document all activities during the course of the investigation.

10. *Hold the laws of search and seizure, and privacy in high regard.*

Never violate Constitutional requirements. Judges will throw out any evidence obtained illegally in violation of the Constitution.

11. *Just answer only the question you were asked.*

Never give more information than you are asked for. It is important to remember that you must always answer your questions as brief as possible. This gives the opposing attorney no chance to use the information you have given him against you.

EXAMPLE OF DIRECT EXAMINATION
FOR COURTROOM TESTIMONY

Q. What is your occupation?

A. I am an insurance investigator.

Q. By whom are you employed?

A. Private Investigative Research Company

Q. What is your address?

A. Never give home address—only agency (9227 Haven Avenue, Suite 300, Rancho Cucamonga, Ca. 91730).

Q. Are they licensed by the State of California for the purpose of insurance investigation?

A. Yes, they are. California License *P.I. 15835.*

Q. Are you a licensed investigator?

A. No, I am not (only the firm has the requirement to be licensed in California, and not each individual).

Q. Did you or your company receive an assignment from *ABC Adjusters* to place *John Doe* under surveillance?

A. Yes, (I), (we), did.

Q. Is that person in the courtroom now?

A. Yes. Then indicate the color of shirt, jacket, sweater, dress, or other attire they are wearing. Look at the subject and point this person out. Do not show any outward animosity towards the claimant, but convey the impression that you are there to tell a true story.

Q. What date or dates did you have *John Doe* under surveillance?

A. You then state the dates and times if you are asked. Let's say, for now, it was July 1, 4, and 6, 1993.

Q. Did you have in your possession at these times a video camcorder?

A. Yes, I had a Sony 8mm camcorder camera.

Q. What lenses did you have with you on these dates?

A. I had a standard 20mm zoom lens capability.

Q. How much film did you obtain?

A. Now this may depend on how many days that you took film. So your answer should be something like this: On July 1, I obtained 40 feet; on

July 4, I obtained 30 feet; and on July 6, I obtained 30 feet. A total of 100 feet of (colored) (black and white) film.

Q. Did you take notes of the activity that you observed on those dates?
A. Yes, I did.
Q. Are they in your own handwriting and were they made at the time the activity occurred?
A. Yes.
Q. Do you wish to use these notes while you testify?
A. (Yes) (No).

If you say "yes" and begin to testify, the applicant's attorney has the right to look at your notes. Always remember, never answer a question whether you know the answer or not, if an attorney has your notes. Simply ask for them back. It is best to avoid the use of notes altogether by not bringing them out unless the questions are too exact to do without them. Placing the film cassettes on the table in front of you will help you to remember dates.

When testifying, always remember to answer only the question as it is put to you. If it is the truth, then you should admit whatever the question is. Most investigators, at their first trial, want to volunteer information and this only leads to embarrassment for you and your client.

Q. Will you please tell the court what you observed on July 1, 4, and 6?
A. Give an accurate account of what you observed on that day, i.e., what he did, where he went, and if there was strenuous activity, the name of the object and the approximate weight. You may add that the subject's movements appeared normal and unrestricted. Utilize bathroom scale here, if you were able to personally weigh the described object.
Q. Does the film fairly present the activity that you observed *John Doe* doing?
A. Yes. It took a cross-section of his various activities; then explain as to part of bending, turning neck, climbing stairs . . . whatever happened.
Q. Are you prepared to show your film today?
A. Yes.

The attorney may or may not at this time (or any other time) ask you questions that the attorney may feel are important. When the attorney has completed the questions, he or she will then ask you to show the film. The judge will then either agree or may ask the applicant's attorney if they wish to cross-examine.

For the most part, you will find that you will show your film first and then be cross-examined. If your equipment has been set-up before, then you may ask for the lights to be turned off. If the equipment is not set-up, then a recess will be called for you to set-up the equipment. Now the lights are off and you can turn on the projector, adjust the focus and set the film speed as before you mentioned in your testimony.

At the conclusion, you are often allowed to rewind the film. Place it in the box and either hand it to the attorney or the referee and then return to the witness stand, if directed to do so. Sometimes the referee will ask that you wait until the conclusion of the session before rewinding the film.

Now the cross-examination will begin. No one really knows what questions the applicant's attorney will ask you. Listen to the question and answer accordingly. Do not volunteer information. If you do not understand the question, ask that it be repeated. When under cross-examination by the opposing counsel, always pause momentarily before answering any questions to give your attorney an opportunity to object to the question. Do not make these pauses obvious.

You have just damaged the name of the client the attorney is defending and the attorney will try anything to tear your testimony down in hopes that your film will not be introduced as evidence. The attorney will purposely make mistakes as to dates, and/or times, to throw you off. Be careful! Bend the truth to your advantage without appearing to do so, if you can, but ALWAYS tell the truth and appear to be as impartial as possible. If the claimant occasionally looks restricted in your film, say so—it will add credibility to your testimony.

Q. How long did you actually observe *John Doe* in activity?
A. This will depend. Let's say for now, approximately four hours.
Q. How long did it take you to film *John Doe?*
A. It may have taken you six hours to shoot the film. Your attorney should object to any question that is not part of the actual activity performed. Do not be too quick to give an answer. Give your attorney a chance to object if they so desire.

In summary, remember that you are a professional in your field and you should make every effort to enhance that professionalism.

CONCLUSION

Preparing yourself properly for your courtroom testimony will enable you to be confident in the delivery of oral and demonstrative testimony. You will also be able to identify the importance of being able to "prove" your proper conduct during the incident now involved in court. Effective courtroom testimony can only be achieved by doing your job right in the field, documenting it fully and correctly, and presenting the case professionally to the truth of the fact.

REVIEW

1. Effective courtroom testimony occurs when:
   - A) The investigator properly documented the incident when it occurred.
   - B) The investigator review the report prior to trial.
   - C) All of the above.
2. List five things you should do when served with a subpoena:
   - A)
   - B)
   - E)
3. Describe three ways to make a favorable impression on the jury prior to your testimony:
   - A)
   - B)
   - C)
4. A general rule among opposing attorneys is: "If you can't attack the facts of the case, attack the deliverer of the facts." You can minimize the effectiveness of this attack on you by:
   - A) Remaining calm and professional throughout cross examination.
   - B) Having good knowledge of the facts of the case.
   - C) Having prepared for cross examination during pre-trial preparation with attorney.
   - D) All of the above.
5. What is proper attire for effective courtroom testimony?
6. What should you do if you make a mistake while testifying and you are still on the stand?
7. What are some considerations on marking diagrams during a court presentation?
8. You have just finished testifying, and the judge has directed you to step down. What should you do and where should you go?
9. Your subject takes the stand and commits perjury. What should you do?
10. Your partner takes the stand and commits perjury. What should you do?
11. The opposing attorney asks you a question which is not clear. What should you do?
    - A) Try to answer the question you think is being asked.
    - B) Remain silent and wait for the attorney to object.
    - C) Inform the court and opposing attorney that you do not understand the questions.
    - D) All of the above.
12. What are the primary reasons that jurors wear identification badges?

13. How many jurors does the opposing attorney have to confuse to cause a "hung jury"?
14. Briefly explain what "investigator talk" is and how it impacts a juror.
15. After the opposing attorney asks you a question, you should briefly pause before answering so that:
    A) You can assimilate your thoughts.
    B) The attorney has time to object if the question is inappropriate.
    C) You are sure the question is completed.
    D) All of the above.
16. The best way to avoid having an ill-prepared attorney is to have an in-depth pre-trial conference.
    A) True
    B) False

GLOSSARY

Abandonment:	To give up a claim or to leave one's spouse or child.
Abduction:	Taking a child from the custody of a person absent a court order.
Abet:	To encourage another to commit a crime.
Abortion:	To produce a miscarriage.
Abscond:	To hide from the jurisdiction of a court in order to avoid a legal process.
Accessory:	Helping in an unlawful act, one who through absentia helps another to break the law.
Accessory Before the Fact:	One who helps another to commit a crime, even though he/she is absent when the crime is committed.
Accessory After the Fact:	One who harbors, assists, or protects another person knowing that the person has committed a crime.
Accomplice:	One involved in a crime with others.
Acknowledgment:	The act by which a party goes before a competent officer or court and declares that he/she has voluntarily performed a certain deed.
Acquittal:	To be exonerated of a crime by the court.
Action:	An ordinary court proceeding where one party seeks to uphold his/her rights under the law.
Adultery:	Voluntary sexual relations between a person who is married and another person than the offender's spouse.
Acronym:	A word made from the initial letters of a term or phrase.
A.D.W.:	Assault with a deadly weapon.
Affidavit:	A voluntary sworn statement.
A.K.A.:	Also known as . . .
Alias:	An assumed name.
Alimony:	An allowance a spouse pays to the other spouse while living apart after a divorce.
Allegation:	An assertion made without proof.
Amicus Curiae:	Friend of the court.
Annulment:	The act of making void.
Apprehend:	To arrest and take into custody.
Arraignment:	To inform a person of charges brought against him/her so a plea can be made.

Arson:	Willful burning of property.
Assault:	To unlawfully attempt to harm another by physical force.
Attest:	To witness in writing of a fact.
Autopsy:	An examination of a body after death.
Bail:	To release a person from jail by guaranteeing that he/she shall remain within the jurisdiction and call of the court. The bailbond which must be posted is a sum usually proportioned to the seriousness of the crime, and it may be forfeited if the defendant does not appear when called (bounty hunters find those that skip bail).
Ballistics:	Science of guns and bullets.
Battery:	Unlawful touching of another.
Bigamy:	When a person has more than one living spouse.
Bill:	A formal declaration of particular things in writing. This term has multiple purposes in law.
Blackmail:	To extort money by threat of exposure.
Bogus:	Counterfeit.
Booked:	To be recorded in police records.
Bookie:	One who accepts bets on sporting events.
Booster:	A professional shoplifter. When booster equipment is used, a crime is usually upgraded to burglary.
Brevity:	Briefness.
Bribery:	Payment given to influence behavior or testimony.
Brief:	A summary of the law relating to a case which is prepared by the attorney's for both parties to a case and handed to the judge.
Brothel:	House of prostitution.
Bug:	To electronically wire a communications line or room and listen to the conversation and or message being transmitted.
Bunco:	To cheat or swindle.
Burglary:	Entering any house, room, apartment, tenement, shop, warehouse, store, mill, barn, stable, outhouse, or other building, tent, vessel, railroad car, locked or sealed, cargo container, whether or not mounted on a vehicle, trailer or coach, any house car, inhabited camper, vehicle when the doors are locked, aircraft, mine, with the intent to commit any larceny or any felony is guilty of burglary.
Caliber:	The diameter of a bullet.
Capias:	"That you Take." General name for writs that order the officer to arrest defendant.
Capital Punishment:	Crime punishable by death.
Case:	To survey the scene or a crime before its commission.

Certiorari, Writ of:	An order by a Superior Court directing an inferior court to send up to the former some or all the records of a case tried in the inferior court for review of trial.
Chattel:	Any article of personal property.
Citation:	A writ, issued by a court, ordering a person to appear and perform a certain act.
Civil Action:	Legal action brought by an individual because of a *wrong doing* in regards to personal or civil rights.
Codicil:	An addition to a will.
Coercion:	To compel by force or threat.
Cohabitation:	To live together as spouses.
Collusion:	A secret between two or more persons for fraudulent or illegal purposes, usually to defraud another.
Complaint:	A formal accusation that commences a legal action.
Condone:	To forgive or overlook.
Con Man:	Confidence person.
Conspiracy:	An agreement by two or more persons to commit a criminal act by unlawful means.
Contempt of Court:	Behavior that challenges the authority of a court or obstructs the execution of court orders.
Conveyance:	A document that transfers title.
Correspondent:	A person (of either sex) accused of adultery with a respondent in a divorce action.
Corpus Delicti:	The body or elements of a crime.
Counsel:	An attorney.
Covenant:	An agreement in writing by which someone pledges to someone else that something has been done or shall be done or that certain facts are true.
Criminal Action:	A legal action brought by the state for a suspected crime.
Criminology:	The science of crime; criminal investigations, the penal system, etc.
Cryptography:	The science of secret codes and writings.
Default:	Nonperformance of a duty or an obligation.
Defendant:	The party accused in a civil or criminal action.
Demur:	To raise an objection in point of law, and rest or pause upon it, referring its decision to the court.
Demurer:	In court procedure a statement that the opposing party has no sufficient basis in law despite the truth of the facts advanced.
Deponent:	One who gives testimony under oath.
Deposition:	The written testimony of a witness under oath before a trial in the presence of a court reporter.
Desertion:	The voluntary leaving of a spouse.
Detention:	The holding of a person in custody.

Disorderly Conduct:	Minor offenses which tend to endanger public peace, safety, or morals.
Divorce:	The dissolution of a marriage. The spouse seeking the divorce petitions the court for a divorce, and is thus called the petitioner. The spouse answering the petition is called the respondent.
D.O.A.:	Dead on Arrival.
D.O.B.:	Date of Birth.
D.O.R.:	Discharged on own recognizance, no monetary bail usually given to first time offenders on minor violations.
Embezzlement:	To take one's property by fraud.
Embracery:	To attempt to corruptly influence a juror.
Enticement:	The act of coaxing.
Entrapment:	Inducing a person to commit a crime or wrongful act not contemplated by him/her.
Equity:	A system of jurisprudence and tribunals, separate from the common law courts, the purpose of which is to render the administration of justice more complete by affording relief where the courts of law cannot give it.
Et Al.:	And others. Used after the names of plaintiffs and defendants to indicate that other persons are involved besides those specifically mentioned.
Exonerate:	To acquit or clear of an accusation.
Execution Against Property:	A judgment has been obtained, the attorney for the plaintiff issues an execution against the property. The execution means that the marshal is ordered to carry out the judgment of the court. Municipal court judgments must be executed by the county marshal. All superior court judgments are executed by the sheriff. Some city court judgments are executed by the marshal, others by the sheriff.
Ex Parte:	One-sided.
Expert Witness:	One who knows a special skill or knowledge about a subject that he/she is called to testify on.
Ex Post Facto:	After the fact.
Extortion:	To take by force or fear money, valuables, from a person with his/her consent.
Extradition:	To surrender a person charged with a crime from one government or state to another.
False Arrest:	The unlawful forcible restraint of a person without his/her consent.
Felony:	A crime or offense more serious than a misdemeanor punishable by one year or more in the state prison, sometimes a fine (or both) and possibly death.
Fence:	A person who receives stolen property.

Foeticide:	Criminal abortion.
Forgery:	Changing or making of any document with the intent to defraud.
Fratricide:	Killing of a brother.
Fugitive:	A wanted criminal.
Garnishment:	A process whereby money is attached that belongs to a debtor, but in the hand of a third party.
Grand Jury:	A jury of inquiry who is summoned and returned by an officer to each session of the criminal courts and whose duty it is to receive complaints and accusations in criminal cases, hear the evidence adduced on the part of the state, and find bills of indictment in cases where they are satisfied that a trial ought to be held. They are first sworn and instructed by the court. This is called a "Grand Jury" because it comprises a greater number of jurors than the ordinary trial jury of petit jury.
Grand Larceny:	Stealing of money or property of another that is usually in excess of $400.00 or $100.00 in citrus deciduous fruits.
Grantee:	The person to whom property is deeded.
Grantor:	The person who transfers property to another.
Habeas Corpus:	A court order to bring a prisoner before the court so that the legality of his/her detention may be decided.
Homicide:	Unlawful killing of a human being by another person.
Hostile:	Unfriendly.
I.D.:	Identification Document.
Illegal:	Unlawful.
Immaterial:	Not pertinent to the question (not germane).
Incest:	Sexual intercourse between related persons.
Indictment:	A written accusation by a grand jury charging a person with a crime for which he/she must be tried in court.
Infraction:	Any crime punishable by fine only.
Injunction:	An order by a court of equity prohibiting a defendant from committing an act which is injurious to the plaintiff.
Inquest:	Inquiry by a coroner's jury into a sudden or questionable death.
Intent:	To aim, plan, or want to commit an act.
Intersect:	To cross.
Interrogate:	An accusatory questioning regarding an issue or event.
Ipso Facto:	By the mere effect of an act or of a fact.
Jeopardy:	The danger of conviction and punishment which a defendant in a criminal action incurs when a valid indictment has been found. Double jeopardy is pro-

hibited under the constitution, that is, a person may not be tried twice for the same crime.

John Doe: A fictitious name for a person whose name is unknown. Jane Doe for a female, and Baby Doe for an infant.

Jury: A group of persons selected by law and sworn to decide on the evidence put before them.

Justifiable Homicide: Homicide committed in pursuance of the law as when an executioner kills a criminal sentenced to death.

Kidnapping: To forcefully abduct or detain a person against his/her will and move to another county, state, or country.

Kleptomania: An irresistible impulse to steal.

Larceny: Unlawfully taking property belonging to another. Grand larceny is established when the property exceeds $400.00 (487 p.c.) petit larceny is established anything less than this amount.

Lessor: One who grants a lease.

Levy: The execution of a judgment.

Libel: To maliciously ridicule or breed contempt against another person in writing or by pictures (written defamation of character).

Lien: To put a legal claim on property of another.

Line-Up: To put an accused on view of a witness for the purpose of identification.

Manslaughter: The killing of another human being without malice.

Mayhem: The act of willfully depriving a person of a member of his body, or disables, or disfigures, or renders it useless, or cuts or disables the tongue, or puts out an eye, or slits the nose, an ear, or lip, and or both.

Misdemeanor: A crime that is less than a felony, punishable by up to a year in the county jail and a fine or both.

Modus Operandi: (M.O.) Method of Operation.

Murder: The killing of a person with malice and forethought (premeditated).

Negligence: The general class of civil suits arising from the defendant's failure to exercise reasonable care.

Nolo Contendere: Plea in a criminal case where the defendant states he/she will not contest the case against him or her.

Ordinance: A law or statute used to designate the enactments of the legislative body of a municipal corporation.

Panel: A list of names required by competent authority to serve as jurors for the trial of a particular action.

Parole: A conditional release from prison.

P.C.: Penal Code or probable cause.

P.D.: Police Department or Public Defender.

Pathology: Study of diseases.

Penology:	Study of punishments and prisons.
Per Annum:	By the years.
Per Diem:	By the day. Also used to designate the monetary compensation paid by a client on a daily basis when on a case. Government rate, usually lower than private.
Perjury:	Every person, having taken an oath that he/she will testify, declare, depose, or certify before any competent tribunal, officer, or person in any of the cases in which the oath may by law of the state of California be administered willfully and contrary to the oath, states as true any material matter which he/she knows to be false . . . is guilty of perjury. Affirmation is also included for those who do not believe in God. Perjury is a felony.
Petitioner:	One who initiates a divorce action.
Petty:	Small or minor. Petty larceny is less than $400.00.
Pimp:	A procurer for illicit sexual relations.
Plaintiff:	The party who starts a legal action.
Polygraph:	The lie detector.
Portrait Parle:	An oral or written description of a person, place, or thing (spoken picture).
Post Mortem Lividity:	Blood flow to lowest point of gravity in a dead body.
Precedent:	A previous decision in a similar case.
Prima Facie:	So far as can be judged from the first appearance or at first sight.
Probate Court:	A court having jurisdiction over estates of deceased persons superior.
Probation:	The type of punishment whereby a convicted person is put under the jurisdiction of probation officers for a stated time instead of being sent to prison.
Prostitute:	A woman or man who participates in sexual relations for a fee.
Pyromania:	An irresponsible impulse to set fires.
Pyromaniac:	One who starts fires.
Quasi:	"Almost." It distinguishes between two or more approximately identical things. Such as a quasi-contract is "almost" a contract, yet it does not possess the full characteristics of a contract.
Recidivist:	A habitual criminal.
Respondent:	One who answers a divorce action.
Rigor Mortis:	Stiffening of muscles of a dead body.
Robbery:	To take personal property of another by use of force or fear.
Ruse:	Pretext, skillful plan.
Sabotage:	Willful and malicious physical damage or injury to

	physical property or unlawful acts of force or violence or unlawful methods of terrorism as a means of accomplishing a change in industrial ownership or control or effecting any political change.
Sane:	A normal mental condition.
Search Warrant:	A written order issued by the appropriate court for the search of a particular location for a particular item(s) named in the warrant.
Seduce:	To entice a woman or man to commit adultery by bribery or false promises.
Simulate:	To pretend or assume the appearance.
Slander:	Oral defamation of character.
Sodomy:	Sexual conduct consisting of contact between the penis of one person and the anus of another person.
Solvent:	Being able to pay one's debts and obligations.
Statute of Limitations:	Time in which an action must be commenced or the defendant cannot be brought to trial.
Stipend:	Allowance, as in salary.
Stipulation:	To settle by agreement.
Subpoena:	A written order to appear in court or before other authorized officials at a given place and time.
Subpoena Duced Tecum:	Same as subpoena, but requiring party to produce certain personal property, such as hospital records, bank records, attendance records, etc.
Sub Rosa:	Confidentially, in secret: literally, under the rose, because the rose was the emblem of the god Horus, *mistakenly* regarded by the Greeks and Romans as the god of silence.
Summons:	A notice for a person to appear in court to answer an action against him/her.
Supreme Court:	Highest (state or federal) court of appeal.
Suspect:	A person believed to have knowledge of a crime.
Suspicion:	A belief based on facts, but which does not amount to proof.
Sustain:	To support or uphold.
Tender:	An offer.
Testimony:	Statements of a competent witness under oath.
Testator:	One who makes a will.
Theft:	To take the personal property of another without his/her consent. With the intent to permanently deprive.
Tort:	A civil wrong or injury.
Toxic:	Poisonous.
Transcript:	A copy of a court order.
True Bill:	An indictment handed down by a grand jury.

Trustee:	A person who holds (lawfully) the property for the benefit of another.
Usury:	Unlawful interest on a loan or debt, lonesharking, shylocking.
Uxoricide:	The murder of one's own wife.
U.C.M.J.:	Uniform code of military justice. Code of rules and regulations used by the United States military.
Venue:	The neighborhood, place or county in which an injury is declared to have been done or fact declared to have happened. Any county, city, location in which a document is notarized.
Verdict:	A decision rendered by a jury.
Vice:	Immoral practice.
Waive:	To surrender a right.
Warrant:	A writ or order issued by an authorized person directing an action for an offense.
Wiretapping:	Unlawful wiring of any electronic communications line.
Witness:	A person who has first hand knowledge of an event.
Writ:	A formal written order in the name of the people issued by a court.

Appendix A
EXAMPLE OF CASE PREPARATION

CASE REPORT
November 12

CONFIDENTIAL

Private Investigations & Consultations

Case Report

TABLE OF CONTENTS

Date: November 12

To: The Litigation Team

From: David

Re: Case Report, City Division, Sheriff's Department

This report as an introduction into police misconduct complaints reported by numerous citizens in the unincorporated area. The complaints are against deputies from the County Sheriff's Department.

The SO has targeted this unincorporated area of northeast County, at the order of County Board Supervisor. The approximate 1/2 square mile of the SO has concentrated on is primarily an African American and Latino working class neighborhood. The African American gang members who live in the area are members of the gang.

The first part of this report consists of a summary by residence from four (4) of fourteen (14) residences involved in a pre-dawn raid on June 6. The raid involved one-hundred and seventy (170) SO deputies together with twenty (20) federal agents and 17 Police Department officers. The SO force included deputies from divisions along with deputies from the Gang Task Force.

The raid resulted in eighteen (18) arrests involving attempted murder of a police officer, conspiracy to commit murder, narcotics and outstanding warrants. All the murder related charges were quickly dropped leaving only a few charged with possessing small amounts of cocaine to be prosecuted along with those outstanding warrants. Presently, we lack statements from most of these individuals.

The raid left a wake of destruction in the targeted homes where citizens, young and old, were left terrified, threatened and angry. Along with the numerous false arrest complaints, others allege physical abuse. During the raid a pregnant minor lost her fetus as a result of a spontaneous abortion from being thrown to the ground. Others, including grandmothers, complained of being threatened with guns to their heads and to the heads of their children, abusive verbal assaults by deputies who screamed profanity and racial slurs at them, and the destruction to the interiors of their homes.

Tape recorded interviews, signed witness statements, still photos and video tapes were taken at five (5) of the homes which were searched during the June 6 raid. There was another raid on many of these same homes on June 26 and another on August 17. We also have the aftermath of those raids on video, but we have not interviewed the victims as of yet. The video tapes not only document the physical damage to the homes, but also the physical and emotional damages suffered by those who narrate their stories.

The second part of this report consists of a summary of documentation given to me by Don, a resident of the targeted area. Don has circulated a petition concerning police misconduct which is signed by approximately 200 individuals who claim to have been abused by Sheriff's deputies in the area. However, there are no indications as to exactly where or when these incidents occurred.

Don has also filed a "class action" claim with the county three (3) weeks ago on behalf of himself and sixteen (16) others regarding various acts of physical abuse and harassment. Two (2) of those individuals were beaten and charged with assault on a police officer and drug possession. There are over one dozen witnesses for both incidents who claim these attacks were unprovoked. Summaries of those incidents are included in this report, but most of the individuals involved have yet to be interviewed.

Case Report

10/12

Page 2

Internal Investigations of the SO has investigated this claim and have transferred some of the officers involved. Don presently feels that the situation has quieted down considerably since an article featured the citizen complaints of police misconduct in the named area earlier this year.

Don also has a pending federal suit against deputies concerning a false arrest he experienced. The case is set for trial in January, before the magistrate. Don is representing himself pro-per.

This report contains: a summary of statements, photos, copies of search warrants, various news articles, and a copy of Don's petition.

Tamara

June 6: (1st incident) House Trashing (video and still photos). Interviewed on video
    and audio cassette with a signed statement.

At 5:00 a.m., deputies broke through the front door of Tamara's apartment where
she lives with her son and her boyfriend, David. As the deputies came through the
front door, David jumped out of a second story window and ran away. Tamara was
ordered out of bed at gun point. She pleaded with the deputies not to hurt her
because she was pregnant and that her baby was by the bed.

One of the deputies told Tamara to leave the bedroom or else she would be killed.
Fearing for the safety of herself and her child, she slowly got out of bed and walked
toward the living room. As Tamara reached the living room, she again pleaded several times, "Please, I am pregnant!" She then heard a deputy say, We don't give a
fuck!" One of the deputies grabbed Tamara by her arm and threw her to the floor
where she landed on her stomach. While still on her stomach, a deputy pulled her
arms behind her back and handcuffed her.

Tamara, who was naked from the waist down, asked a deputy if she could have
something to cover herself. The deputy replied, "Fuck you, sit down and be quiet."
Tamara was then lifted off the floor and thrown onto the living room couch. At some
point later, the male deputy retrieved a pair of male undershorts from the bedroom and put the underwear on Tamara himself.

After questioning, Tamara told the deputies where $2,300.00 and a shotgun was
hidden in the bedroom, both of which they confiscated. A capsule with cocaine residue was allegedly also found resulting in Tamara's arrest for sales. Tamara did not
receive any receipts for the money or the gun.

Upon arrest, Tamara's apartment was left unsecured resulting in various items
stolen including jewelry.

Approximately one month later, Tamara experienced a spontaneous abortion at
five months gestation.

Terence

June 6: House Trashing (video and still photos). False arrest. Interviewed on audio
cassette with signed statement.

Between 0500 and 0530, Terence was in bed with his fiance, Veronica, and was
awakened by loud voices saying, "Sheriff, Sheriff!" The deputies came into the bedroom and ordered Terence and Veronica to freeze and to get up. Terence informed
the deputies that he was nude and that Veronica was nude from the waist down.

One of the deputies stated that if they didn't get out of bed he was going to shoot.
They both got out of bed and put their hands up at which time they were taken to
the living room. Veronica was finally allowed to cover herself while Lee was put to
his knees and handcuffed in the nude. They also brought in Latonja, a resident in
the back house, and continued to search the entire house.

The deputies asked Terence where the guns and drugs were. He told them that
there were none. The search warrant was for gang related items. Terence states that
he is not a gang member. The deputies confiscated Veronica's photo album and a
bebe gun.

The deputies also searched vehicles parked on the property by breaking into them
even though Terence told the deputies where the keys were. The deputies broke a
window of a Cutlass, and ripped out a trunk lock of a Cadillac, rearranged the plug
wires, and disconnected the gas line. The deputies also left numerous scratches on
both vehicles.

Terence was arrested for attempted murder of a police officer but the charges were
later dropped.

Veronica

June 6: House Trashing (video and still photos). Interviewed on video and audio cassette with a signed statement.

Veronica's statement is consistent with Terence's statement except for the following: Veronica's son, Dante, was brought into the living room and placed on the couch. She confirms that Terence is not a gang member. She also confirms that the deputies damaged the front door and dumped the contents on the floor of every closet and drawer throughout the house. Veronica also reports that the deputies threatened to shoot her dog and continued to tease and intimidate the dog until it urinated on the carpet.

Latonja

June 6: House Trashing (video and still photos). Interviewed on video and audio
cassette with a signed statement.

Latonja was asleep with her two (2) year-old son at approximately 0500 hours when
she was awoke by the noise of her front door being broken down. A few moments
later she states that several men pointed their guns at her head and told her to freeze.

Latonja was wearing a tee-shirt and underwear when she was ordered out of the
bed at which time she realized the men with the guns were deputies. Latonja was
not allowed to put on anymore clothes.

The deputies asked Latonja if her boyfriend, Dereck, was a gangbanger and if
she knew where he was. Latonja stated that her boyfriend was not a gangbanger and
that he was presently on duty in the military reserve.

Latonja was then made to stand outside in the cold with her son. At some point,
Latonja and her son were taken into the front house living room where she remained
for over an hour with Terence and Veronica.

Upon returning to her home, Latonja noted that her front and back door were
splintered and glass broken, her bed was turned on end and clothes were scattered.
Contents of drawers were also scattered including pictures and letters. A $50.00 bot-
tle of Jazz cologne had been opened and poured over the bed.

Latonja gave her boyfriend's truck keys to the deputies so that they could search
it, but never received the keys back. The deputies confiscated a bag of "oilsoak"
which is commonly used to soak up oil from the garage floor. The deputies stated
that it was "cut" used in diluting methamphetamine.

Latonja asked one of the deputies as they were leaving who was going to be responsible for the damage. One of the deputies responded, "As far as we're concerned,
the house is now just as it was when we found it. We didn't do anything." Another
deputy handed her a claim form and a copy of the search warrant.

Vurnetta

June 6: House Trashing (video and still photos). Interviewed on video and audio
cassette with a signed statement.

At approximately 0500 hours, Vurnetta was awakened by the noise of men yelling
obscenities and pounding at her front door. As she rose from her bed, she heard
the sound of glass breaking and wood splitting. Vurnetta heard voices coming from
the living room where her son, Lee, was sleeping. She heard the same male voices
scream, "Don't move mother fucker or I'll kill you!"

When Vurnetta went into the living room, she states several of the approximately six (6) or seven (7) deputies pointed their weapons at her in a threatening
manner. Vurnetta was told to put her hands on her head and leave the house. The
deputy that led her out used his baton to knock some crystal pieces from the coffee
table to the floor and then crushed them with his boot.

Vurnetta's family including sons Lee, James, and Jack and her daughter Melodie
were herded out to the front yard wearing only dirt while handcuffed. From the
front yard, Vurnetta could hear glass breaking and heavy objects hitting the ground.
Vurnetta and her daughter asked a deputy what was going on. Vurnetta states that
he replied with obscenities and racial slurs.

The damage to the interior of Vurnetta's home included: broken front windows
and door, drapes torn and thrown on the floor, furniture overturned, pictures torn
from the walls, and all contents from all drawers were strewn throughout the house.
Vurnetta states the deputies did not confiscate anything from her home as a result
of the raid.

Earlene

June 6: House Trashing (video and still photos). Interviewed on video and audio
cassette with a signed statement.

Earlene was awakened at 0500 hours by a loud banging coming from her front
door and male voices yelling. Next she heard the crunch of the front door as it was
being broken from the main structure!" Earlene then heard voices yelling, "Sheriff,
freeze mother fucker. If you move, I'll kill you!" These remarks were made to her
son, Willie, who was asleep on the couch in the living room.

Earlene states that there were seven (7) or eight (8) male and one (1) female deputy in her living room point their pistols and shotguns at her and the rest of her
family. Earlene, Willie, daughter Sherry who was seven (7) months pregnant at the
time and her boyfriend Michael were all taken outside while only wearing underwear or nightgowns. All but Earlene was made to lie face down in the dirt.

Earlene was ordered back into the house to secure her dogs. One of the deputies
stated that if her dogs got loose, he would shoot them (during another raid on June
26 deputies did shoot one of Earlene's dogs while in her living room). Earlene stated
that she went back outside and just stood there and watched as the deputies ransacked
her home of twenty (20) years.

The family ordered her back into the house where deputies up-righted overturned
furniture so that they could sit down. Earlene states the deputies began to yell at
her son Willie and Phillip calling them, "Gang members and Punks". One deputy
said the young men were "lightweights" and that the deputies were going to import
some real gang members to "kick your ass."

One of the deputies stated that they were lucky because they were _____
_____ deputies and, "If you were from the _____ area, we would just
take you out into the alley and shoot you. It would be just another gang shooting."
The deputies then made Earlene's son Willie, Phillip and her daughter Sherry line
up against the wall where a deputy took their pictures while holding name placards.

The deputies confiscated several .22 rounds and one 9mm round of ammunition
from the house. Upon leaving, one of the deputies handed Earlene a claim form, a
receipt for the ammunition, and a search warrant.

The damage inside the Earlene home included: shelves cleared and drawers emp-
tied with their contents strewn on the floor, Earlene found her watch and medications on the front lawn. Her water and stereo equipment were damaged. Two vehicles
which were parked out front were also damaged during the raid.

Tamara

June 27: (2nd incident) Illegal entry, tow and failure to take a complaint. (Interviewed on audio cassette with signed statement.)

At approximately 1100 hours, Tamara was visiting friends, Terence and Barbara. Tamara heard her car alarm go off and opened the front door to look. Tamara saw her car door open with two deputies standing beside her car. There was another young man in the back of their unit.

The two deputies came to the door and asked her who the car belonged to. Tamara responded that it was hers at which point both deputies entered the house. Tamara told them that they were not given permission to enter and then attempted to call their watch commander about what was going on. The deputy kept trying to take the phone from her hands and finally pulled the cord from the wall.

The other deputy told Tamara and Terence that his brother, Kevin, had run from them and that they were going to pay for it. The deputy then searched all the rooms of the house. During the warrantless search, the deputy stated, "When someone runs from me, this is what is going to happen." The deputy also threatened to tow Tamara's car if she didn't shut up.

After searching the house, the deputies went outside and searched Tamara's car. Tamara called the _____ station and talked to a sergeant. The sergeant requested to speak with one of the deputies after Tamara explained the situation. The deputy told Tamara to tell the sergeant that he was busy and would talk to him when he got back to the station. Tamara told the sergeant what the deputy said at which time the sergeant told Tamara, "Well, don't call me again. I don't want to talk to you."

The deputy also stated the reason they were there was drugs. The deputies then had Tamara's car towed because they alleged Kevin had been driving it and then ran from them and that he was an unlicensed driver. Tamara paid $79.00 to get her car from impound.

At the time, Tamara told the deputies that the car had not been moved in the last 24 hours. She also called the sergeant back and informed him of the tow. The sergeant stated to Tamara, "I told you not to call me again," and then hung up on her.

Tamara

1st Week of July: (3rd incident) Illegal tow with damage to interior of vehicle (photos). Interview on audio cassette with a signed statement.

Tamara was driving her vehicle on her way to visit a friend when she had a flat tire. Tamara left her car for about five (5) minutes to go and get someone to help her change her tire.

When Tamara returned, several deputies were around her car. Tamara asked the deputies what they were doing. One of the deputies stated, "Someone fled from this vehicle on foot." Tamara told them that she was alone in the car and that she parked it because of the flat tire. The deputies then impounded her car.

Several days later, Tamara called the _____ Sheriff's station and was told that her car had not been impounded. She was told to come in and get a release form. Once at the station, a deputy at the desk told her that he was having trouble locating her car. He also told her that her car was not impounded, but stored because it had been abandoned.

After finally receiving a release form, Tamara went to the storage yard, paid the fees and retrieved her car. Tamara states that the interior of her car had been damaged including: turn signal broken off, arm rest removed, stereo and equalizer removed, exposing wires, driver's seat broken, and stereo speakers from the trunk had holes punched in them. Tamara did not receive any documents from the sheriff's department or the storage yard concerning the damage.

Don

August 18: False arrest and excessive force (Needs to be interviewed).

At 02:45 hours, Don was driving his car through his neighborhood when a _____ Sheriff's unit pulled along side of him and shined his spotlight in his face. Don stopped his vehicle and asked the deputies, "What are you shining that light in my face?"

At that point, another sheriff's unit pulled up behind Don's vehicle. One of the deputies got out of his vehicle, drew his gun and said, "God dammit, I'll show you what the hell I'm doing . . . mother fucker!"

Don had left his vehicle when a deputy approached him, grabbed his left arm and twisted it behind Don's back until a bone popped and his wrist watch broke. The deputy then threw Don's face down on the sheriff's unit and said, "God dammit, you don't tell me what to do . . . I'll tell you what to do any god damn thing I want to and there is not a damn thing you can do about it. Now stretch your hands on top of the car."

The deputy then searched Don and threw the contents of his pocket on the sheriff's unit. A deputy from the second sheriff's unit then said, "Evidently you have never been busted by this sheriff's department before. We do things differently around here . . . it's my way and there is not a damn thing you are going to do about it." At that point, the deputy began to twist Don's arm again and said, "Your a smart ass, huh?"

The deputies told Don that he could go. Don picked up his belongings and asked the deputy, "May I please have your name badge and number?"

The deputy backed away from Don while covering his badge with his flashlight and said, "I'll show you how I mind, god damnit, I am going to arrest you!"

When Don asked why, the deputy replied, "Drunk and disorderly."

Don was given a field sobriety test and passed. He was then handcuffed and placed in the back of the deputy's unit. Don was then driven to several residents where the deputy and his partner attempted to arrest individuals with outstanding warrants. Don was left sitting in the unit which was parked directly in front of front doorways, while the deputies went to the houses to attempt their arrest. Don states that if there had been a shooting, he would have been caught in the cross fire.

The next morning, a detective informed Don that he was being charged with "assault on a police officer, and that he was being released O.R. The following day, the same detective told Don that the district attorney rejected his case.

Don's federal claim is before the magistrate and is set for jury trial January 7. The magistrate has told Don in open court that he has won every motion he has brought. The magistrate also told the county counsel, Roger, that Don was a very good witness and that he believed everything Don was alleging. The magistrate commented in court that the case sounded like, " . . . shades of South Africa." The magistrate also told Roger, "Their own station didn't believe the deputies charges since they never filed the case."

The county has offered $1,500.00 which Don refused. He has asked the Litigation Team to represent him in his case and amend all other Sheriff's misconduct cases we might be able to bring forward. The county is attempting to keep Don from naming the Sheriff as a defendant because they claim that Don's case is an isolated incident.

Rose

June 6: House Trashing (needs to be interviewed).

At 0500 hours, deputies destroyed Rose's front security door, broke a kitchen window, and destroyed clothing, dishes, suit cases and jewelry, some of which was missing after the warrant search. In addition, the deputies destroyed 20 feet of fencing, a garage door, and various other items.

During the raid a fourteen year old girl was told, at gun point, to raise her blouse. Another sixteen year old male was arrested and then later released after three (3) days in jail where he was beaten by deputies. This same young man was also beaten by deputies on June 6.

Donald

Ronald

August 3: Excessive force and false arrest (needs to be interviewed).

During a meeting of police abuse victims in the front yard of Don's home, two (2) units of the sheriff's station drove by and yelled harassing remarks at the group through their loud speakers which was witnessed by a reporter and photographer. Many of the individuals present were already afraid of retaliation by deputies for talking with the reporter.

During the meeting, eight (8) deputies handcuffed Donald and then beat him into unconsciousness with clubs and flashlights while kicking and dragging him. This incident was witnessed by approximately forty (40) individuals. The deputies claimed to have found drugs on the ground near Donald and charged him with possession for sales. He is presently incarcerated and believed to be mentally incompetent as a result of this beating.

Donald's twin brother, Ronald, was also beaten in front of his mother's home and was witnessed by several witnesses. The deputies also searched his mother's home destroying many items. After the search, $1,500.00 in cash turned up missing.

During another incident, Ronald was strip searched on the street by six (6) deputies, one of which was a sergeant. When witnesses complained to the _____ station, an individual who described himself as a captain, was extremely rude and told the complaining parties that he had no intention of doing anything about the complaint. According to Don, this was not an untypical response. Don states that usually when they attempt to file complaints at the _____ station, the complaining parties are usually threatened and cursed at.

Lewis

September 9: Excessive force, false arrest (needs to be interviewed).

During an arrest for alleged possession for sales, Lewis was searched, handcuffed and placed in the back of a sheriff's unit without incident. A deputy then arrived on the scene (the deputy had threatened and harassed Lewis a few days before this incident in front of witnesses).

The deputy pulled Lewis out of the sheriff's unit, threw him to the ground and started beating him. The deputy yelled at Kelly, who was watching, "Get your ass back into the house" and that she had not seen shit or heard shit.

The deputies then chained Lewis's feet (hog tied), picked him up by his ears, and threw him face down back into the car. He was then hit in the head several times with a flashlight. The deputy then held Lewis by the head and kneed him with his knee in Lewis's jaw. The deputy then threw Lewis back on the ground and kicked him in the ribs and back. The deputy then jumped on his back with both knees, pulled his head back by pulling his hair and said, "This is not nigger hair." Later at the _____ sheriff's station, the deputy hit Lewis two (2) more times in the mouth with his fist.

Lewis is presently in custody on charges of possession for sales and assault on a police officer. He is requesting the Litigation Team to represent him on his criminal and civil cases. I have received a list of twelve (12) individuals who witnessed the attack on Lewis.

PETITION FOR INTERNAL AFFAIRS
COUNSEL MADE UP OF PRIVATE CITIZENS

We, the undersigned, do hereby protest the actions of the Sheriff Department in regards to its harassments and abuses of the private citizens in our community and do hereby petition for an Internal Affairs Committee made up of private citizens.

We have had the following abuses and harassments directed toward us as follows:

NAME and ADDRESS of PERSON ABUSED and HARASSMENTS DIRECTED TOWARD US as FOLLOWS;

Please write your name and address legibly in one space and check the type of abuse or harassment you have been subjected to in the space beside your name:

1. Had the spotlight shined in your face while you were driving?
2. Had the spotlight shined in your face at any time without driving?
3. Been subjected to unlawful search and seizure?
4. Were you treated roughly and handled wrongfully?
5. Have you had drugs and/or weapons placed in your pockets or on your person or in your vehicle?
6. Have you been falsely arrested?
7. Have you been stopped without probable cause?
8. Have any other abuses or harassments been placed on you? If so, what were they?

Name: _____ Address: _____

Type of Abuse/Harassment: _____

Appendix B
BUSINESS STATEMENT FORMS

PIRC PRIVATE INVESTIGATIVE RESEARCH COMPANY

INVESTIGATION • INFORMATION • EDUCATION

CA Lic.# 15835

RETAINER AGREEMENT

This agreement is made this _____ day of _____, 19_____, at Rancho Cucamonga, California, by and between _____ of _____, hereinafter designated as "Client", and Private Investigative Research Company, a company owned by Michael G. Mendoza, located in Rancho Cucamonga, California, hereinafter designated as "Investigators",
Witnesseth:

Client, in consideration of services rendered and/or to be rendered by Investigators to Client, retains Investigators to gather facts, items, and information that would assist Client in

_____

_____

_____

and empowers Investigators to take all steps deemed appropriate, necessary, and advisable by Investigators, such as, but not limited to, instituting various legal investigations, interviews, information evaluations and case reviews that would assist Client in effecting a compromise of a case, or litigating a case, or bringing a case to any agreed upon conclusion.

Client agrees to pay a retainer fee to Investigators in the amount of $_____ prior to Investigators having any obligation to proceed. Thereafter, if Client for any reason should instruct Investigators not to proceed further, a minimum of $_____ of said retainer fee shall be non-refundable to Client and be retained by Investigators as their compensation. Should Investigator's charges at the time of termination exceed the aforesaid minimum, the amount charged by Investigators shall be the amount owing by Client. Investigators acknowledge receipt of $_____ against the retainer and Client acknowledges that $_____ remains due and owing toward the full amount of the retainer and that same will be paid within _____ days after the understanding that the retainer is not a "flat fee and costs", but rather that Client may become obligated to Investigators for further fees and costs which will be billed to Client at the agree rate plus actual cost expended by the Investigator. The term "costs" includes, but is not limited to, filing fees, film and developing services, recording tape and supplies, transportation and parking, and incidental monies expended in connection with an investigation.

Client agrees to pay the following charges:

INVESTIGATION TIME $_____, plus costs

9227 HAVEN AVENUE • SUITE 300 • RANCHO CUCAMONGA, CA 91730-5450
TEL: (909) 466-1935 • FAX: (909) 483-5247

Retainer Agreement
page 2

Payments on account are due when a statement is rendered and if not paid when due, Investigators shall have no further obligation to proceed on Clients behalf, unless Client elects to accept installment payments on account in a minimum amount of $_____ per month.

It is agreed that all Investigator's fees and costs that remain unpaid 30 days following a statement thereof to Client at his or her last known address shall bear simple interest at the legal rate, and in the event of litigation for collection of any amount owing hereunder, the party receiving judgement shall be entitled to reasonable Attorney's fees plus costs of action.

IN WITNESS WHEREOF, the parties have hereunto set their hands on the date and place first written above.

_____   X_____
Michael G. Mendoza, / Owner   (Client)
Private Investigative Research Company

PIRC

CA Lic.# 15835

PRIVATE INVESTIGATIVE RESEARCH COMPANY

INVESTIGATION • INFORMATION • EDUCATION

Employee's Time Accounting Form

Case _____ Time Start_____ Time End_____

Mileage Start _____ Mileage End _____ Total _____

Expenses $_____ For_____

_____

Brief Description of Activity _____

_____

_____

_____

_____

Date _____ Signature _____

9227 HAVEN AVENUE • SUITE 300 • RANCHO CUCAMONGA, CA 91730-5450
TEL: (909) 466-1935 • FAX: (909) 483-5247

PIRC° PRIVATE INVESTIGATIVE RESEARCH COMPANY

INVESTIGATION • INFORMATION • EDUCATION

CA Lic.# 15835

FACE SHEET

NAME _____ DOB _____ CDL/ID _____

ADDRESS _____

PHONE _____ OCCUPATION _____

BUSINESS   MESSAGE
PHONE _____ PHONE _____

NAME/ ADDRESS/ PHONE OF FRIEND OR RELATIVE _____

_____

ENTER CODES: 1 _____ 2 _____ 3 _____ REF _____

DATE _____ INVESTIGATOR _____

9227 HAVEN AVENUE • SUITE 300 • RANCHO CUCAMONGA, CA 91730-5450
TEL: (909) 466-1935 • FAX: (909) 483-5247

PIRE.

PRIVATE INVESTIGATIVE RESEARCH COMPANY
INVESTIGATION • INFORMATION • EDUCATION

CA Lic.# 15835

CASE HISTORY LOG

Name _____ Case# _____ Date _____

DATE ENTRY   **ITEM/CONTACT/DOCUMENT OR "TO DO" MEMO**

_____

_____

_____

_____

_____

_____

_____

_____

_____

_____

_____

_____

_____

_____

_____

_____

_____

_____

_____

_____

_____

_____

9227 HAVEN AVENUE • SUITE 300 • RANCHO CUCAMONGA, CA 91730-5450
TEL: (909) 466-1935 • FAX: (909) 483-5247

CA Lic.# 15835

CASE BILLING SHEET

CASE NAME _____ BILL TO _____

DATE	REMARKS	BILLED	REC'D	BALANCE

PIRC. PRIVATE INVESTIGATIVE RESEARCH COMPANY

INVESTIGATION • INFORMATION • EDUCATION

CA Lic.# 15835

TIME ACCOUNTING SHEET

DATE_____ NAME _____

CASE NAME	REMARKS	START	STOP	HOURS

9227 HAVEN AVENUE • SUITE 300 • RANCHO CUCAMONGA, CA 91730-5450
TEL: (909) 466-1935 • FAX: (909) 483-5247

PIRC PRIVATE INVESTIGATIVE RESEARCH COMPANY

INVESTIGATION • INFORMATION • EDUCATION

CA Lic.# 15835

TELEPHONE LOG

DATE_____ INVESTIGATOR _____

CASE NAME	TELEPHONE#	(NAME) PERSON OR COMPANY CALLING	START	STOP	TOTALTIME

PURPOSE/ REMARKS _____

_____

_____

_____

_____

DATE_____ INVESTIGATOR _____

CASE NAME	TELEPHONE#	(NAME) PERSON OR COMPANY CALLING	START	STOP	TOTAL TIME

PURPOSE/ REMARKS _____

_____

_____

_____

_____

9227 HAVEN AVENUE • SUITE 300 • RANCHO CUCAMONGA, CA 91730-5450
TEL: (909) 466-1935 • FAX: (909) 483-5247

PIRC PRIVATE INVESTIGATIVE RESEARCH COMPANY

INVESTIGATION • INFORMATION • EDUCATION

CA Lic.# 15835

GENERAL INVESTIGATIVE PROCEDURES

1) IN-PERSON INTERVIEWS

A. First fill out the personal information sheet (face sheet) as completely as possible. If the subject is a witness, put the clients name or the case number in the "ref" space.

B. Take a photograph of the subject unless they refuse. Label the photo with a placard stating the subject's first initial and last name and case number if possible.

C. Record all statements on micro cassettes for later transcription and/or retention.

D. Write out all statements and have the subject review, change (if necessary) and sign them.

E. Enter all information into the computer in letter/report form and be sure that it is PIRC letterhead compatible. Address all reports and letters to the client. The first paragraph should start with the words "As per your instruction the following was..."

F. Fill out time accounting sheet including expenses (include receipts) and mileage.

G. Create new folder and issue PIRC number if not already accomplished.

H. Make dated entry on case history log sheet indicating action taken/work accomplished. BE BRIEF!

2) TELEPHONE INTERVIEWS

A) Telephone interviews are to be handled basically as an in-person interview with the following exceptions:

   1. The telephone number that was used to contact the subject, and any other applicable numbers, will be recorded on the face sheet in the narrative section, unless it is a business home or message number. In those instances the numbers will be recorded in the spaces provided.

   2. Record the phone number and the actual time on the phone on the time accounting sheet in the remarks section.

   3. All correspondence will be formatted as if an in-person interview.

9227 HAVEN AVENUE • SUITE 300 • RANCHO CUCAMONGA, CA 91730-5450
TEL: (909) 466-1935 • FAX: (909) 483-5247

BIBLIOGRAPHY

Broder, James F., Schur, Peyton B. *Investigation of Substance Abuse in the Workplace.* Boston: Butterworth-Heinemann, 1990.

"Checking Out Prospective Mates". *USA Today.* Dec. 1990, Vol. 119, No. 2547, p. 5.

Chow, Robert. "Private's Eyes Stakeout Ends in Death". *The Orange County Register,* Wednesday, February 13, 1991.

Golec, Anthony M. *Techniques of Legal Investigation,* 2nd Ed. Springfield: Charles C Thomas, 1984.

"Internal Affairs Sting Worked—Too Well," *The Los Angeles Times,* Jan. 26, 1992, p. J6.

"Like to Act? Police May Have a Role for You," *The Daily Bulletin, c/o The New York Times,* 1992.

O'Hara, Charles E., O'Hara, Gregory L. *Fundamentals of Criminal Investigation,* Rev. 5th Ed. Springfield: Charles C Thomas, 1988.

Excerpts from *Publication Manual of The P.I. Resource Catalog,* Thomas Investigative Publications, Inc., 1995 Ed., (1995).

"Private Investigator's Influence on American History." C.I.P.I. Journal, Summer 1993, Vol. 1, No. 1, pp. 1, 4.

Rush, Donald A. and Siljander, Raymond P. *Fundamentals of Civil and Private Investigation.* Springfield: Charles C Thomas, 1984.

Sennewald, Charles A. *The Process of Investigation: Concepts and Strategies for the Security Professional.* Boston: Butterworth-Heinemann, 1981.

Smith, Edward. *Practical Guide for Private Investigators.* Boulder: Paladin Press, 1990.

"Spying Raises Issues of Trust, Ethics," *Press Enterprise,* Jan. 24, 1994.

Treaster, Joseph B. "Two FBI Agents Killed in Miami." *The New York Times,* Saturday, April 2, 1986, pp. 1, 8.

INDEX